AN UNEASY EMBRACE

T0373716

/ AFRICAN
/ ARGUMENTS

African Arguments is a series of short books about contemporary Africa and the critical issues and debates surrounding the continent. The books are scholarly and engaged, substantive and topical. They focus on questions of justice, rights and citizenship; politics, protests and revolutions; the environment, land, oil and other resources; health and disease; economy: growth, aid, taxation, debt and capital flight; and both Africa's international relations and country case studies.

Managing Editor, Stephanie Kitchen

Series editors

Adam Branch
Alex de Waal
Alcinda Honwana
Ebenezer Obadare
Carlos Oya
Nicholas Westcott

SHOBANA SHANKAR

An Uneasy Embrace

Africa, India and the Spectre of Race

HURST & COMPANY, LONDON

IAI   International African Institute

Published in collaboration with the International African Institute.

First published in the United Kingdom in 2021 by

C. Hurst & Co. (Publishers) Ltd.,

83 Torbay Road, London, NW6 7DT

Copyright © Shobana Shankar, 2021

All rights reserved.

Printed in Great Britain by Bell and Bain Ltd, Glasgow

The right of Shobana Shankar to be identified as the author
of this publication is asserted by her in accordance with the
Copyright, Designs and Patents Act, 1988.

A Cataloguing-in-Publication data record for this book
is available from the British Library.

ISBN: 9781787385696

This book is printed using paper from registered sustainable
and managed sources.

www.hurstpublishers.com

CONTENTS

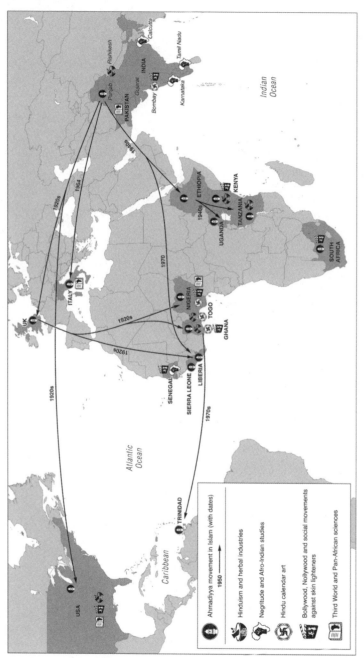

Some exchanges between Africans and Indians, c.1900 to the present

PREFACE

The idea for this book started with a friendship. A Sri Lankan couple—Christian missionaries living in Kano, Nigeria—became like family to me. We spoke to each other in Tamil, though our dialects were different, and we enjoyed meals made with our vegetables like moringa that grew well and were widely available in Nigeria. We felt different, with roots in South India and no commercial endeavour, different from the vast majority of other South Asians in West Africa. We had come for a different purpose, and not even the same purpose as each other. The couple worked with Nigerian Christians to spread the gospel in a Muslim city. I was a New York-born doctoral student conducting research on people like them. Nigerians often assumed we were biologically related. It crossed my mind, with some worry, that I could be mistaken for a missionary.

That fear that I could be perceived as a representative or harbinger of a foreign power or proselytisation has never left me. How many Indian settlers in Africa acknowledged that Africans might perceive them as avatars of alien dominance or occupation, even if not in the same imperialist mode as with the British or French? In the past, many Indians arrived on African shores not from India as a nation but rather from a colony that today is splintered into multiple countries. They probably did not think

PREFACE

of themselves as one people, just as my Sri Lankan friends and I could hardly be called the same, until Africans did just that. I lived in the old city of Kano, spoke Hausa, and spent most of my time at the homes of Nigerian friends, but they knew I belonged to another family, another people. They believed I was Indian even if I did not come from India.

The history of African-Indian entanglements is not tied narrowly to nation states. Races, civilisations, peoples—these came before nationalities existed in Africa and South Asia and still have significance today. They capture differences having little to do with geographical place but rather notions of essential character, which try as we might to avoid, shape how many people see the world. Essentialisation between Africans and Indians is a kind of a racialisation, which raises an uncomfortable topic because race seems both direct and confusing. It may be tempting to explain this as an imposition of Euro-American power. But the historical evidence does not support that facile explanation. The power of race-making does not only rest with whites. This book grew out of my own discomfort, not only with race, but also with religion, ethnolinguistic identity, caste, occupation, and nationality. I suspect many people do not share any such ambivalence, but it would be wrong to deny that race informs ideas of and encounters with others outside the West.

I am grateful for research support from the American Institute of Indian Studies, Council of American Overseas Research Centers, West African Research Association, West African Research Center, Nehru Memorial Museum and Library, Africa's Asian Options at Goethe University, and Stony Brook University. Thanks to my wonderful hosts: Ousmane Kane, Mariane Yade, Stefan Schmid, Rirhandu Mageza-Bethel, Frank Schulze-Engler, Sophia Thubauville, Ruth Achenbach, Veit Bachmann, and Stefan Ouma. At the International Centre for Theoretical Physics, Valerio Cappellini was an excellent guide to the archives

PREFACE

and library. In India, I had the honour to interview the late Dr U. P. Upadhyaya of the Tulu Lexicon Project in Manguluru. Opportunities to present portions of this research were invaluable. At the Cornell University History colloquium, Judi Byfield and Durba Ghosh offered excellent suggestions. Thanks to Mike Gomez at New York University, for comments during my presentation at the African Diaspora Forum and support for this project all along the way. The African studies community at the University of Florida—including Fiona McLaughlin, Terje Østebø, Benjamin Soares, Leonardo Villalón, and Luise White—were generous hosts and critics. I was fortunate to get insightful feedback from Mamadou Diouf and Manan Ahmed at the Columbia University seminar. Thanks to Zekeria Ould Ahmed Salem and Sean Hanretta at Northwestern's Institute for the Study of Islamic Thought in Africa, and to Wale Adebanwi at the African Studies Centre at the University of Oxford. Nwando Achebe and Jamie Monson at Michigan State University were welcoming as well.

I am fortunate to have had the opportunity to work with Raga Makawi and Stephanie Kitchen. Alice Clarke, Miles Irving, Lara Weisweiller-Wu, and Rose Bell deserve much credit for their patience and professionalism. Much appreciation also goes to the anonymous reviewers whose suggestions helped me see the bigger picture.

Many thanks to Omar Ali, Ned Alpers, David Amponsah (whose forthcoming work on West African-Indian religious worlds deserves mention), Abamfo Atiemo, Visham Balroop, Oliver Coates, Faisal Devji, Sylviane Diouf, Roquinaldo Ferreira, Barbara Frank, Kabiru Haruna Isa, Sri Jayanthi Kumaraswami, Dennis Laumann, Mara Leichtman, Karen Leonard, Wendell Marsh, Nara Milanich, Renu Modi, Ebenezer Obadare, Narayana Osei-Nyarko, Derek Peterson, Naaborko Sackeyfio-Lenoch, Yousuf Saeed, Lahra Smith, Goolam Vahed, Meera

Venkatachalam, Mansour Sora Wade, Tracey Walters, and Albert Wuaku.

To my parents, sister, aunts, uncles, and cousins who have supported me, my gratitude is endless. This book is not endless, thanks to Marcus.

NOTE ON TERMINOLOGY AND LANGUAGE

The terms related to race, ethnicity, and caste in this book each have complicated histories, but at the risk of oversimplification, some explanation of the ones I use most often may be useful.

After the murder of George Floyd on 25 May 2020 and the Black Lives Matter mobilisation that followed, the *New York Times* and Associated Press explained they would capitalise the term "Black" to recognise the shared experience of Blacks around the world. I do the same here.

Africanité and *négritude* are both terms that arose in Francophone Black philosophical, intellectual, and cultural studies to affirm the qualities of being from the African continent or a descendant of the diaspora and to honour Black identity, history, cultural characteristics, and ways of knowing. Léopold Senghor, the first president of Senegal, features prominently in this book as he was a key founder of the *négritude* movement by which he distinguished Africanness from Arabness, Europeanness, and Indianness. He worked with Aimé Césaire, Léon Damas, and others in the 1930s.

Afrocentric or *Afrocentrism* is the centring of African and African diasporic perspectives. The term has other definitions that

NOTE ON TERMINOLOGY AND LANGUAGE

emphasise its origin in a reaction to European intellectualism that denied that Africa had history and denied Black contributions to world civilisations.

Pan-Africanism is an ideology or a spectrum of related ideologies that elevates the connectedness of Africans and African-descended peoples by ancestry, customs, and identity as a basis for unification or by return to Africa. Different thinkers elaborated various elements of Pan-Africanism or espoused it in diverse projects including Marcus Garvey's "Return to Africa" movement. *Pan-Asianism* and *Pan-Islamism* similarly attached cultural identities to the idea of homeland, in the latter case revolving around the Ottoman Empire during World War I.

Aryan and *Dravidian* are terms for language families codified by European Indologists starting in the eighteenth century. Indo-Aryan languages represented one branch and Dravidian another, the latter assumed to be present in India before the arrival of the Indo-Aryans sometime around the second millennium BCE. While Aryan-descended languages are in Northern India and Dravidian in Southern India, there are cross-fertilisations. The terms became racialised though they did not themselves convey any sense of skin colour (*varna*) or caste (*jati*).

Words for castes—Brahmin, Kshatriya, Bania, and Shudra—originate in the Laws of Manu written in Sanskrit around 200–300 CE. These designations in ancient texts do not connote skin colour.

INTRODUCTION

More than 3 million people living on the African continent today trace their roots to the Indian subcontinent.[1] Despite their relatively small number, the presence of Indians weighs heavily for many Africans. Kenyan writer Ngugi wa Thiong'o began to see it when he published his childhood memoir in 2006: "There it was, staring at me right from the pages of my narrative. It starts from home, through school, college and after".[2] When he was a child, he witnessed Africans and Indians live separate lives—"hardly any social contact"—or worse, fights between kids and the abuse *jungli*, Hindi for wild or uncivilised, hurled at African workers by *dukkawallahs*, the Indian shopkeepers. When he went to university at Makerere in Uganda, he had personal contact with Indians. With dorm living, classes, sports, and politics, he found that "doing things together is the best teacher of race relations". The racial and class resentments may have become easier to ignore in the minds of students of his generation in the 1960s, with idealistic notions of Afro-Asian solidarity. For his mother, on the other hand, the land of her ancestors—used as a Hindu funeral pyre—would never be the same:

To her dying day, she believed and swore that on some nights, she would see disembodied Indian spirits, like lit candles in the dark, wandering in the forest around the cremation place. She talked about it as a matter of regular material fact and she would become visibly upset when we doubted her.[3]

Like ghosts, resentments return to haunt Africans and Indians. In India, after African unsuspecting immigrants were attacked by a mob in 2014, African leaders protested to the Indian government. Trade agreements and overseas studentships were threatened.[4] Not long after, South Africans began to learn of how the Indian-born Gupta brothers "captured" their country and its ruling party, the African National Congress, through deceit and corruption, "inflaming racial tensions in a country still struggling to recover from decades of apartheid".[5] Any goodwill of the anti-apartheid movement was shattered—the Guptas insulted Black workers as "monkeys", while Blacks taunted random Indians as "Guptas". "White people were better than these Indians", many Blacks grumbled. Women teased Indian men about dating them for their "financial stability". In West Africa, where the Indian diaspora is much smaller, there are similar feelings of anger towards Indians. When the government of India installed a statue of Gandhi on the campus of the University of Ghana, Legon, in 2016 (after financing the new presidential palace and without consulting faculty or students), a protest movement began. #GandhiMustFall, in the mode of #RhodesMustFall in South Africa, called for an economic and intellectual boycott.[6] Activists rejected African governments' coziness with Indian politicians and businessmen, and repudiated the high-caste Hindu Gandhi's racism towards Blacks in South Africa and towards Dalits, India's "untouchables". For Africa, argued one of the movement's leaders, "[B. R.] Ambedkar is more relevant ... than Gandhi", referring to the Dalit politician who challenged the Mahatma on caste reform.[7] Caste, however, is not what Indians want Africans to see.

INTRODUCTION

There have been moments of common struggle, but conflicts between Africans and Indians emerge and recede like the tides. This book explores how Africans and Indians make and see their differences. What do race and racism mean in their relationships, in conflict and moments of solidarity—in Afro-Asian solidarity and non-violent global social movements against racial oppression? Responding to critics who call attention to Gandhi's racism during his career in South Africa (1893–1914), historian Ramachandra Guha argues that they make an intellectual error by imposing "an American concept (and reality) on a place with a different history".[8] This accusation depends on several flawed assumptions—it takes for granted that ideas and practices are territorially bound, that race has a singular origin, and that Africans and Indians are somehow immutably not modern. African-Indian history offers definitions of race that are far more than "inherent, heritable, persistent or predicative characteristics ... which thus had a biological or quasi-biological basis".[9] Race is a symbol of a divisive moral contest between two postcolonial peoples who have contributed to global struggles for self-determination. At the same time, race is also a foundation for unity.

To take seriously indigenous ideologies and practices of difference and the relevance of race in the non-Western world, this book must contend with the sorts of critique Guha makes and must acknowledge the studies that have exposed the folly of attempts to categorically dismiss race. Amongst the significant works are those by Suraj Yengde and Isabel Wilkerson, that show that race and caste are inextricably knotted in the modern world.[10] With Africans and Indians amongst the largest diasporas in the world, their entanglements have embedded the race-caste crucible the world over. I focus on African-Indian entanglements touching South Africa, India, the United States, Ghana, Nigeria, and Francophone Senegal, but of course the map could be widened.

Race in African-Indian entanglements became an inescapable issue in the twentieth century, when the Indian Ocean and Black Atlantic worlds collided. Indian forced labour and economic mobility in Africa, driven by European imperial expansions, contributed to a global racial system. The work of Pan-African communist intellectual W. E. B. Du Bois reflects an ambivalence about "black and brown alliances".[11] Even as he was hopeful, he was the most famous commentator amongst others who were concerned about India in the Black world. In the Black Atlantic, where racial imagination and protest became iconic,[12] India and Indians found themselves in a new ideological realm. Africans and the African diaspora constructed strong and dynamic Pan-African and Afrocentric movements to fight racism and develop race consciousness. Decolonisation and self-determination forced open questions about African-Indian differences and inequality, defined by Euro-American racial hierarchies and discord over caste, religion, sex, and skin colour that simmered beneath the rhetoric of Afro-Indian solidarity permeating global networks. Race, even as its meaning seemed hard to disentangle in the litany of resentments that Ngugi grew up observing, had to be confronted directly.

Herein lies the central theme of this book—the remaking of race in particular cultural projects that Africans and Indians undertook to address their pressing problems and priorities as postcolonial peoples. As in Ngugi's Makerere days, when he and his classmates lived and learned in close quarters and everyday intimacies, the African-Indian cultural experiments I examine constructed kinships amid tensions—creative, competitive, and nonconformist—that unfolded with specific intent in West Africa, as if to escape history in Eastern and Southern Africa. These cultural movements were also not fully in the hands of political leaders, but rather in a cultural economy initiated by Africans before a sizeable Indian diaspora arrived. Atlantic Africa beckoned to

INTRODUCTION

Indians and India with an explicit consciousness of race in Pan-Africanism, Afrocentricity, and popular devotionalism in indigenous religions and Islam, even before Kwame Nkrumah and Nehru ushered in the Asian-African Conference and Non-Alignment Movement. That conventional starting point has a rich prehistory of a vibrant cultural imagination that gave meaning to African-Indian political relations in popular discourse. An epoch of African-Indian discovery that has been overshadowed by later political events reveals the dynamic and intricate construction of difference and intimacy in the shadow of Euro-American power.

***

Over many centuries, the monsoons had taken migrants across the Indian Ocean in many directions, leaving the impression that fluid and cosmopolitan social and cultural relations arose in a pre-Atlantic—and perhaps according to some histories a pre-racial—age. African slaves and soldiers rose to great power and prestige in Gujarat and on the Deccan Plateau, intermarrying with Indians and creating Afro-Indian communities.[13] On the Swahili coast, Muslim Indian traders had settled into the social and cultural milieu.[14] From the extant evidence (largely related to powerful people and popular saintly figures), it is difficult to develop a broader history of early African-Indian social categories and intercourse.

Rather than categorically denying or disqualifying any notion of race in these early encounters, it is maybe more useful to imagine what existed instead. Did Africans and Indians have a concept of immutable biological difference in the same vein as European racial ideologies of the nineteenth century? It is perhaps too convenient to explain this as a purely European invention imposed on colonised peoples. Forms of essentialisation of people-groups (akin to race) and hierarchical organisations certainly existed. Terms for barbarian (such as *mleccha* in the Vedas, and the root of Hutu in Kinyarwanda) show concepts of group superiority. Terms about physical difference—defined by blood, ancestry, or origins—including *haratin* and *gnawa* denoting Blackness and slave descent in Mauritania and Morocco, *varna* (skin colour) and *jati* (caste) in India, are many centuries old.

These forms of differentiation do not suggest that Africans and Indians understood social difference and inequality as inherited or fixed. Rather, they were necessarily reproduced through social and economic practices like slavery, marriage, and inherited occupational stratification, in which some fluidity and ambiguity persisted (for example, skin colour did not automatically consign a person to any particular status in earlier centuries in India, though it was noted as a social fact). Essentialisation in some slave societies, particularly in Islamic Africa, hardened into categories that closely approximate to modern racial stigmatisation—with differentiated *bidan* (white) and *haratin* (Black) social groups. On the other hand, in medieval India, African free and slave mobility did not harden into a racialised Blackness as African men serving in royal militaries and political leadership rose to great status, recruited more African soldiers and slaves, and married local women in the Deccan and Gujarat regions.[15] Added to these migrants, known as the Habshis (from the word Habasha for Ethiopia), were the Siddi, migrants from Africa who arrived during the colonial era and settled into Indian communities without as much assimilation through intermarriage. Nonetheless, these African diasporic layers almost dissolved and re-dispersed into Indian society.[16] Caste in India differed from caste in Africa, which is often overlooked. In Ethiopia, history reveals a political evolution of occupational restrictions stemming from the punishment of religious dissenters who were excommunicated by the Orthodox Christian monarchy before the early modern period.[17] In the Senegambia region, Islam has not erased caste but instead led to associations of impurity with blacksmiths and griots, who are believed to have harnessed malign powers.[18]

Many of the sources related to slavery and caste in the Western Sahel come from Arab and European chroniclers. Their ideas about caste were incubated during the era of encounters with Indians and may have been imported into later descriptions of African endogamous social groups to explain rigid strictures on intermarriage and occupation.[19] Cultural interaction, translation, and mistranslation make disentangling non-Western discourses of difference difficult. Indeed, European racial ideologies are traceable to the appropriation of knowledges and practices of power of colonised peoples. Aryan, Bantu, and Dravidian were language classifications that became racialised. The Hamitic language classification reveals how European racial ideologies themselves emerged from multicultural Abrahamic religious discourses. European racial ideologies were heterogeneous, until the Christian idea of universal humanity waned and the scientific racial logic of immutable and hierarchical human differences became the dominant strand of thought in the nineteenth century. The British did not simply bring categories of Aryans, Semites/Hamites, Dravidians, and Bantus from Britain to India and Africa, but also between and amongst the imperial domains, creating a "three-way interchange of ideas".[20] Racial ideas moved between these regions. The Hamitic myth has had a longer life outside Europe, just as the Indo-Aryan myth of civilisational dominance has in the Indian subcontinent and in the diaspora, Iran, and elsewhere.[21]

The Atlantic and Indian Ocean worlds were distinct, to be sure, but not detached from one another. Ascribing American or other origins to ideas and practices of race seems quaint, naive, and ignorant of the evidence of the co-constructedness of a much older polycultural racial logic. The interpenetration of indigenous and European ideologies of hierarchy and exclusion has had the power to foment violence in such episodes as the Zanzibar Revolution, genocides in Rwanda and Darfur, and caste-based killings in India. Historian Bruce S. Hall argues, "Rather than explain race away, its recurrent role suggests that it has been successfully articulated to other social and political forces, which means that we need to understand how race can play a central role in explaining bigger things".[22]

African-Indian racial discourses are visible most often in the "smaller things". Indian migrations in East and Southern Africa—as indentured workers in the Indian Ocean islands and South Africa and "free" passengers—were many, but they became collapsed and figured by the *dukkawallah*, or shopkeeper, who was the object of the disaffection Ngugi remembered. The negotiations between Africans and Indians were heavily filtered through British efforts to control the dynamics between them, and racial notions were particularly useful to the imperial government. In Jon Soske's survey of the stereotypes of Indians throughout Eastern and Southern Africa, a reliable caricature of the Indian merchant appears across different communities. Many Africans reported they believed Indians were especially devious in their business acumen, besting almost everyone.[23] British imperialists and white settlers feared Indian economic competition and saw Indians as filthy and despotic—in contrast to the African depiction of Indian acumen. The British ranked Indians as inferior to Africans, whom they described as lazy.[24] They encouraged African-Indian rivalry and competition, hoping to exercise control over both.[25] Both Africans and Indians were subject to racist discrimination and were encouraged to practise racism towards each other, which is not to say they had no independent agency. Indeed, in West Africa, where encounters with Indians were sporadic until well into the twentieth century, African associations of Indians with wealth and commerce were not absent, but they were connected with mysticism and magic to explain Indians' perceived ability to accumulate wealth outside their own country. Indian materialism, in West African perspective, has been informed by a different collective memory of migration, in the slave trade and longing for home.[26] At the same time, Hinduism attracted West African nonconformists and renegades who wanted to tap the powers of new deities.[27] These "smaller things" are invisible in the British colonial sources, especially those concerning the settler colonies.

We know little of how Indian ideas shaped the diaspora's interactions with Africans—how ideas from India carried over into Africa. The experience of "crossing the black water" (*kala pani*) that meant the loss of caste for Hindus did not apply evenly, as the Indian diaspora was heterogeneous in religion, caste, class, and opportunities within different colonies.[28] Privileged Indians held on to caste in South Africa and Kenya.[29] One wonders how much this shaped the views of Gandhi, who also may have been aware of the Sufi Muslim Habshis in Gujarat. The Mahatma's birthplace, Porbandar, is not far from Junagadh District, where many Siddi communities reside. Further to the east is the well-known pilgrimage site of Ratanpur, the resting place of the Sufi saint Bava Ghor, who was an African settler in India and patron of the agate trade.[30] Many Habshis were Muslims, so religious segregation might have prevailed, although Hindus also visit the Bava Ghor shrine. What Gandhi knew of this history is unknown, yet once in South Africa, where Gandhi was confronted directly with the notion of African-Indian commonality as a political possibility, he wrote in 1893 to the Natal parliament "that both the English and the Indians spring from a common stock, called the Indo-Aryan".[31] He meant to illustrate Indian superiority over Africans, whom he considered insufficiently civilised for political participation. Two decades later, an Indian migrant to the United States, Bhagat Singh Thind, espoused a similar view of Indian racial origin when he sought to secure US citizenship on the basis that he was Aryan. His claim was denied. While some Indians challenged this view, the wider pattern was Indian separation from Blacks in Africa, North America, and the Caribbean. In Jamaica from the nineteenth century, Indian-Black separation was self-determined, Verene Shepherd shows, especially when the Indian population remained relatively small. British colonial documents describe Indians who regarded Blacks as "hopelessly polluted" and who refused to send Indian children to Black schools, especially Christian ones. Black women held "an aversion" to Indian men. Again, the caste and sexual stereotypes of British observers cannot be dismissed, though the attention to gender relations adds a significant dimension to the racial dynamics. Closer physical proximity seemed to bring more conflict and cultural supremacist attitudes. As Shepherd continues, "One of the most important variables which determines the presence or absence of conflict between Indians and Blacks is the economic variable".[32]

The racial system in which Africans and Indians had to contend with each other placed them in a strange balance between (often) desired segregation and integration that threatened economic competition. The benefits of this fragile condition to British imperialists are clear, but it is likewise useful to African polemicists against Indian economic success and exploitation of Africans. This tripartite racial structure has been documented in certain colonies like Kenya, but does not explain the role of race in the encounters elsewhere in Africa and around the world, particularly after decolonisation. The British authorities did not invent African and Indian concepts of origins, religious superiority and difference, bodily pollution, bloodlines, and sexual aversion. These older themes, which may not all have been synonymous with race, gained attention in the postcolonial cultural traffic between Africa and India, revealing greater levels of interest, intimacy, and even surprising inversions.[33]

INTRODUCTION

***

Decolonisation, with the independence of India and Pakistan in 1947, Egypt (which had nominal independence from Britain in 1922) in 1952, Sudan after the Suez crisis in 1956, and Ghana in 1957, brought African-Indian conflict into greater relief. In the midst of struggles for self-rule, anti-Indian riots in Durban in 1949 led to the loss of many lives, rape, and the destruction of Indian property. The Mau Mau Rebellion in Kenya in the 1950s forced Indian settlers to choose sides, either supporting African self-determination or siding with the British imperialists. In the midst of this, political aspirants created a movement for Afro-Asian solidarity on the global stage. The role of the new Indian government in challenging South African apartheid at the United Nations from 1946 was an early public salvo.[34] The Afro-Asian Conference in Bandung followed in 1955. Twenty-nine African and Asian countries met in Indonesia and issued a ten-point communiqué that, along with Non-Alignment, established a strategic alliance of new independent nations navigating together the Cold War and other postcolonial problems. It established "Afro-Asianism", an "ill-defined term" conveying a "cold-war ideology of diplomatic solidarity as well as a more general phenomenon of intercontinental exchange and interracial connection".[35] The historian Christopher J. Lee notes that the risks of oversimplification of Bandung and its afterlives have been amplified with the 50-year commemoration of the event that coincided with the launch of the New Asian-African Strategic Partnership in 2005.

In 1947 the government of India saw decolonisation in Africa as a pivotal issue for the future post-imperial world. The complex problems surrounding the Indian diaspora in Kenya, Tanganyika, South Africa, and other parts of the Indian Ocean certainly challenged Nehru and the Indian National Congress government to respond. These Indian leaders and diplomats were committed to stated ideals of "ethical globalism" and "non-racialism", but these inchoate ideas were informed by caste politics in India, until everyday experiences of racism and white supremacy outside the country, especially in the settler colonies of Australia, Canada, and South Africa, gave Indians abroad a new language for the articulation of anti-racist politics.[36] These lessons were occurring outside settler colonies too, where Black racial ideologies framed public discourse and popular politics.

The reverberations of changing African-Indian politics across the African continent have rarely been considered. Did Gold Coasters and Nigerians look at Kenya and worry that their nationalist movements, which faced numerous internal fractures, might be riven with problems of religious and ethnic unification as in India? The question of non-African entrepreneurs, the Lebanese and Indians, surely factored into the efforts to indigenise ownership and control of businesses in West Africa.[37] We know little, either, about how Africans in French and Portuguese colonies understood Indian independence and territorial unification in relation to their own situations.[38] African-Indian history has been replayed on too small a stage, within the Indian Ocean, and certainly not in an Africa-wide arena or a Pan-African one in which Africans sought unity across colonial and national boundaries vis-à-vis Indians and India.

In another respect, Afro-Asian solidarity was choreographed theatre, as historian Gerard McCann writes, and Africans were, at least at Bandung, stage-managed.[39] Nehru worried about paternalism, but the problem was not simply that Africans seemed to play side-parts to Asian leads. Solidarity has too often meant elite alliances. McCann focuses on the lesser-known voices of hundreds of Africans, including James Gilbert Markham, a West African journalist in Burma who toured African and Asian territories and developed his political priorities through national and international lenses. Africans and Indians have been shaped in their outlook by local and translocal experiences and have translated these into political visions such as non-alignment, socialism, and trade unionism that include a larger cast of actors beyond the likes of Nehru and Nkrumah. These newly emancipated citizens became invested in the political projects of independence through their translocal encounters and imaginations.

Politics of this period, particularly global bonds in McCann's view, were "brittle".[40] Yet some were not. Pan-Africanist anti-racism endured and expanded, albeit in new formulations. Martin Luther King Jr. and the African National Congress famously deployed Gandhian non-violence to resist white supremacy. The civil rights struggle in the United States and anti-apartheid organising in South Africa expanded on multiracial and transnational solidarities built on older global social movements.[41] Less well known are the Dalit Panthers, formed in Bombay in 1972. Their platform imagined a brethren joined across the Indian subcontinent, Africa, Cambodia, the United States, and Vietnam.[42] At the same time, Afrocentric intellectuals across Africa and the African diaspora in the Americas debated the place of India, particularly South Indian Dravidian peoples, in Black history, as they worked to rewrite intellectual global history as a crucial part of decolonisation. In 1967, Senegalese scholar Cheikh Anta Diop reviewed the history of caste in ancient Africa and India with a careful eye, to distinguish between caste and race: "the study of the caste system in India holds a wealth of lessons: it allows one to judge the relative importance of racial, economic, and ideological factors".[43] Academic Afrocentrism has been largely dismissed by white Western scholars.[44] Likewise, Pan-Islamism across Africa and Asia has received little interest outside the frame of Islamic reformism. According to Cemil Aydin, Islamic globalism intersected with anti-racism: "the rendering of Muslims as racially distinct ... and inferior aimed to disable and deny their demands for rights within European empires" and helped "create the Muslim world for their own strategic purposes and positioned it in everlasting conflict with the West".[45] While there are many ideas of India within Africa,[46] and perhaps only a vague idea of Africa in India,[47] African-Indian intellectual history has not received proper scholarly treatment, given the biases of Western Anglophone lenses.

Race and racism have produced essentialisms meant to counter white supremacy,[48] but non-Western racial myths or fantasies are diverse, complex, and no more reactionary than Western racial ideologies. European race-making contained many fabulations, including the Christian notion of fallen peoples and the concomitant (millenarian) seed of race renewal that was used to justify expansionism and exploitation. Colonised peoples' notions of race are no less authentic and are not simply products of white supremacy.[49] They have produced competing utopian and universalist visions of an ideal society.

Racial reckoning is a constant condition of African-Indian intellectual history in which #GandhiMustFall and other movements are episodes. The growing power of China and India has precipitated alarmist and even cautiously hopeful cries about a new "scramble for Africa".[50] Some African political strategists recommend that "Africa should emulate Asia".[51] These arguments are not new and support the challenge of some scholars to look beyond the presentist preoccupation with neoliberal economic development in favour of focusing on African-Indian entanglements in spheres outside economic history.[52]

The #GandhiMustFall movement began in Ghana, where anthropologist Jemima Pierre encountered popular notions of race as irrelevant.[53] #GandhiMustFall activists focused on Gandhi's writings and speeches and his life in South Africa, chronicled by Africa-based scholars like Ashwin Desai and Goolam Vahed, and B. R. Ambedkar. Many observers have missed African intellectuals' dissent in #GandhiMustFall, reducing it to knee-jerk politics against Indianness writ large: "Gandhi is a metaphor for the Indian presence in Africa and histories of both Indian racism as well as commercial wealth ... while Gandhi becomes increasingly sidelined in the maelstrom of Indian politics, in Africa he has come to stand in for the Indian presence".[54] Indian writer Arundhati Roy, defending African protests against Gandhi and against Indian racism, argues that African activism is more sophisticated for its perceptiveness about the exclusionary practices that Indians themselves seek to mask: "In India, casteism has flown under the radar of international scrutiny for so long—a Project of Unseeing helped along by even the best known, most respected intellectuals and academics".[55] Indian historian Rajmohan Gandhi refutes many of Roy's claims, citing evidence that Gandhi, as early as 1908, called for the "commingling of the different races of South Africa", even while his priority remained rights for Indians.[56] Such defence of Gandhi's racial ideas does little to rectify the outright dismissal of African critiques of Indian racism as economic grievance. Race is generally avoided, and "cultural difference" is preferred in India, where racism is "a problem without a name".[57] Discussions of race have been confined to a small circle of Indians, activists, and writers, and the Indian government categorically rejects the conflation of race and caste.[58] It forestalls critiques of casteism and communalism. The sidelining of African dissent as somehow reactionary or naively influenced by "American impositions" denies its intellectual merits and reflects the existing hierarchies in "brown over Black" in global knowledge production.[59] Yet African historiography is an excellent vantage point for a postcolonial critique of India.

#GandhiMustFall—its layered meanings as an African-Indian dialogue and distancing—contains the seeds of a new kind of history of African-Indian entanglements, one that focuses on intellectual and cultural negotiation and competition. Ngugi's transformed ideas about India and Kenyan history came in part from his role in the Afro-Asian Writers' Association. Its journal *Lotus* allowed non-Western writers to create a sense of a postcolonial interracialism that was seen as the "vanguard of modernity". This view of being at the centre of contemporary transformations is distinct from the idea that African-Indian cultural interactions are somehow "parallel" or "alternative" modernities to a Western one.[60] Intellectual and cultural history outside the West decentres Europe, which Ngugi and others felt was often the third party in the room in African-Indian relations. Decentring the West in African-Indian knowledge and cultural production does not mean ignoring the West or the inequalities it created between Africans and Indians. Rather it offers a glimpse of how Africans and Indians regarded themselves in relation to each other as part of "how power is exercised and practiced in a globalized world".[61]

***

I have written this global intellectual history using conceptual approaches and methods beyond the traditional focus on literate elites, their writings, and the influence of their ideas. Instead, the epistemologies discussed here are framed in African-Indian entanglements that occurred in many spheres outside explicitly anti-imperial or nationalist politics. Decoloniality offers a possibility for historicising the relationships with the overdetermined categories of the Indian merchant and his African dupe.[62] Decoloniality refuses lazy "habits of perception" about Africanness and Indianness that too often reduce complicated processes of identity-making by a crude shorthand to give the impression that identities are fixed and easily knowable.[63]

I focus on intermediaries who constructed idioms and ideas within and about African-Indian history.[64] Intermediation occurred in the space between the Black Atlantic and the Indian Ocean and through the circulation of people and goods. This book also attempts to centre African perspectives, alongside others, to address the problem McCann raises about where the "African" is in "Afro-Asian" history.[65] Each chapter asks who the African and Indian are. The cultural studies scholar Isabel Hofmeyr identifies multiple layers in narratives of the Indian Ocean, that order African-Indian discourse from the "high" nostalgia and romance for the lost worlds of Afro-Asia to the "low" of comedy and jokes, where stereotypes and satire are expressed.[66] Africans and Indians rarely used words such as solidarity. Solidarity, like "race relations", is a European-inflected social scientific concept. African and Indian collective identities emerged through religious expressions, dress, performance, leisure, and art. These modes have largely been ignored in African-Indian histories focused on secular themes. While Gandhian politics has received a great deal of attention, the many branches of Afrocentric and Pan-African thought have not been taken seriously enough by many Euro-American-centred scholars.[67]

The sources consulted here are scattered in archives and repositories and themselves reveal the circulation of the ideas from and about African-Indian negotiations to all corners of the world. They include government records in Britain, Ghana, India, Nigeria, and Senegal. I also consulted records of universities and educational institutions, including the International Centre for Theoretical Physics (ICTP), founded by Pakistani Nobel Laureate and Ahmadi Muslim Abdus Salam. The South Asian and African networks of the ICTP network led me to faculty at historically Black colleges and universities in the United States. African faculty were the conduits to another set of relationships to religious itinerants—Muslim, Christian, Hindu, and indigenous religious practitioners—who wrote their life histories or gave oral accounts. Popular cultural organisations—local dance and singing groups—led me to media personalities and filmmakers. The interconnections across and between institutions and informal networks show a world of African-Indian cultural, intellectual, and political initiatives that have sustained communities with real and imagined belonging that truly spans a cultural geography that has not yet been mapped.

This book begins by examining cultural circulations between the Black Atlantic and the Indian Ocean. The flow of books, images, iconography, and word-of-mouth stories sometimes preceded physical encounters for most people. The migration of Indian missionaries of the Ahmadiyya Muslim movement to West Africa is directly traceable to imperatives borne of cultural consumption (Chapter 1). Tracing how this cultural economy developed across Africa through the first part of the twentieth century, I suggest that African exclusion from this cultural economy in the era of Indian independence generated some of the intense conflicts between Africans and Indians in the 1940s and 1950s. African anti-Indianism was not merely economic grievance against Indian shopkeepers—it arose also from a deep resentment of being denied the kind of modern goods and standards of living that Indians had or appeared to have in India and in Africa (Chapter 2). British media censorship coupled with Indian self-segregation created new forms of exclusion that particularly offended urban Africans and those who were literate, mobile, and worldly. Continued exclusion in the midst of decolonisation and efforts at desegregation and Africanisation after independence in much of the continent around 1960 help to explain some of the sudden rise of violence against Indians. In the same period that Idi Amin's Asian expulsion was perceived as Afrocentric, Léopold Senghor and other West Africans embarked on Afro-Indian university projects designed to include Dravidian South India as part of the Black world (Chapter 3). In this implicit challenge to Amin and the Organization of African Unity (which did not take up the question of minorities), Afro-Dravidianism created a new possibility.

INTRODUCTION

As fault lines began to form between African nations and with refugees fleeing Africa, other South Asian exiles—often religious minorities with academic expertise—flowed into Africa to institutions of learning, including the Pakistani Ahmadi migration into West Africa in the 1970s (Chapter 4). Pakistani Nobel Laureate, Abdus Salam, worked closely with African and African-American scientists, but the Black scientists' desire for a separate Pan-African scientific institute shows how postcolonial transnationalism was complicated by race and religion. Earlier configurations of multiracial Islamic politics no longer seemed salient by the 1980s. Instead, religious experiences and the arts gave form to African cultural autonomy and critical humanism, with the establishment of Hinduism amongst West Africans (Chapter 5) and the growth of Senegalese and Nigerian filmmaking and dance through collaborations and competition with Indian arts on the world stage (Chapter 6). Ghanaian Hinduism did not express Western fascination with Eastern spirituality, but instead became a way to preserve indigenous African religions and remake Hinduism without casteism for Indians and Africans, against the backdrop of Indian exclusivity elsewhere in Africa. West African challenges to Indian racial aesthetics of beauty—predicated on fair skin and straight hair—have led Indian women to more vocally reject restrictive gender norms, colourism, and racism.

The book concludes by reflecting on how African-Indian politics of difference has been both historically productive and exploited. It has provided an intersectional language of dissent and nonconformity. At the same time, the Modi government in India and the right-wing Hindu establishment have sought to use African-Indian difference and hierarchies as evidence of Indian universalism and as justification for Indian paternalism towards Africa. They refuse to acknowledge how Africa has challenged and shaped India. Even Indians who reject right-wing Hinduism fail to appreciate the complexities of race, caste, and gender oppression in India, thereby accepting politically expedient versions of history and missing possibilities for alternative futures. Wilful blindness is a spectre hanging over the political future of the Global South.

This exploration across vast and too-often separated regions, each with their own enormous literatures, has necessarily required some omissions. This book does not treat the African diaspora in India, for example, although it offers glimpses of how their presence was used to connect Africans to Indians. Further, I focus here on West Africa and the Black Atlantic in the acknowledgement that the Indian Ocean littoral has already benefited from excellent detailed studies.

Afro-South Asia presents existential problems for Africans and Indians about postcoloniality, minorities, territoriality, epistemology, education, and cultural preservation. This book reveals popular grassroots interactions and perceptions as well as "high-level" governmental rhetoric and actions, with government actors seeking sometimes to capitalise on the everyday intimacies of Africans and Indians in order to construct "solidarity", or difference, as alternate realities, depending on their political objectives. This process is not unlike the way Idi Amin and others used everyday distance and separation to justify the Asian expulsion. My approach to larger patterns and local histories may leave some dissatisfied, but by focusing on these different scales, the book may offer unique perspectives on the realities and possibilities of coexistence and engagement—ways of

1

A CULTURAL ECONOMY BETWEEN THE
BLACK ATLANTIC AND INDIAN OCEAN

Introduction

Judging by the numbers, the history of African and South Asian migrations is vast. The best estimate of the toll of the transoceanic trade in African souls—taken across the Indian Ocean, Mediterranean, and Red Sea on the one hand, and the Atlantic Ocean on the other—stands at at least 20 million over roughly one millennium.[1] Indian indentured labourers, whose dispersal began largely with the British abolition of slavery in 1833 and lasted for about one century, accounted for nearly 1.2 million migrants to 19 different colonies in Africa, the Caribbean and South America, and Eastern Asia and the Pacific.[2] These figures do not even include the passage of "free" people. And, of course, in the demographic and economic calculations of it all the cultural dimensions are often overshadowed.

Yet new cultural landscapes were built by these migrants, giving rise to new identity- and world-making exemplified by Pan-Africanists Martin Delany, Edward Wilmot Blyden, Marcus

Garvey, and others, who, using different logics and methods, connected Black peoples to an original African homeland. Pan-
Indianists included Mohandas Gandhi and members of the Ghadar
movement in Canada and the United States led by Punjabi Sikh
labour leaders. In different ways these activists connected the
struggles of Indians abroad to conditions back home under British
rule. Even if we map out a Brown Atlantic shaped by waves of
migrants with a distinct literary-cultural paradigm,[3] it is impossible
to ignore the fact that transoceanic Black cultural imagination
predated that of Indians. How did Black cultural consciousness, as
a modern counter-culture of the Black Atlantic, as the scholar Paul
Gilroy first articulated, intersect with, include, influence, and
exclude Indians? This history comes into clearer view when we
focus on cultural politics amongst oppressed peoples, rather than
purely on economic factors and prominent actors like Gandhi.

***

When the barrister Mohandas K. Gandhi arrived in South Africa
in 1893 for a short-term assignment that turned into a 21-year
stay, he had little idea about an exciting transplant from the East
that had arrived in West Africa several years before him. An
image of an "exotic dancer" had made its way from the Pacific via
Europe to cities in Atlantic Africa. The performer, who went by
the stage name "Maladamatjaute", hailed most likely from
Samoa, although she came to represent the East as an exotic and
unknown type.[4] Her studio photograph came to West Africa
from Hamburg, where the performer had recently arrived as the
wife of a German game hunter. Her husband had travelled to the
Pacific to collect animals for Carl Hagenbeck, an animal merchant whose customers included P. T. Barnum and other zoo-
keepers and the German colonial government, which had purchased camels for its military campaign to conquer Southwest

Africa.[5] Hagenbeck, who had journeyed extensively in search of wild animals and successfully staged reindeer with Laplanders, was convinced that "ethnographic exhibitions would prove lucrative".[6] So, besides the photo of his wife pictured with snakes, there were images of Nubians, "devil dancers" from Ceylon, Somalis, South African "Hottentots", Patagonians, and others. Maladamatjaute's photo is similar to another in Hagenbeck's memoir, of Indian dancing girls; all of the ladies held their hands in distinct gestures (*mudra*). The photo of the Samoan girl with snakes, however, enjoyed enormous popularity and was reproduced many times.

West African and Indian printing presses churned out chromolithographs of Maladamatjaute, or ones reminiscent of her, a fascination that was not matched in the West by the early twentieth century.[7] While the snake charmer's image turned up in 14 countries and 41 cultures, a traffic of its reproduction grew uniquely between the Gold Coast in West Africa and India: a Kumasi trader in the central Gold Coast had an old copy and ordered thousands to be reproduced by the Shree Ram Calendar Company in Bombay in 1955.[8] In the calendar artwork in India, the depiction of animals and humans together or half-human, half-other deities was common, and developed from local styles like the Kerala mural painting tradition called Kalamezhuth.[9] Raja Ravi Varma (1848–1906), perhaps India's most famous illustrator, transferred Kerala ritualistic production from immovable walls to portable surfaces. He opened his own printing press in Bombay in 1892, and some of his first and best-known chromolithographs were of the goddess Lakshmi and the virtuous mother Shakuntala featured in the epic *Mahabharatha*.[10] His artistic renderings, which were well-promoted throughout the British Empire, showed women engaging in "feminine activities" such as self-decoration, holding flowers, playing the *veena* (a stringed instrument), or simply waiting. The tradition he created in calendar art inspired depictions and adaptations of Maladamatjaute that attracted West African buyers.

The interest in Indian iconography amongst West Africans arose from a similar use that Indians and Africans put to images—to catch the watchful eye of powerful deities. Mami Wata had been venerated in coastal and riverine Africa and the Black Atlantic before the snake charmer photograph appeared, but the early twentieth century was a high point in her cult. Christianity had challenged the worship of indigenous deities (especially female ones),[11] but the rich visual culture of Mami Wata and Vodun absorbed their challengers. The idea of India was also taken in, as it was intimately connected to the sea as unknowable, endless, and unfinished.[12] Thus India could represent in an immediate way water, wealth, beauty, and potential danger, making the incorporation of Hindu images a unique experience where few indigenous African deities had had such visual exposure, instead being kept secret.

What does a goddess and her spawned images have to do with Gandhi? The idea of India in West Africa, embodied by exotic women—of the flesh and of the spirit, from across the water—richly dressed, with flowing hair, bejewelled and mirrored, and the gentleman in a black suit, white shirt, and tie could not be more different. Perhaps they were never seen nor even understood as the same, because Gandhi did not appeal to the same imagination or emotions as Maladamatjaute and Lakshmi did. Moreover, the respective uses and consumption of these "Eastern" personae—icons in ritual devotion versus Gandhi in photos from the Boer War or his newspaper *Indian Opinion*—were not only altogether different but also belonged to separate spheres of action: summoning the supernatural on the one hand, versus "slow reading" or supplicating before the colonial government on the other.[13] West Africans had their gentlemen-activists—men like Edward Wilmot Blyden and Victor Casely-Hayford who watched and wrote about Gandhi—but others amongst them sought Indian icons that were female or semi-human. Moreover, the desire to see and be seen was tied to religious experiences like Hindu *darshan* (seeing and being seen by deities or a blessed person) as an adjunct to mural-making, sculpture, and painting before print technologies, which created a new economy of sensing the sacred.[14]

The point is not merely that these different faces of India existed across the continent and never met. Rather, there is a notable contrast, even conflict, between how to live with India and Indians. Atlantic Africa absorbed them into a spiritual and sensual iconography, in which a feminine or sexually ambiguous creature was understood as having special power over any human, male or female, Black or white, especially as they moved across the sea. This power was female and directed towards fertility in a cult that mapped across Atlantic Africa and Central Africa, where overseas trade was seductive and destructive, but also, crucially, where the physical presence of Indians was small. This spiritualism contained both the familiar and the foreign, this world and others, human and non-human: a container that in many respects conflicted with the persona of Gandhi as an exemplar of the Indian diaspora in South Africa—distant, pure, and didactic. Even before he appreciated the "interconnectedness of African and Asian interests [without] an amalgamated identity",[15] Africans expressed some admiration not of him but of his achievements, rather than his character or his culture. A far more complex cultural economy developed around images, religious pamphlets, and eventually Muslim Indian missionaries in West Africa, simultaneous to Gandhi's work in South Africa.

Atlantic African thinkers alongside Gandhi

Why Gandhi did not make as strong a first impression in West Africa as other Indian personae must be understood within the world of Black Atlantic thought in the late nineteenth and early twentieth centuries. A strong sense of self-reflection and self-construction permeated West African intellectual currents during this era, and ideas of others were mediated through this sense of the self. More particularly, as Pan-Africanism grew as a global ideology, West Africans did not consider African relationships to Asia and Asians solely in the vein of a singular figure like Gandhi. West Africans knew of Gandhi and his Indian constituents in South Africa through news of the Empire covered by the West African press. The newspapers, however, were not solely concerned with politics. They covered topics in fragmentary and politically disunified ways in the early colonial period, compared to those conveyed by the press decades later.[16] India did not represent a political idea so much as a mystical one, even as West Africans recognised the wider implications of the Boer War in which Gandhi and other Indians organised to support the British and British taxation in India.

A leading architect of West African understanding of world affairs was Edward Wilmot Blyden, the founder of Pan-Africanism. He was born in St Thomas, Danish West Indies, in 1832, and having been denied admission to theological colleges in the United States due to his race he moved to Liberia, founded by the American Colonization Society. Blyden's work in West Africa was extensive, ranging from writing regular newspaper articles to teaching Greek and Latin at Liberia College and other subjects at Fourah Bay College in Sierra Leone. He also served as the Liberian ambassador to Britain and France. In his numerous books, articles, and speeches, the theme of Blacks in world history and their relations to other races was central. In his book *The Negro in Ancient History* (1869), Blyden traced the origins of the Black race from Ham, Noah's son, in the Old Testament, acknowledging their "decivilization" in more recent times compared to their past glories. Yet all societies have their "retrogressive racial types", he noted, but as regards Africans, foreign slavery had fallen upon them more than any others. However, as a race, comparable only to the Chinese in their worldwide dispersion, "God has watched over and preserved these people through all the vicissitudes of their unwritten history, and no doubt for some great purpose of mercy toward them, as well as for the display of his glory of his own grace and providence".[17] Blyden avowed that the African personality was unique and, like other races, arose from a mystical origin.[18] A divine hand, even, was guiding the African race into the future, he claimed: "we may expect to have a full revelation of this purpose and glory as soon as the Gospel is known".[19] Blyden did not restrict his argument to religion, nor even to Christianity; along with it, he saw indigenous religions and Islam as vital, maybe better than Christianity, for the African personality. This view of race could be applied to Indians, as arising from their own mystical origin and with their own traditions.

His Pan-Africanism created a vision of Africa's redemption that made Gandhi in South Africa seem perhaps useful, but not prophetic or profound. The Zulu-language Anglican journal, *Inkanyiso Yase Natal*, shows the earliest evidence of African perceptions of Gandhi. It reported that the Supreme Court's overruling of the Natal Bar's prohibition on his legal practice was a victory for non-whites to compete alongside whites in work and supported his arguments about the inconsistency of the franchise for colonised subjects across the Empire.[20] Gandhi's profile grew as he started the newspaper *Indian Opinion* in 1903 and the Phoenix Settlement in 1904, adjacent to John Dube's Ohlange school founded in 1900, but always parallel and apart from Africans. Though Gandhi and Dube admired one another, both espousing "race pride",[21] they did so from afar. Indeed, when in 1912, Krishna Gokhale, former president of the Indian National Congress, visited South Africa, Gandhi escorted him to Ohlange to meet Dube, but, in his own paper, *Indian Opinion*, erased himself from the visit. Dube's paper, on the other hand, noted Gandhi's presence at the African school and suggested that "natives should perfect" their own African National Congress, with the hope of having leaders like Gokhale and Gandhi to negotiate with the British.[22]

The South African Gandhi's own words confirm his separation from and denigration of Africans as unready for participation in modern life compared to "civilised" Indians and Europeans.[23] Africans for their part also saw Indians as separate and not quite modern, especially in the idolatry of Hinduism. From the perspective of Indian history, the African years of Gandhi's career shaped his convictions to later become a moral leader. Yet, from the vantage point of African and diaspora history, Gandhi was indifferent or, worse, retrograde. He selectively engaged with Black leaders. Amongst them, he did not seem to know of Blyden but instead praised Dube, and Dube's inspiration, Booker T. Washington. These men proposed a model of Black uplift—based on Christ-like living, practical education towards self-reliance, and diligent labours—that was also approved by European colonisers like the German regime in Togo. Their views, apparently unknown or of little interest to Gandhi, were the subject of intense debate and disagreement amongst Black intellectuals and activists.[24] Views similar to Gandhi's on Black politics and civilisation had already been dismissed by his own contemporaries like Blyden, W. E. B. Du Bois, and others. Meanwhile, as Louis Harlan, the Southern white biographer of Washington argues, the Tuskegee founder's views were closer to those of "enlightened European colonialists", which gained him an offer of employment from Cecil Rhodes's British South Africa Company in Rhodesia to "raise, educate, and civilize the Black man".[25] Washington advised the education commissioner of the Union of South Africa, formed in 1910, to take a firm hand over Black education in the former Boer Republics, even as far as to limit Christian influence:

Since the blacks are to live under the English Government, they should be taught to love and revere that government better than any other institution. To teach them this, they should receive their education and training for citizenship from or through the government. It is not always true that the Missions teach respect for the rulers in power.[26]

Washington took an interest in a number of African causes, but usually in concert with white officials or through ghostwriters, as in the case of his commentary on the abuses in Congo.

Gandhi's expressions of admiration for Washington and his ideologues like Dube inserted him, albeit passively, into a heated and wide cultural and intellectual context in which African disinterest in him and the Indians he represented must be understood. Washington's ideas and willingness to work within existing power structures were not universally shared, being but one strand of Black thought and politics at a time of great Black political awakening that Gandhi saw too narrowly from Phoenix across the way from Ohlange. Focusing on Gandhi's racism towards Black South Africans obscures African political complexity and multiplicity of thought about race and power in the early twentieth century. Aspects of Gandhi's politics did not attract Blacks, either in South Africa or the diaspora, because his engagement with Black politics was superficial.

Non-violence was not weighed by Africans within a simple opposition between peaceful and militant approaches to white oppression but concerned the preservation of the body. Black virility, in the view of Blyden, was measured by fertility, not violence or its absence. He argued that Blacks had to actively defend themselves against non-African influences that were corrupting and depleting the "African personality".[27] He painted a picture of ancient African communal existence in a verdant idyllic rural landscape populated by polygynous households. Amongst Blyden's criticisms of Christianity, in spite of his own church ordination, was his argument about its detrimental imposition of the nuclear family structure on women. He read Christianity's purpose in Africa to "rule bodies, not save souls" as in many ways trying to hold back the full growth of Africans, in the sense of reproductive, cultural, and economic freedom. Blyden's focus on cultural autonomy over political freedom did, at times, lead him into contradictory positions, such as the promotion of British interests in Africa, but his views, disseminated in print throughout Africa, appealed to a sense of African plentitude and richness. He expressed a concern for African fertility and well-being, like Mami Wata worship, albeit in a different political idiom for literate African audiences.

Gandhi's insistence on purity and chastity, which became obsessive in later life, may have somehow matched the rhetoric of the ardent Christian Dube, but did not fit the objective of West African Mami Wata worship and Blyden's Pan-Africanism. Even some Indians, like influential writer Bankim Chandra Chatterjee, worried about the emasculation of "the once vigorous Aryan race" and that Hindus would be "spectacularly vulnerable to the Abrahamic faiths" if they did not give up devotionalism and become more militant.[28] Perhaps for this apparent difference of muscularity in religions, Gandhi stressed that Africans as Christians had their own "priests" and Indians their own, but he had no more than a superficial idea of Black Christianity, which included a martial religiosity in the early twentieth century, or other African religions. As African-Americans faced lynch mobs and other post-Reconstruction terrors, and saw the destruction of Native American communities as a portent, prominent leaders like Ida Wells and W. E. B. Du Bois called for "manly resistance" and the protection of Black women and property.[29]

The African spirit, which Blyden felt was best expressed in African traditions and better through Islam than Christianity, contrasted starkly with "the tendency of the West Aryan genius ... to divorce God from His works ... Man is an end, not a means".[30] While Gandhi highlighted the common Aryan roots of Europeans and Indians, Blyden saw no likeness, but instead demoted European Aryans below the morally superior Africans, whose genius in godly devotion marked their major contribution to human history, along with their rectitude in the face of materialism and moral decay. While Gandhi celebrated African obedience to Christianity as a sign of civilisational progress, Blyden identified it as a danger to Africa, a cultural violence which he wrote about as a call to arms during the European scramble for Africa.

In their writings, Blyden and Gandhi seemed to agree on the need for oppressed peoples to purge their recent histories and tap into indigenous institutions. But the difference in their views of how religion should be "disciplining" was fundamental and revealed why Africans did not immediately accept Gandhian non-violence but instead had to "adapt and modify" it.[31] Blacks did not consider themselves as prone to violence and in special need of self-control. Nor did they share Gandhi's prescriptions about purity, defined in decidedly Hindu terms and including self-denial, sexual abstinence, and other self-imposed impoverishments. Even Dube, Gandhi's neighbour, saw Black entrepreneurialism and middle-class aspiration as the best way forward. Dube, like many Black leaders both conservative and more radical, emphasised bodily healing and striving for prosperity, not ascetic renunciation.[32] Black leaders from across the political spectrum from Blyden to Sierra Leonian settler James Africanus Horton, who promoted the creation of an African middle class made in the mould of Britain's own, defined Black success in terms of material and bodily strength. Horton was less well known across the Atlantic, but, like Blyden, was one of very few Black thinkers to reject racism on the ground that Africans and Europeans were biological equals. He believed Africans' gift to be biological and bodily strength, attested by their resilience to survive the slave trade.[33] He did not rely on a religious argument about equality before God. These Black thinkers formed no "monolithic unity"

but were "prophets of modernization", whose politics were prona-
talist and perhaps more prescient of African politics than Gandhi's.

Gandhi's early positions were uninspiring in the wider world
of African debates at the time, and little evidence suggests any
meaningful African connection to him or his ideas before 1914.
His vision evolved over years, mostly after his departure from
South Africa, and gradually gained acceptance as Black perceptions of him grew and changed. Some African-American
Christians, like their white counterparts, came to see Gandhi as
a Christ-like figure from the mid-1930s when his followers visited the United States and images of Gandhi's resistance campaigns circulated.[34] Later Black leaders—in Africa and the diaspora—were more fulsome in their praise of Gandhi, just as he
became more interested in Africans years after his departure from
South Africa. The transformation of African views about Gandhi
is largely ignored, though emphasised about Gandhi himself
amongst those who defend him against claims of racism.[35]

While satyagraha could be translated into Christian sacrifice, it
did not satisfy the whole imagination of power and disempower-
ment embodied in a complex universe of African thought, from
muscular Black resistance to Mami Wata's magical abilities.
Gandhian resistance was to become a metanarrative for anti-colonial and later anti-racist resistance, but vernaculars like Mami
Wata worship continued to give expression to the desire for fertility and wealth, but also the dangers inherent in richness and prosperity, white and Black, male and female, indigenous and migrant,
that were reflected in West African-Indian entanglements.

Great migration masala

Black Atlantic cosmology, alive to spiritual power, became linked
with India and Indians in a distinct but related strand of Pan-
Islamism. Blyden, who was not a Muslim but had a scholarly

understanding of the Arabic language and Islam and immersion in Muslim communities in West Africa, came over the course of his career to promote Islam amongst Blacks for its liberatory potential.[36] He drew attention to special themes including Africans in Islam's founding and establishment, through the figure of Bilal, the Prophet Muhammad's faithful companion and caller to prayer, African Islamic literacy, and the visualisation of a political nation in Islam. These themes were the ingredients of a new African-Indian nexus in the Atlantic world.

In England, as the snake charmer's image began to move across the world, Atlantic Islam was evolving into a distinctive ideology.[37] The Liverpool Muslim Institute was founded by a British convert to Islam, William Henry Abdullah Quilliam, along with a handful of other converts. The Institute offered a unique meeting place for Muslim subjects of the British Empire, and the Institute's ideology made an explicit connection between Islam and racial equality. Quilliam converted to Islam in the course of his studies in Morocco and maintained a lifelong commitment to Africa, particularly to the Islamisation of the continent. He saw Africa as where Islam's "light first shone" and decried the continent's Christianisation, as did Blyden when warning about missionary education in West Africa. The two men's shared interests brought them together in 1892, following the death of a Muslim West African soldier in England whose final rites were conducted by Quilliam. When the British Muslims approached Blyden, he was surprised but accepted their help in the interest of improving West Africans' access to education.[38]

Western education was embraced by both Blyden and Quilliam explicitly because it had been rejected by what they understood to be too many Muslims throughout the British Empire, from India to Sierra Leone. Both men believed that it was possible to "Islamicise" British education, if Western-educated Muslims began to serve in the colonial government to press for recognition of Muslim interests, such as the sovereignty of the Ottoman Sultan and freedom to undertake pilgrimage. Quilliam felt that by remaining in separate Islamic institutions, Indian Muslims had failed to get appropriate educational qualifications and therefore could not disprove the British view of Muslims' inability to modernise and organise to participate in representative government; like Blyden, he feared that Africans would make the same mistake. Both men—Muslim and Christian—used Christian converts to warn against non-whites becoming cheap imitations of the British. Muslims could instead absorb England and the West to embody the highest form of civilisation in the modern world. This became a message sent around the world through the Liverpool Institute between West Africa, South Africa, Australia, India, and further East.

Quilliam (and other white converts to Islam) symbolised this possibility. They were not benefactors to West Africans so much as seekers of higher truth to which the world had been blinded by European imperialism and white supremacy. The Liverpool Institute, by intertwining Islam and racial equality, attempted to render white converts spiritually certain and racially ambiguous. Quilliam signified his conversion with a new name and attire and accepted the honorific of Shaykh-al-Islam from the Ottoman Sultan Abdul Hamid II. The Briton virtually represented the Sultan to argue for Muslims in the British Empire, and was deputed by the Ottoman potentate to travel to West Africa in 1894 to consecrate the mosque built in Lagos by wealthy businessman and philanthropist Mohammad Shitta, who was also recognised by the Sultan for his service to Islam with the title of "Bey". Quilliam's trip through West Africa was an occasion for Africans to express cultural and racial pride. The Sierra Leonian Mohammad Gheirawani wrote that no longer could Islam be denounced as the "religion only of inferior races": "What will they say now when great Englishmen are bowing down under the rays of the Crescent?"[39] Quilliam, in 1905, also influenced the Ottoman Sultan's titling of Blyden as "Bey" for his work in education, leading Blyden to remark on the once unimaginable: "Here you have a body of British Muslims assembled in the second city of the British Empire congratulating an African Negro on being decorated by the Sultan of Turkey. This event will live in history".[40]

Quilliam's visit to West Africa also interested non-Muslim Africans including Christians and others involved in social welfare, especially education. David Brown Vincent, a Baptist leader in the Niger Delta who changed his name to Mojola Agbebi, met with Quilliam and was also in contact with the American Muslim convert Alexander Russell Webb, who served as editor of *The Moslem World* newspaper. Agbebi's own convictions—"his repudiation of Christianity as a Western religion" and his Ethiopianist belief in the African continent as the scene of Christ's second coming[41]—fit in with a Black Christian strand in the Pan-Islamic multiracialism of the Liverpool Institute. Another notable Afrocentrist, Kelfallah Sankoh, born Isaac Augustus Johnson, who had started his career with the Dress Reform Society in Freetown, which promoted the taking of African names and wearing of local dress, spent several months at the Liverpool Institute following Quilliam's visit to West Africa.

The Liverpool Institute remapped routes of travel and inscribed spaces with new religious significance. Its vice presidents' locations were assiduously listed in publications—Morocco, Nigeria, Sierra Leone, South Africa, Burma, India, Hungary, Greece, and Australia.[42] Migrants between these places promised the growth and gathering together of the Muslim populations. *Islamic World*, *The Crescent*, and other serials and pamphlets described Muslim students and businessmen succeeding in foreign institutions and in colonial cities like Cape Town and Perth. Foreign correspondents contributed news from throughout the world of a Muslim world under construction, from the migrant labourers to mosques marking the arrival of new religious communities. Important news was the arrival in Liverpool in 1906 of 50 men from India's northern provinces— noted as "Afghans, Pathans, Afridis, and Pashtuns"—on their way to Nigeria, where they were employed in Zungeru, then the capital of the Northern Protectorate, which was predominantly Muslim. More than mere imperial servants whom the British probably assumed shared a common "oriental" ancient bloodline with Nigerian Muslims (in the racial thinking of the day),[43] these men were possibly cultural mediators whose letters, repro-duced in the Liverpool Muslim Institute's *Crescent* newspaper, fostered an imagination of the *umma* reconstituting itself. In the vein of Blyden's call of Africa for Africans, Quilliam wrote of "Asia for Asians", challenging readers to see intra-Muslim con-flicts as the product of European propaganda.

This "rendezvous of Islam", as Quilliam described the prom-ised unification under the mantle of the Ottoman sultan,[44] infused a sense of return and redemption to unite Muslims, echoing Afrocentric and Ethiopianist expressions of Christians in Africa and the African diaspora. Blyden the Christian was the unique intellectual bridge *between* Islamic and Black nationalism, which he achieved through his writings, relationships, and insti-tutions such as schools designed with the purpose of fulfilling an anti-Christian mission in Africa. His work as Minister of Education in Liberia included the creation of learning systems to undo or counteract the education of white Christian missionary societies and philanthropies in Africa and the diaspora. A sur-prising successor of sorts to Blyden was the Ahmadiyya Indian Muslim movement, begun in Punjab in British India in 1889.

Mirza Ghulam Ahmad, the Ahmadiyya founder, was a reli-gious teacher who claimed to be a prophet and messiah. The sect was embroiled in controversies from the beginning. Muslims considered Ahmad and his followers heretics, and Christian missionaries, whom the Ahmadis denounced for misleading people about Islam, disagreed openly with Ahmadis. In spite of, or perhaps because of these attacks, the Ahmadiyya had a tremendous impact as an Islamic missionary movement, especially where suspicion of Christian intentions ran high.

The mission gained momentum when one of Ahmad's followers, Khwaja Kamal-ud-Din, a young Punjabi lawyer, left India and revived the Woking Mosque in Surrey as a second centre for Islam, after the Liverpool Institute, in Britain. He and others travelled in Europe and some African and Asian territories throughout the 1910s, to "counteract the bad image Islam had acquired in the West" as tensions between Europe and the Ottoman Empire escalated.[45] The Ahmadiyya sect survived a split into two branches, the Lahori and the Qadiani, over Ahmad's succession in 1914. The Qadiani branch took the reins from the Liverpool Institute and expanded its reach further, beyond Asia and Europe, where the bulk of missionaries had been sent before World War I.[46] The expansion of the Qadiani branch of the Ahmadiyya came with a more urgent call to resist Christianity, particularly evangelism, which European conversions to Islam had exposed as a failure. On this point, other Muslims, even including Salafi leader, Muhammad Rida (who disavowed the Ahmadis), concurred, leading to his opening of a Salafi missionary school in 1912.[47] "Christian plans for dominance of the Cross all over the world have been brought to nought", wrote Ahmad's successor, who was anointed Khalifatul Masih, about its foreign missions: "the wind is beginning to blow from the East to the West".[48]

Duse Muhammad Ali, an immigrant-activist of Egyptian and Sudanese heritage who grew up in London, was a frequent visitor to the Ahmadi-run Woking Mosque.[49] Ali, though he knew little about Islam according to one biography, believed that Islamic identity and worldview provided the geopolitical, cultural, scientific, and economic basis to bring prosperity to Africa.[50] His book critiquing British policies in Egypt and Sudan received praise from participants at the first Universal Races Congress in London in 1911, which served as the basis for his launch of the journal *African Times and Orient Review*. The paper became a platform for unification of the non-white races, a cause he took up in occasional collaboration with Marcus Garvey, the Jamaican-born Pan-Africanist whose Universal Negro Improvement Association in the United States worked to bring Blacks back to Africa. Garvey took Ali's messages to heart when launching the UNIA formally in New York in 1914. The organisation's slogan "One God, One Aim, One Destiny" directly supported the cause of promoting Islam in African-America, even though Garvey was not himself a Muslim.[51]

There were early hints of tension between Ahmadi Indian missionaries and Pan-Africanists in London. Ali, a Sunni, first met the Ahmadi lawyer Khwaja Kamal-ud-Din in 1913 and found him unappealing; Ali's biographer cautions against reading too much into Ali's description of the "heavy-set", dictatorial, and perspiring Punjabi. Indeed, the Indian needed the Sudanese Sunni to give legitimacy to the despised Ahmadi. Ali advised Kamal-ud-Din to appear non-sectarian so that Sunnis could be persuaded to worship at the Woking Mosque. The Ahmadi followed his advice, evidenced by the calculated blurring of lines between the Lahori and Qadiani branch for some years, and the collaboration between the Sudanese and Indian by publishing in each other's papers to promote unity across races and sects. Ali's writings show his attempts to challenge not only Europeans but also Indians who held negative views of Blacks. In one article, he refuted the Darwinist theory of evolutionary progress amongst the "darker races" by citing Black leaders, from the Prophet Muhammad to Toussaint L'Ouverture, Frederick Douglass, and Booker T. Washington.[52] Even as "unlettered" peoples, these men were naturally gifted thinkers whose intelligence contradicted pseudo-scientific ranking of racial intelligences that had made Indians like Gandhi feel superior to Africans. The Ahmadi could scarcely afford to argue.

There can be little doubt of Duse Muhammad Ali's influence on the Indian Muslim mission. In February 1920, the first missionary of the Ahmadiyya movement to the US, Mufti Muhammad Sadiq, arrived in Philadelphia from England, and shortly thereafter so did Ali. Like Gandhi in South Africa, Sadiq was indignant to find the authorities treated him with suspicion. He was held in detention for his inability to prove he belonged to a bona fide mission and for practising a religion that allows polygamy. The spiritual head of Sadiq's mission, Khalifatul Masih Bashiruddin Mahmud Ahmad, asked the government of India for help:

> I was shocked to learn that he was detained not under suspicion for having 2 wives but merely because he belongs to a religion which permits polygamy. This is interference with religion and is highly unjust. They have detained our missionary who is a British subject only because he believes polygamy to be permissible, while their own missionaries are going about freely in British India preaching their own religion and establishing their missions, schools and colleges wherever they please. When American missionaries are enjoying perfect freedom in British India and have the same privileges as other Indian subjects of the British Government, nay, in some cases they enjoy even greater privileges than the Indians, is it not only fair and just that Indian British subjects should have the privileges in the United States as their missionaries enjoy in British India?[53]

Ahmad requested that the British retaliate by threatening to "expatriate" all American Christian missionaries in India if the American government did not resolve the matter. He observed: "to prevent a man from preaching Islam merely because he holds polygamy to be permissible is nothing short of persecution for religious views, which is condemned by all civilised countries, among which the United States of America claim to occupy the foremost place".[54] After three weeks in detention, Sadiq "immediately began proselytizing Americans on behalf of Islam ... and found African Americans especially receptive to his mission".[55]

A sizeable proportion of the West African slaves brought to the Americas over several centuries were Muslims. Though little memory of Islam existed in many African-American communities, by the early twentieth century Islam represented a return to African origins.[56] Indeed, a fascination with African origins—in Africa and "Asiatic" or "Moorish" peoples—grew amongst the several strands of Islam and neo-Islamic religious movements developing in Midwestern cities including Detroit, Chicago, Gary (Indiana), and in smaller towns, around the time Sadiq arrived.[57] Black Islam embedded in its religious teachings the rejection of whites' power to name, denigrate, and foreshorten Black civilisation in world history and futurism.

Within a few short years the Indian Ahmadis had built these Black intellectual strands into their message that Islam represented the only truly egalitarian way of living in the world. In 1924, Ahmad began his addresses to the Conference on Living Religions within the Empire in London by remarking that "people of all ranks and classes" belonged to the Ahmadiyya movement, bringing together high- and low-caste Indians and embracing Africans, predominantly in the west of the continent; and in America, from Chicago, the mission had spread to Trinidad, Brazil, and Costa Rica.[58] What brought together peoples from every race, religion, and nationality in the movement was prophecy, that is, the promise of a messenger, "the opening through which all nations may obtain a vision of their Lord".[59] By describing the Ahmadiyya founder leader as a Persian by race, a Muslim born in India under a Christian government, the Khalifatul destabilised the idea of a singular racial identity of the sect's founder, evoking instead a sense of displacement and arrival.

The Ahmadiyya creed began to share a sense of moral urgency with Pan-Africanism, Pan-Islamism, and the American-origin, Indian-founded, Ghadar movement for workers and religious rights established in 1913. All had in common a "flexible idiom in which various ideological statements could be made".[60] The "phenomenon of travelers" that the Ghadarite movement had been, in appealing to economic migrants in America and around the world, waned, but a new force grew in missionaries of Islam who could heal and unite the oppressed and outcast. Blyden foresaw this with Black Christians coming from America to West Africa. After the waning intensity of the Pan-Islamism of the Ghadarites in the early 1920s, observers noted that a special element endured: "It is claimed that the convictions of Moslems should be respected not because Moslems are discontented with the worldly prospects of Islam, but because they are moved by a distinctive religious certainty, which they are not at liberty to disregard", wrote one Christian missionary in India.[61] The threat of Islam as an ideological unification of non-whites seemed to be its moral certitude.

Being a Muslim in 1920s America meant belonging to a distinct cultural universe. Immigration had created a new polyglot population knit together by an "alternative spirituality that was grounded in local reality" as Islam became a public practice.[62] The Muslim communities that Sadiq founded in Chicago, and Duse Ali in Detroit, were a patchwork, with settlers from Syria and other former Ottoman lands in some neighbourhoods and Indians and African-Americans from the rural South living together in others. African-American Muslim converts, as members of the Moorish Science Temple, Nation of Islam, and other sects, "lost" their Americanness (hence the original name, Lost-Found Nation of Islam) through their renaming (typically replacing their Christian names), sartorial displays of fezzes, turbans, and flowing robes, and embrace of an "Asiatic identity".[63] The American orientalist fascination was one played upon by Sadiq, who fulfilled expectations, and Ali, who wore a fez and performed Islamic identity in other ways. Recalling an early impression of Islam's utter foreignness in America, Malcolm X told a story of his dark-skinned friend who wore a turban and was seated in the whites section of the restaurant without hesitation or fear of violence.[64] While American racial and cultural confusion surrounded Indians as "Hindus", who were supposed spiritual experts with the ability to read minds and bend reality, Muslim Indians identified not with Indian Hindus but with Blacks.[65]

The Muslim cultural universe in America also had its own hier-archies. Most Indians, having darker skin than Syrians or Lebanese in America, did not occupy a high status amongst immigrants. Unable to find factory jobs as Arab Muslims did, many took to peddling exotic goods and spiritual items like holy water, incense, relics, and perfume.[66] Sadiq's dress, the standard "uniform" of Ahmadis around the world, marked him as a mis-sionary, not a businessman. This distinctive feature of their move-ment directly challenged any prevailing idea of Indian commer-cialism in both urban America and the British Empire. In the decades before Sadiq arrived, Indian peddlers selling "fancy goods" and notions had penetrated deep into America and other parts of the West.[67] But the Muslim missionary found a new purpose as part of a religious economy with Black entrepreneurs, who were empowered to proselytise and lead congregations of their own. In the 1920s, African-American Ahmadiyya mosques sprang up in Cleveland, Pittsburgh, Cincinnati, Dayton, and smaller cities.[68] Black Muslims and new religionists like Noble Drew Ali, founder of the Moorish Science Temple in the immediate vicinity of Ahmadiyya mosques, found the "storefront churches and street universities" to be a "rich intellectual scene", as they faced ostra-cism and competition from Christian churches seeking to attract more congregants streaming into the north from the south.[69]

Tensions also divided Muslims. Mosque-building, for example, brought out many differences—sectarian, social status, and otherwise—despite the emphasis Sadiq and others put on the importance of Muslim public spaces. Major conflicts also arose over the apparent heterodoxy of the Moorish Science Temple, the Nation of Islam, and the Ahmadiyya, with some immigrant Muslims, such as the Sudanese Satti Majid in the 1920s, attempting to discredit these non-conformist branches despite their wild popularity. The growing number of converts showed the strength of "links between Islam and the models of African American liberation" that Pan-Africanists like Duse Mohammad Ali, Marcus Garvey, and Sadiq promised.[70] One of Sadiq's successors, Mutiur Rahman Bengalee, who lived in the US from 1929 to 1940, made one of the strongest statements on Islam's superiority over other religions in fighting race prejudice.[71] Ahmadiyya Indian views stood in distinct contrast to those of Indian migrants like Gandhi and Bhagat Singh Thind, who claimed that Aryan ancestry meant an alliance with whites.

As the movements started by these men splintered into different factions and even dwindled away, with the Nation of Islam continuing to grow and eclipse others, one common theme endured. Islam became racialised through a transcontinental project connecting Asia, Africa, Europe, and the Americas. It affirmed Blackness as history and future in mosques from Woking to Wabash, from Liverpool to Lagos. In blurring the lines between Arabs, Ottomans, Eastern Europeans, Indians, Ethiopians, and other Africans, it challenged the strengthening Euro-American physiognomic science of race using older notions of bloodlines and other invisible markers of heredity and descent. These older ideas even included the racist Hamitic myth in which Blacks, as descendants of the fallen son of Noah, were doomed to slavery, but gave it new lustre by making Blackness a badge of religious honour with redemptive power to which oth-

43

ers could convert. The reverberation of this Islamically inspired Black politics back across the Atlantic to the Indian Ocean revealed still more dimensions of its potency and malleability.

Blackness and Islam in West Africa

Sadiq or another Indian Muslim missionary may not themselves have understood how to expand the Ahmadiyya using Pan-African networks to West Africa. Rather, it was Africans involved in neo-Islamic movements that paralleled and intersected with worldwide currents who saw a certain value in the Ahmadiyya. The connection was made by British military recruits from the Hausa region of Central Sudan, which had for decades experienced Sufi-led jihads and a thoroughgoing Islamisation of society and politics. These soldiers were conscripted to serve in the British colonial armies and arrived in the Gold Coast, where they spread interest in Islam in communities situated near the Atlantic where Islam was relatively new. One notable convert, Binyameen Sam, a Gold Coast man who had been educated at Methodist schools, converted to Islam through the Hausa, whose "barracks" Islam, similar to the kind of popular devotion Nile Green observes in British India, represented a novel mixture of protection-seeking, entertainment, and miraculous stories. Islam became the basis for a new educational system through English-language texts and preaching.[72] Sam, together with Adoagyir Mahdi Appah, a member of a ruling Fante family, founded a school at Ekrawfo in 1896, just two years after Edward Blyden, Abdullah Quilliam, and Sultan Hamid II honoured Mohammad Shitta of Lagos and helped open the mosque.

In addition to the Hausa, other Black migrants, such as the Afro-Brazilians who built the Shitta Bey Mosque, helped connect West African communities through Islam. Many Brazilians were expelled to West Africa or voluntarily moved there during the era of insurrections between 1807 and 1835.[73] Of the roughly 8,000 Afro-Brazilians who migrated to West Africa from 1820 to 1899, many were Muslims themselves, but even amongst the Catholics, Islam remained an "emotional" attachment.[74] For some, fulfilling their dream of returning to Africa, Islam was honoured as a true religion of Africa, a belief echoing Blyden, Garvey, and others. Afro-Brazilians brought to Lagos a distinct perspective on "the central intellectual issues of race and civilization resulting from the encounter with European imperialism and religion";[75] they valorised the "West African coast as the classical origin of the finest in Afro-Brazilian culture".[76] Classical culture meant a mélange of African ethnicities, languages, and cultural expressions, but also Freemasonry and the English language. For these Afro-Brazilians, the highest expression of the "Black race" was this coastal culture, not defined by Europeans per se, though they enjoyed good relations with the British. As tradespeople, builders, merchants, and traders, Afro-Brazilians had an outsized role in building middle-class prosperity. They were regarded favourably by the British authorities and enjoyed freedom of mobility between cities in Nigeria, the Gold Coast, and Sierra Leone. An Afro-Brazilian Lagosian acted as the conduit between the Indian Ahmadiyya and the Ekrawfo Muslim community in the Gold Coast in 1921.

Muhammad Lawal Basil Agusto was the founder of the Muslim Literary Society, which collected English-language publications for literate Muslims and those "unlettered" Lagos Muslims in need of moral guidance.[77] It is rumoured that Agusto obtained Ahmadiyya literature from Dr Oguntola Sapara, a Sierra Leonian Nigerian who began as a printer's apprentice and, in exchange for labour for British medical officers, was sent to London and Edinburgh for formal schooling in medicine and midwifery.[78] Sapara's travel to England and interaction with Khwaja Kamal-ud-

Din at the Woking Mosque has been cited as the first point of Lagosian contact with the Ahmadiyya. Following his appointment as the first African Assistant Colonial Surgeon, Sapara contributed enormously to public health in Lagos and beyond, especially to smallpox control efforts, which saw him go "undercover" in the Sopona cult to study how priests drew in fearful seekers and perhaps infected them.[79] The orisha of smallpox, known by different names including Sopona or Sakpata, was one of the most powerful in Afro-Brazilian religions, revered in Candomblé and as a Catholic saint but always regarded as an African "classical" deity.[80] Sapara, as a doctor, traveller, and one-time cult member, acted as a conduit of knowledge, bringing in Ahmadiyya publications to a unique circle of Lagosians. Some were members of the Muslim Literary Society and Muslim Juvenile Society, who, after reading literature from India, invited an Indian missionary around 1916 to reside in Lagos.

Yet a Muslim missionary, Maulvi Abdul Rahman Nayyar, did not arrive until 1921. Once he did come, he got to work quickly, making stops across West Africa from Lagos to Saltpond and Freetown. It was in Saltpond that the Ekrawfo Muslims heard from an Afro-Brazilian about the Ahmadiyya, but it might not have been the sect's texts or teaching that caught Africans' attention then. Saltpond, a port town, was where the first Fante communities performed the Fancy Dress masquerade-parade, reportedly introduced by Afro-Brazilians in the 1920s, who were also said to be the first tailors in the area.[81] One new character represented in Fancy Dress was the "Red Indian", a figure seemingly representative of the American Plains warrior from films and images, perhaps from American Christian mission schools. The Red Indian figure sported feathers (typically peacock feathers from Austria and India), beads, and bows and arrows; but the figure, who was always accompanied by a military-style regiment, also sported a large turban, the signature mark of the Ahmadi missionary, that caught the eye of local British officers. The Secretary of State for the Colonies questioned the sect's intent, believing that "Mohammedans did not have organised missionaries".[82] Another British officer, McClauson, explained that the "Ahmadiyya is a 'modernist' movement, which endeavours to impart a more spiritual meaning to the more grossly materialistic tenets of Islam". The converts, he wrote, were "mostly of feeble intellect" and their missionaries "mostly mild brown old gentlemen with white beards and green turbans, wandering about".[83]

To the contrary, the Indian missionary Nayyar was more a lightning rod for West African initiatives than a leader himself. In Lagos, almost immediately after his arrival, conflict erupted. Some members disagreed with his approach to the Qur'an as being too literal, while others disliked financial control by an outsider.[84] The dislike of foreign control became so great that in 1939–40 a large faction of the Ahmadiyya, under the leadership of the lawyer Jibril Martin, left.[85] Many of the offshoots of the Ahmadiyya were highly organised and influential; indeed, Martin, who was a member of the Nigerian Youth Association, officially represented Lagos before the British colonial government.

In the Northern Nigerian environment, Nayyar slipped in with very little notice and seemed to keep it that way for many years when his replacements arrived, despite the fact that the majority Muslim population decried Ahmadi heterodoxy from the beginning. Nayyar made his first trip to Northern Nigerian cities in 1922.[86] His arrival might have been prefigured by Northern Nigerian scholars and traders who collected Ahmadi publications, apart from those that came via the coast, perhaps from Cairo.[87] Another story is told of a Lagos man's prophetic dream of a white Muslim ("with a skull cap") from across the sea who would bring a new religion to Nigeria, that presaged Nayyar's arrival,[88] though this could have also been Quilliam, given the meaning of whiteness. The authority of Nayyar was not disputed, it seems, by any of the Northern Nigerian Muslim emirs, most of whom surely denied the central foundational claim of Ahmadi prophecy; nevertheless, they all tolerated the presence of the Ahmadiyya for more than two decades.[89]

Perhaps the most direct impact of Nayyar's presence was in the Gold Coast, where African Ahmadis became ardent missionaries who spread their faith beyond Saltpond into the Twi-speaking regions of Wa and Kumasi. Schools were a centrepiece of these evangelical activities, as children of all creeds were welcome. The English-medium schools provided a new sense of the world that upended what had been taught in Christian missionary and British colonial schools. The Ahmadiyya frightened Christian missionaries in India and in the US, who feared the interracial unity of Muslims threatened to make the Christian West irrelevant.[90] In Africa, the Ahmadi schools treated Christian teaching as a form of violence against Islam and "poisonous propaganda".[91] Ahmadi missions from West to East—in Sierra Leone, the Gold Coast, Nigeria, and "East Africa", which got less focus—operated independent newspapers and other media. In Nigeria an Ahmadi printing press made books for use in government schools, and in Ghana the Ahmadis started the first formal Arabic language school. The content aimed to "correct" Christian mis-education—about Islam, the West's superiority, Jesus's fate on the cross and his death in India (an Ahmadi belief), and, increasingly, precolonial African history, notably Islamic history. The malleability of the Christian Bible in non-Christian Indian hands appealed to indigenous local and vernacular understanding.

The Ahmadiyya's extensive print culture economy connected West Africa and India, to where Ahmadi missionaries, including Sadiq and Nayyar, sent notices and news. Lahore was a centre for Muslim media, and the newspaper *The Moslem Outlook* was uniquely connected to Ahmadiyya missions in London and Cape Town. By the mid-1920s, Ahmadi reporters were clearly trying to educate and conjoin Muslim Indians to other Muslims and Black people everywhere. American slavery became a common theme in *The Moslem Outlook* in the 1920s. One article titled "Islamic Culture: Causes of its Rise and Decline" was written by a Muslim reformer who claimed there was "no analogy in the Islamic world to slavery on American plantations".[92] Another article reported on the lecture of an American Christian reverend on "The Negro in the Modern World", and the comments by the barrister Sheikh Abdul Qadir, who was knighted in 1927 and chaired the meeting:[93]

> Millions of negro slaves were brought in ship-loads from Africa during the 17th and 18th centuries to work on the American plantations ... Since their emancipation the negroes were inspired with new hopes and ideas. They have discovered that they can equal the whites. But there are oppressive and restrictive laws, prejudice and hatred against them, which deprived them of the opportunity for training and work.

The lecturer claimed that Black Americans believed that Gandhi "was the greatest coloured man of the world; but they had no faith in the doctrine of nonviolence". A debate ensued about the "left wing" Black supporters of Marcus Garvey and his "extremely violent views", and the "extreme right wing represented by Booker Washington [who] trusts in good sense of the whites".[94] The author, who remained anonymous, summarised Garveyites' position thus: "there could never be a reconciliation between the negroes and the whites according to this school, which had got a large following in Africa".[95]

In 1927, Abdul Fayaz Khan Sahib Ahmady wrote a lengthy piece titled "Brotherhood of Man" in *The Moslem Outlook*, making reference to African slaves in India as evidence of the principle of equality embedded in the very foundation of Islam:

There is no gainsaying the fact that the majority of Muslims of India are those recruited from the original inhabitants of the country—the Pariahs and untouchables. But yet as soon as these people embraced Islam, they were admitted into the society, with the same fairness and magnanimity, as if they were Syed for ages. Malik Kafur, who as history tells us fell in love with a blue-eyed fair-complexioned princess of the imperial *harem*, hailed from the rank of low class Hindu. The General, who commanded the Pathan Army during the days of Sultana Razia, was no other than a Black Abyssinian ... In India we find a dynasty known by the proud title of slave dynasty came as they were from the status of slaves. In short, as we proceed, through the pages of the Islamic history, the same example of Equality and Brotherhood will meet us in every page. It is indeed a unique feature of Islam, and we challenge the followers of other persuasions and creeds to show a better example, or at least a like of it, from their history, and from their sacred literature. The salvation of the depressed classes lies in Islam and Islam alone.[96]

Ahmady suggests African ancestry of some Indian Muslims and also claims a common bond between low-caste Indians and African slaves. Razia Sultan, the Muslim princess who fell in love with an Abyssinian slave, would become a staple of Indian cinema. The themes of interracial brotherhood and romance were aimed at the Hindu caste system, but also the urgent contemporary problems of conversion campaigns underway in Lahore and other parts of Northern India by the Hindu Arya Samaj organisation.[97] The themes were radical for the time, when the segregation of the Indian diaspora in East Africa was beginning to irritate Africans. By contrast, the Ahmadiyya curriculum in Africa drew attention to African-Indian intimacy and kinship.

Ahmadiyya print proselytism shows Pan-Africanism intermingling with Pan-Islamism. Drawing attention to Africans in India connected the Atlantic and Indian Ocean worlds. Racial nationalism appealed to the plight of Muslims, low-caste and untouchable people, and the darker skinned—by implication those who did not have Aryan roots. Ahmadis and perhaps other Indian Muslims began addressing Indian political questions through a racial prism. At the same time, Black Atlantic newsprint nationalism emerged from Lagos: "From the turn of the century well into the 1920s, Lagosian newspapers regularly documented the lynching of Black North Americans and the racial forms of cooperation mobilized by them in order to escape murder and oppression, including 'repatriation' to Liberia. Lagosian newspapers exchanged many letters with Black North American newspapers".[98] *The Moslem Outlook* adopted this strategy to frame Indian dialogue with Blacks around the world.

Conclusion

Gandhi's significance to Africa is shaped more by his later mythologisation and less by his life in South Africa. Instead, in the interwar years in the Black Atlantic, Pan-Africanism and Pan-Islamism created a powerful African-Indian cultural symbiosis, a racial religious consciousness that inspired new modes of self-expression, styles of clothing and construction, writing, and rhetoric. This "coloured cosmopolitanism" developed a transnational scope with circulations that were far wider and more multidirectional than previously understood.[99] Africa stood at the centre, not just for Blacks but for Indian Muslims too. The Ahmadiyya were amongst those who "stole" from Garvey, an accusation levelled at many Black leaders by H. G. Mudgal, an Indian who came from Karnataka to the US by way of Trinidad, and served as editor for Du Bois's *Negro World*.[100] In 1930, Mudgal warned that Europeans were "trying to create a mythical racial term" by their use of the category of Aryan, and held out hope for young Indians to reject caste and race "snobbishness".[101]

Through a critical race consciousness emerging in the flow of ideas between America, West Africa, and India, Blackness was being redefined not only in opposition to whiteness but affirmatively as a critical humanism. This was not a colour-blind politics of non-racialism, but rather a critical racialism in which Black/Asiatic racial knowledge was deliberately promoted through mythical epistemologies of ancient migrations, mixing, and millennialism. These threads anticipated Afrocentricity, expressed in the arts in Francophone *négritude*'s framing of *métissage* (mixing) and in the scientific "proofs" of Africa as the birthplace of humankind affirmed by Senegalese intellectual Cheikh Anta Diop and others. This cultural economy, operating outside the spheres of any kind of formal relationships between Africans and Indians, gained new visibility as the anti-imperial struggles became more defined and targeted against the West. Undoubtedly, African and Indian migrations through the West intensified their encounters and invested them with new urgency as political independence stood on the horizon.

2

FEARS OF INDIAN INDEPENDENCE

Introduction

In 1943, Sir Frederick Lugard, the former British Governor of Nigeria and representative to the League of Nations and International Labour Organization, spoke with Abubakar Imam, the editor of the main Hausa-language newspaper in Northern Nigeria, *Gaskiya Ta Fi Kwabo* (The Truth is More than a Penny), to take the pulse of African opinions on British rule. Imam described the fear of discussing decolonisation: "If you talk this over to the average Administrative Officer in Northern Nigeria, they think of you as another Ghandi [sic], a trouble maker".[1] When asked if Nigeria was another India, he answered not yet, because propaganda in the newspapers and the lack of education amongst the masses had kept many Nigerians ignorant. He urged Lugard to use his influence in Britain to allow social development in his part of Nigeria:

> Since a country can progress with Islam as its faith, there is, as far as we can see, no reason whatsoever why that line of progress should not be encouraged in the Moslem areas of Northern Nigeria,

53

especially as in that area anything Islamic, nay, anything Eastern, is what is respected, at any rate up to the present time. A Northern Nigerian will accept more easily what is eastern than western.[2]

Imam asked for more opportunities for Nigerians to travel to the East, but Gandhi's India is not what he meant. He meant Arabia, where some Northern Nigerian emirs had recently flown to perform hajj, or perhaps Japan, where Muslim anti-imperialists and African intellectuals studied the measured modernisation of the traditional monarchy.[3] India—even as a model of resistance against the British—did not offer much hope to Muslims like Imam. Whether Nigeria should even aspire to be an India, with its imminent independence but seemingly irresolvable Hindu-Muslim conflicts, was in doubt.

Even at the height of his power, the Mahatma was still just a man to many Africans. The reason was not simply that Northern Nigerians, who had a reputation for their loyalty to the British in contrast to their neighbours in the South and other Africans, did not want to ruffle any of the colonial master's feathers. Religion, specifically Islam, represented a source of difference from and ethical superiority over European imperialism. The Gandhian movement, by this time fully committed to non-violence and to *swadeshi* (economic independence from foreign imports), was but one kind of political possibility. Africans also understood Muslim Indian nationalism through Ahmadiyya missionaries, whose leaders promoted independent Muslim statehood. One of the most prominent Ahmadis, the barrister Zafrullah Khan, presided over the All-India Muslim League in 1931, and despite theological disagreements with other Muslims helped nurture the idea of Pakistan.[4] A theocratic state held out a real possibility for some Africans, who did not see Indian nationalism in the ways the British did or in the way Indian nationalists sought to export it.

Gandhi's influence was indeed great, but the question of India and Indians in Africa and African-Indian relations with the coming end of European empires was not viewed by Africans in any singular way. While the Indian diaspora in Africa represented a new kind of problem, African independence was being articulated not only through a push for economic independence but also through expressions of cultural autonomy and self-respect that were being thwarted by British efforts to quash anti-colonial protest and Indian protectionism over its idea of Indianness. The nature of African-Indian entanglements became a distinct sphere of resistance to exclusion and superiority in everyday life, while the political rhetoric of Afro-Asian solidarity in the 1950s masked many of these grassroots negotiations.

Danger in a growing diaspora

African-Indian tensions in East Africa were rising in the interwar years because of increasing numbers of Indians arriving and their changing economic fortunes.[5] In Kenya, Indian labourers who had worked on the British railway and other colonial schemes began to open small shops (*dukka*) that were supplied by European importers and wealthier Indian merchants, allowing them to gain a stronger economic foothold. Tanganyika, which changed from having a German colonial government to becoming a League of Nations Mandate Territory under British administration after World War I, saw its mainland Indian population grow. Whereas in decades past Muslim Indians had lived on the island of Zanzibar, Indian railway workers now opened small shops in rural areas on the mainland. Throughout Eastern Africa, whites feared competition with the Indian-origin population in import businesses and land acquisition. The discourse of a British government "protecting" Africans from

Asian predations filled the newspapers by the 1920s.[6] In Kenya, Sana Aiyar notes, Indian leaders responded with different kinds of arguments—about their civilising influence on Africans and their protection towards them—to prove they had historic and positive connections to Africans, and to refute British depictions of their rapacious greed for African wealth and land.[7]

In Ethiopia, Indians joined the global protest against the 1935 Italian invasion of Ethiopia. As one of two African states that had remained independent in the early twentieth century, the invasion unified African anti-colonial activists, African-American communities, and Indian leaders like Gandhi and Nehru. Mass demonstrations against the British in India were turned towards the cause of opposing the Italian fascists.[8] British officials worried that resident Indians in East Africa might show vocal opposition, which had to be tamped down, "lest the appearance be given that [the] government of India supports Ethiopia".[9] The relationship between Ethiopia and India stretched back thousands of years. Many of the Africans descended from slaves, warriors, and others who travelled to India in the medieval era from the Horn of Africa. In the nineteenth century, many Indians from Gujarat, working as merchants as well as unskilled craftsmen and labourers, began settling in Aden and then Ethiopia—they were able to establish trading businesses under the Emperor Menelik II's rather open policy towards foreign exchange and networks.[10]

Yet behind the unity against European occupation, a dark cloud was brewing. Many Indians in Ethiopia were Muslim, which appears to have worried Haile Selassie once he was reinstalled in 1943 after the Italian occupation. Two years later, the Ethiopian government ordered the expulsion of an Indian and a Yemeni who were given ten days to vacate the country.[11] The Indian had lived in the country for 42 years. The British government in India was told that both men had been discovered to be members of a secret fanatical Moslem society, working against Ethiopian interests and interfering in local politics. The Indian has been granted a further delay because of a civil case brought against him by an Italian, but is being prevented by the local authorities from going to Addis Ababa to defend his case in High Court.[12]

The Christian Ethiopian government had tolerated Muslims as long as interreligious relations were asymmetric and clearly defined—Muslims were classified as "Muslims living in Ethiopia" until 1974.[13] And the sense of rising Muslim activism worried the Ethiopian and British authorities, given the wider regional politics from Egypt to Arabia. Moreover, the rising calls amongst Indian Muslims for a two-state solution exposed intra-Muslim conflicts—in 1935, the writer Muhammad Iqbal had recommended that the Ahmadiyya sect start their own separate state, which prompted questioning from Nehru about Muslim unity.[14]

Muslim Indians in Africa began to worry that a Hindu-dominated India would leave them permanently displaced. In 1941, for example, two Muslim Indians in Nyasaland exchanged correspondence about their bad situation: "it is certain that the condition of the Indians is in no way better than that of the Jews in the world. The colour distinction in the minds of the white races has not diminished one bit".[15] The analogy to the Jews was an increasingly common turn in Muslim Indians' arguments about the unique displacement they suffered.[16]

Certainly such talk heightened fear of Indian colonisation in Africa. In a communiqué from 1944 intercepted by the Egyptian censors, an Indian identified as Dr Nazir Ahmed appeared to invite Ahmadi missionaries to evangelise in Ethiopia. He wrote:

In this country God has arranged for the improvement and reform of the inhabitants after bringing a great change twice in a century. The original inhabitants of this country have become a ruling nation and possess power and dignity. They do not like to see the white nation and keeping in touch with them. The question of liking Indians and Asiatics and keeping their service is under consideration. For example I have been given the position of Civil Surgeon here.

Moreover we are enjoying the liberty of a free nation under their easy and simple laws. There is a great demand in this country for skilled and qualified mechanics, doctors, physicians, compounders, stenographers, typists and ordinary clerks ... All needy persons particularly belonging to the Ahmadya [sic] Movement should communicate with me by air mail through Nazir Ahmed Aama and Kharja (Supervisor of General and Foreign Affairs), so that arrangements could be made for obtaining their permits to enter this country. All correspondence should be made by Airmail as it takes more than three months by seamail. The Allmighty Lord is creating favourable circumstances for the spreading of the Ahmadya movement in this country, which is very widespread for getting employment. All the officers of this government have become unpleasant and doubtful of the white nation. Even Indian officers serving under the white ruling nation are not liked by them. There is so much abundance of money here and food stuffs are so cheap, as has never been seen in any other country.[17]

The invitation was for more Indians to come to Ethiopia to seize on rich opportunities, including to exploit the anti-white feeling after the Italian occupation. When the Indian government sent a "goodwill" mission to Ethiopia in 1948, with the stated purpose of building on the "general good impressions of Indians in Ethiopia, more so than in other countries",[18] the Indian delegate warned that the "Indian Muslims are giving financial assistance to the Arab League". The Ethiopian representative in turn emphasised that if any "drastic action were taken against the Muslims", it should be seen as anti-Muslim, not as anti-Indian.

In West Africa too, Muslim Indians, amongst the relatively small diaspora there, began to claim they were being targeted by Africans and being forced to assimilate. The Ahmadiyya's past pronouncements of a shared cause with Africans gave way to complaints to the British of their mistreatment in the Gold Coast and Nigeria. In the 1930s, M. Nazir Ahmad, the Indian Ahmadi in charge of the Saltpond mission, defended his freedom to preach in Northern Ghana, amongst historically Muslim African communities. An Ahmadi convert, Salihu, the son of the Liman of the town of Wa, became the focus of riots that broke out to stop the Ahmadis from continuing their activities in Wa. Despite British sympathy for the Ahmadiyya, the colonial chief commissioner reported with some concern that this was the first time he knew of "religious differences being the direct cause of a riot in the Gold Coast".[19] Disfavour for the Indian mission grew. For his part, the Liman denounced his son in a letter, calling him a "confusionist" and "the key which opens all disorder".[20]

The presence of the Indian Ahmadis was escalating the chaos and British involvement in African-Indian affairs, where there had once been relatively peaceful relations. In 1947, in Zaria Province of Nigeria, Mr F. R. Hakeem, an Ahmadi Indian missionary, wrote a letter to the British Resident to complain of a recent ban on his sect from praying in its own separate mosque. The emir of Zaria for his part lodged his own complaint, and explanation, with the British authorities, reporting that the Nigerian Ahmadi community had long had a divisive effect due to its insistence on multiple Friday prayers (*qutba*), control over its own mosque, denouncing of non-Ahmadi Muslims, and imposition of directives from the sect's leadership thousands of miles away.[21] The emir of Zaria, after consulting with other Muslim leaders and fearing the agitation of the *ulema* (scholars), felt he had to "assert his position as a religious leader and to put right things which they considered had gone wrong".[22] He saw his measure not as a ban but rather an effort to unify Muslims, whom the Ahmadi missionary had attempted to divide by publicly announcing that "any Muslim not following him [the Indian missionary] was dead".[23] To put the rights of the Ahmadiyya, who numbered only 31, over those of the nearly 500,000 Muslims of Zaria would be a failure, he argued, on the part of British authorities who had vowed to protect Islam if Muslim rulers remained loyal to the colonial government.

The tactic of the missionary Hakeem in pleading his case to the British authorities on the grounds of religious freedom is telling. He wrote that the Northern Nigerian Muslim rulers "act like poison and say they are an antidote. They are an enemy to society and an enemy to Islam. Their hearts are void of sympathy but they conceal themselves".[24] Decrying the emir's Maliki interpretation of jihad as violent struggle, the missionary recounted how he and his sect had long supported Britain's "peaceful rule", citing the pamphlet "The British Government and Jihad" penned by Mirza Ghulam Ahmad in 1907, to prove his point. He also cited his own letter published in a Nigerian newspaper denouncing the African workers' strikes that had rocked Nigeria in 1945. The Indian painting of Africans as dangerous jihadists did not work with the British officials, who resolved the conflict by requiring the Ahmadis to join the single Friday prayer to be allowed in town, led by a new imam appointed by the emir.

Indians in Africa had to acknowledge African authority, but around the continent many Indians continued to petition the British for special dispensation. Indians often appealed to the British on the grounds of potential African violence, making the most of Indians' international reputation for non-violence. In Kenya, during the Mau Mau struggle against colonial occupation, some prominent Indians supported the fighters and defended violence as the last option; even Nehru took this position, albeit with some consternation. Yet many other Indians felt under physical threat from the Mau Mau and sided with the British and African loyalists. They joined the Home Guard, beating and stealing from Africans in retaliation.[25]

The political strategy of situational separatism was hardly new. Gandhi deployed it decades earlier by emphasising the "civilisational" and racial superiority of Indians over Africans in South Africa. Indian racialisation of militant resistance in the era of Indian independence was a feature of the self-righteousness and victimisation that Indians were cultivating.

Economic grievances were also growing. Even in West Africa, grumbling about Indian shopkeepers regularly appeared in African newspapers. Fluctuations in the prices of everyday goods available in Indian shops impacted large segments of the population, whereas fewer Africans were able to shop at the more expensive European and Lebanese shops.[26] Cultural competition and the fear of Indian cultural domination were significant too. Indians spread throughout the British Empire were no longer simply migrants working in African colonies, but were those "whom Indian nationalists thought of ... as dispersed fragments of a great Indian nation-in-the-making who had their role to play in the struggle for freedom".[27] India was constituted by those outside through unlikely elements:

> Religion, more than an Indian culture which remained largely undefined, was often seen as the major link between these dispersed communities and the "Motherland". Hindu preachers, both Arya Samajists and "Sanatanists" as well as Sikh priests, and Muslim mullahs often visited these communities, and, in a reverse movement, pilgrims from as far away as Fiji or Guyana travelled to Benares, Amritsar, and other holy places in India. Obviously, before the era of mass air travel, these movements were on a relatively modest scale, but they occurred nevertheless. So, if the notion of "diaspora" did not exist, some of its underpinnings were already there.[28]

Religion, particularly religious nationalism, was not, however, defined simply by primordial attachments, but developed in a cultural economy spread far beyond India.

Even after the slaughter of millions of Jews during World War II, comparisons between Indians and Jews were used to stoke fears of Indian settlement in Africa. A 1953 letter in *The East African Standard*, signed by a "Kenya African" (but blamed by Indian leaders on British propaganda), argued:

> History so I read, says Indians visited the Coast of East Africa during monsoon winds many thousand years ago even before the first white man set foot on African soil. The purpose undoubtedly of their visit, was to purchase slaves and other obtainable goods from the Arabs who were a nuisance by then in Africa. This ungodly game dragged on for many years, the Indian eagerly awaiting the arrival of slave caravans in the coast, risking nothing but money, while the Arab penetrates the interior among hostile Africans, risking both life and money. During the whole of this period, the East Africa coast visitor the honourable Indian friend never thought of developing the country or teaching the primitive African something new worth his visit. I do not see also what assistance or Liberation the Indians in India could give the Kenya African if they never rendered them any in the whole of that period of the dark days ...
>
> The birth rate of Indians, on which I must say a word, is terribly increasing that in a hundred years' time we will have a million and this will just mean more trouble as to where to accommodate them. The Government should take the responsibility of checking and controlling their present birth rate system.[29]

The author goes on to compare the Indian in Africa to the Jew in Palestine, both of whom wanted to "drain these lands to the last drop". The spectre of Indian colonisation began to infect West Africa as well, where anti-Indian feelings were rising in the Gold Coast on the eve of Indian independence. In a secret report, the High Commission in Accra relayed fears that British propaganda of Indian support for the Gold Coast's independence was part of "a well-thought plan by India to colonise Africa beginning with the Gold Coast after the British had left the country".[30] Articles in the *Daily Graphic* newspaper suggested the plot was working. While Britain was still very much part of the problem between Africans and Indians, there was no denying the growing resentment in reckoning with the past.

Desires for cultural independence

While local tensions simmered, the independent Indian government took a strong public stance in supporting Africans' rights to self-determination. In 1946, India withdrew its High Commissioner to South Africa in protest against racial segregation, and Nehru's interim Congress-led government brought the issue of the poor treatment of Indians in South Africa before the General Assembly of the United Nations.[31] Not long after, in 1947, Kwame Nkrumah returned to the Gold Coast from overseas to work with the United Gold Coast Convention party to lead protests against the British government, with Nehru voicing India's support for Nkrumah and what would become Sub-Saharan Africa's first independent nation.[32] A few years later, Nehru would host the acting secretary of the Kenya African Union, Joseph Murumbi, in New Delhi and voice some modicum of support for the Mau Mau.

Yet these overtures did little more than paper over grievances. In South Africa in 1949, the year after the Nationalist Party victory formalised apartheid, anti-Indian riots broke out in Durban. Indians were killed, beaten, and raped, and their property was defaced. Over 140 people died.[33] While the government authorities blamed long-simmering tensions, other reports, including from the Indian High Commission's office, refuted this conclusion, saying that the Nationalist Party had disseminated anti-Indian propaganda with promises that seized Indian property would be turned over to Africans. Both of these explanations ignore the working-class sympathies of some of those who destroyed Indian property.[34]

Afterwards, leaders of the African and Indian political parties felt that the white authorities had manipulated both sides, trying to use the riots to prove that Blacks were violent and unfit for self-rule and to lay the groundwork for repatriation of Indians. The government of India under Nehru, for its part, wanted a return to good, friendly relations and encouraged Natal Indians, as it did with Kenyan Indians, to work with Africans. Though middle-class Indians felt betrayed by Nehru, they worked with the African National Congress leaders in Natal and the Natal Indian Congress to resolve lingering conflicts and normalise relations. African grievances about being blocked from securing transport operators' licences, and the contemptuous attitudes of Indians towards Africans, including their segregation of African cinema-goers, were aired and discussed. Though some of these conflicts were resolved, segregation effectively took the issues off the table and left some festering wounds: "Even though [Natal ANC leader] Champion welcomed Government of India stand on African economic advance and even quoted Nehru at public meetings in Zulu to promote inter-racial harmony, he remained unconvinced of the local Indian middle class and as long as he was its leader, Natal ANC kept its distance from the National Indian Conference".[35]

Tensions grew in Ghana too, despite Nkrumah's solidarity with Nehru. The Anti-Inflation Campaign Committee in Accra, founded by Chief Nii Kwabena Bonne II, organised a boycott of imported goods sold by local Indian shopkeepers, as well as their European and Lebanese counterparts, in 1947. They saw all of these sellers as part of the apparatus that was profiteering off African consumers.[36] On the last day of the month-long boycott, ex-soldiers who had fought for the British in World War II were preparing to present a petition to the British Governor when police shot and killed two men and wounded others.[37] Protests ensued, and the police arrested Nkrumah and several other leaders. The British also struck back with ferocious censorship of the African press, jailing anyone suspected of writing "seditious" articles and blaming communism and Blacks' "racial hatred". They also banned any migrants entering the Gold Coast who appeared to have no visible means of support and, of course, anyone appearing to be anti-British.[38] The immigration surveillance led to restrictions on all Indians other than demonstrably successful businesspeople, thus creating even more reasons for class conflicts between Africans and Indians.

Yet in the Durban and Accra episodes, Africans were voicing more than anger that foreigners sold goods at high prices. The protests of the ex-servicemen in the Gold Coast—as a vanguard in the growing anti-colonial movement—and the Zulus who detested segregated cinema, were both protests against exclusion from a cultural economy. African soldiers numbering in the hundreds of thousands had served in European armies—Allied and Axis—during World War II, and the British Army's employment of West and East African troops to defeat the Italians in the African theatre and the Japanese in Burma, brought to the fore a number of problems: the discrimination non-white soldiers faced, the more meagre rations they received, and, for Africans, their very long distance from home. The soldiers wanted and sometimes got, as a result of their agitations, better food and comfortable clothing, as well as access to sex, alcohol, cigarettes, and entertainments such as newspapers, illustrated books, films, handset radios, and sports equipment.[39] In Burma—a difficult, remote theatre of operations that even British and Indian soldiers complained about—East and

West African soldiers far from home were refused the leave they were promised and subjected to discrimination from Indian soldiers and civilians even more than from the British.[40] While Africans faced scorn from local communities, who spread rumours of cannibalism and rape, Africans also held contempt for Indians. Yet new African-Indian relationships formed, such as liaisons between African men and Indian working women that provided both parties with domestic comforts and physical intimacies. What made life endurable for African soldiers on the frontlines, "comforts funds" like those created for Nigerian forces in 1940, disappeared once they were finally repatriated to Africa. Some returned to the Gold Coast, Nigeria, and elsewhere many years after the end of the war, and were denied recognition, benefits, employment, and the life they had once had.

Indian cultural goods brought entertainment and a certain freedom from the intense censorship the British colonial authorities imposed. After the protests in the Gold Coast, the British cracked down on films to exclude the importation of virtually any films that were not about "British life and civilisation". Just as pictures and printed materials in earlier decades provoked interest and led to the invitation of Ahmadi missionaries to come to West Africa, from the latter 1920s, Indian films became popular not only amongst Indian audiences but also amongst Africans, even more so than the American, Arab, or "African" films that were made specifically to cater to African audiences.[41] Indian films proved to be far more lucrative than others. For their part, Indian cinema operators, whose numbers grew in colonies like South Africa and Tanganyika with large Indian diasporas as early as the 1930s, became embroiled in racial segregation of filmgoers and African protests against their unequal treatment.[42] Indian owners in Tanganyika who stood against desegregation in the theatres found themselves in an alliance with British authorities and conservative Africans, mostly elders, who felt the films could destabilise the moral order. After the nationalist fervour grew in India, Indians used the cinema to publicise their pride. Images of the Mahatma flashed on screens before each film at Indian cinemas. With Indian films becoming more political and popular, film distributors with networks from Southeast Asia to the Middle East and Africa had to plan for the possibility that aggressive censors might stymie their business.

Only fragments of the history of Indian films in Africa and around the world before the 1950s remain, but they reveal changing African-Indian dynamics. Cinema threatened racial segregation and older Africans felt the films challenged traditional authority. Fears about Indians sowing division came from the Empire's cracking-apart and the heavier hand that Britain might take in its remaining African colonies—through violence and censorship. These measures in turn brought about more demand for the cultural goods Africans had come to enjoy. By 1953, the Indian government estimated that its film industry was second in the world after that of the United States—India produced 259 films that year.[43]

The interests of Africans in early Indian films should not be understood apart from those that inspired Mami Wata worship and Ahmadi affiliation. Indian films in the 1930s employed "a visual field between chromolithography, theatre, and other genres".[44] They brought alive the sorts of images that had evoked such a strong response in religious imaginations. Many of the early Indian filmmakers had worked as painters and photographers, in media that drew on Indian myths and religions. Besides the colourful Hindu goddesses and gods, even Islamicate prints, which could not depict human figures, used images of roses, calligraphy, praying hands, birds, and mosques that could be worked into films.[45] A favourite theme, recalling the interspecies snake charmer and Hindu gods and goddesses, was Tarzan Ki Beti (*Tarzan's Daughter*, 1938), adapted from Edgar Rice Burroughs and Hollywood, which in the 1920s and 1930s, "became a locus of debate over the appropriateness of mingling [South Asian and American] cultural traditions".[46] In Senegal and Ghana, by the 1950s and 1960s, African viewers identified a class of Indian god films that reminded them of their own epics and myths.

Cinema soundscapes too were drawn from religious forms, particularly the *ghazal*, the romantic poem popularised through Persianate influences, with refrains that worked especially well in musical cinema. Its long and varied history from pre-Islamic Arabia, with roots in the ode (*qasida*), resonated in much of the world, including in African Islamic devotional poetry in Kiswahili and Hausa. In the twentieth century, African poets used these rhymes to express nationalist themes in a neo-classicism that expressed nostalgia for the precolonial age.[47] The Sufi and Shi'a *ghazal* traditions focused the attentions of singers and audiences towards divine love and, in seeming echo of this theme, many of the first and most popular, like *Anarkali* (1928, about an affair between a Mughal courtesan and emperor), *Yousuf Zuleikha* (1930, *Potiphar's Wife*), and *Al Hilal* (1935, an Ottoman Roman-Muslim love story with an anti-slavery message), were intense and tragic love stories.

These films played in packed theatres, but African viewers were restricted due to limited viewing spaces. Not surprisingly, a common anxiety appeared in many locations throughout the British Empire about whether the uneducated masses could or should comprehend such "cosmopolitan" culture. When cinemas were eventually desegregated, or, in the case of South Africa, used to foster a sense of Indian culture apart from others,[48] Indian importers of films recognised the enormous potential amongst African consumers and thus expanded their imports and cinema openings, although in different ways in these separate markets.

Cinema was not the only cultural arena in which the Indian presence in Africa grew. In the expanding print culture of African cities, Indians, or now Pakistanis, took on a new role in journalism. Ahmadi missionaries in Anglophone West Africa and East Africa undertook intensive efforts in English-language writing and publishing. With newsletters such as *The Moslem Sunrise* published in Detroit and *The Moslem Outlook* published in Lahore, and later briefly in Cape Town, the missionaries added a new dimension to African print culture. These were not solely religious texts but also tools for expanding English literacy. Indian-origin books and other printed matter were exported from the 1930s, but in 1943, the Indian firm Asia Publishing House was established in Bombay and led to an enormous growth in exports of publications in English and Indian languages.[49]

The Indian population in Africa was growing in the years immediately preceding independence: men were increasingly bringing their wives and children to settle, and Indian employees outnumbered their African counterparts. The increase in migrants meant an expanded flow of cultural goods. These changes led to contradictory effects of fear of migration alongside the whetting of African tastes for Indian goods, that were often cheaper and distinct from European and American products. It was debatable what and how much Indians were willing to sell to Africans as consumers.

India's eyes towards the West

Like Gandhi, Nehru realised he could learn valuable lessons from studying happenings on the African continent. In the early years of a decolonising Afro-Asia and the Cold War, solidarity meant many kinds of networks—trade unions, literary collaborations, and anti-apartheid struggles—but they were multidirectional in surprising ways.[50] Nehru recognised the need for India and Indians to tread softly, and soft power meant careful negotiations with African political leaders and potential allies to iron out local issues between Africans and Indians in Africa, while not disturbing the narrative of solidarity between the nations.

The Indian Council for Cultural Relations (ICCR) was founded in 1950 by the first education minister, Maulana Abul Kalam Azad, to play a significant role in establishing India's soft power in Africa. Amongst Azad's work was expanding India's overseas scholarship programme, which started in 1945. Azad had the reputation of being a staunch nationalist who worked closely with Gandhi, and who later in his life often criticised sectarian approaches to communal interests, particularly amongst Muslims. Yet as a young man in the 1910s, Azad was a "celebrated theorist of transnational jihad" as "closely imbricated" with anti-colonial agitation.[51] Western Christian hostility to Islam had shaped his effort to decolonise education in the same way as it had affected Africans like Blyden and the Ahmadiyya.

ICCR scholarships for Africans to come to India in the intervening years between Indian and African independence produced a very secular kind of solidarity. Africans on tour saw factories, public works projects, and universities. They also saw at first hand the caste system and the inequalities it produced. Yet Indian caste did not apply to men like R. Mugo Gatheru, who felt a sense of freedom from the *kipande* (pass) system he endured in Kenya.[52] Less well known was the ICCR's sponsorship of religious tours of Indians to Africa. It was perhaps Azad's "universalistic vision" of the Islamic world that undergirded the religious work the ICCR began in 1954 by organising the trip of a swami (Hindu religious teacher) of the Ramakrishna Mission to explore the possibilities of a humanitarian mission for East Africa and an intellectual one for West Africa. Swami Nisreyasananda, who spent nearly four months travelling around the African continent, reported on the high interest in spiritual matters in West Africa and the challenges in Kenya, where the

Mau Mau emergency had exacerbated tensions between Africans and Indians and seemed to offer little room for cross-cultural dialogue.

The ICCR, forwarding the swami's notes, commented that "the African in East Africa is backward educationally. West Africa—and particularly the Gold Coast—presents a different picture. The percentage of educated Africans is, perhaps, nowhere in Africa to the South of the Sahara as high as in the Gold Coast".[53] Swami Nisreyasananda had met Muslim Ahmadis in both Kenya and the Gold Coast, and based on these meetings recommended strongly that in the latter, Indians should establish a centre that was "completely multi-religious and multi-racial, in which the people gathering for philosophic and religious discussions would have the opportunity of forming their own views".[54] Significantly, the idea of East and West African difference was one echoed by West Africans themselves. One Gold Coaster, an ex-soldier, wrote: "We West Africans are quite different from those from East Africa. I say this because in East Africa there were some whites who had been able to build their own part of the town for whites and a part for Blacks, but we never experienced anything like that in our own country".[55] A similar sentiment, though made in an altogether different vein, was espoused by the former South African minister Oswald Pirow:

> Nehru is just another coolie ... There are some non-whites who, with White education, have made White moral principles their own. One example of this is Booker T. Washington ... There is another sort of non-White—you get them on the west coast of Africa but particularly in India, who accompany a great amount of book learning with a total lack of moral responsibility. An outstanding example of this undesirable type is the Prime Minister of India, Mr. Nehru.[56]

In exploring the possibility of an Indian religious mission to West Africa, the Ramakrishna Mission sought to construct a kinship between West Africans and Indians that was by design distinct from and superior to the race relations in East Africa. This strategy involved a denigration of East Africa as a region and East Africans as "unprepared" for certain kinds of transnational projects. The intended audience of the government-sponsored spiritual mission was multireligious and African and only incidentally included any resident Indians. Following such a proposal would, it seemed from the swami's tour, unite Hindu and secular Indian actors in West Africa with Muslim missionaries to symbolise India's pluralism.

Indian officers building relations in West Africa saw many of the same elements that the swami had. In 1955, the year after the swami's tour, the Indian press attaché, Mahesh Jugran, completed his own tour of Nigeria and the Gold Coast as part of the formal opening of the Indian Commission for West Africa in Accra. He noted a number of key observations. First, he, like others, made a very clear distinction between West Africans and East Africans, claiming that Jomo Kenyatta and "immature youth" would "turn to the path of violence" with little hesitation. Second, he blamed the British for not investing in public works, transportation, or educational institutions apart from a few exceptions—of the road between Lomé and Lagos, he wrote: "it is indeed intriguing to notice the road on the British side of the Custom barrier all in pits whereas across the barrier hardly two yards from the British territory is an excellent road comparable to any first-class highway in the world".[57] Third, while Jugran heard admiration for Nehru, he fielded harsh questions on all sides about India's entry into the Commonwealth despite being a republic, doubts about its food production to date, and religious politics, convincing him that the British controlled the West African media about India. The common refrain about Indians' anti-Muslim sentiments in Nigeria all but confirmed his suspicions:

At every party that the British had arranged for me, I met Nigerians who were as suspicious about India as perhaps a Nigerian nationalist was about the bonafides of the British intentions. Repeatedly when I saw men who accused Pandit Nehru of imperialism in Kashmir, in Goa and in other parts of South East Asia, I could not but conclude that all these receptions and all these parties were a deliberate attempt to impress upon me that the people of Nigeria were not so blindly the followers of India, as was perhaps believed by some people in the world ... there was a strong desire to know about the plans for Pakistan.

A few Northerners dressed in their long Arab-like robes were introduced to me as Muslims and they took me to task for what they described as our shameful treatment of Muslims in India, of our aggression in Kashmir and so on. The usual type of questions, as one heard in Pakistan, were put to me. My trip to the North confirmed this too, that the British were trying their best to introduce the Pakistani idea and perpetuating it in Nigeria. It was indeed a clever game of the British to kill two birds with one stone.[58]

Jugran also recounted the deliberate attempts to embarrass India on the caste problem. One British officer asked him his caste in a meeting with several others: "When I told him that I was born in a Brahmin family he went on to introduce me to all the African guests as a man belonging to the highest caste in India. It provoked Africans to remark that they hoped I was treating my 'untouchables' kindly".[59]

Finding Naseem Saifi, an Ahmadiyya missionary who had been in Nigeria since 1945—before Partition—proved to be useful for Jugran to refute the perception of Hindu discrimination:

I am sure, they [the Nigerians] never expected me to embrace the head of the Ahmadiya [sic] movement in Nigeria, Mr. Naseem Saifi when he was introduced to me as a Pakistani. Fortunately for me this man too did not indicate anything which would have given a hint to strangers that we were a separate people. Apart from his work as an

Ahmadiya Missionary, he displayed the same patriotism, the same unity of India irrespective of its religions, as was expected from any citizen bred and brought up in a secular country. I felt proud of this man and deliberately spent most of my time with him just to indicate that this question of Muslims in India was a bogey started by the British in India.[60]

Though Jugran did not mention Saifi's background in his notes on the visit, the missionary was an important figure known throughout Nigeria for his work in journalism. In 1947, he began regular radio broadcasts via the Nigerian Broadcasting Corporation, focusing specifically on Muslim affairs. He helped spearhead the first English-language Muslim weekly newspaper, *The Truth*, published out of Lagos starting in 1951. This work kept him in close contact with Muslim Nigerian intellectuals and political leaders, as well as non-Muslims like Nnamdi Azikiwe and Chief Obafemi Awolowo, who both had careers as journalists.[61] Saifi joined Nigerian delegations, meeting honoured guests from Ethiopian Emperor Haile Selassie to American boxing champion and civil rights activist Muhammad Ali, who visited Nigeria in 1964. Saifi identified as a Pakistani, as his publication of the book *In Defence of Pakistan*, a collection of his editorials and other writings, revealed, though not until after Jugran's visit. Jugran also probably did not realise, or at least did not acknowledge, that Nigerians' views about India were not shaped entirely by British propaganda but were also constantly reshaped by the Nigerian press, which was itself no unified voice. Saifi, with his connection to this literary world of West Africa, had commanded enormous influence.

It is entirely possible that the Indian government wanted to keep good relations with the Ahmadiyya for other reasons. With Partition and the move of the Ahmadiyya headquarters from Qadian, India, to Rabwah, Pakistan, the Indian authorities discovered a large cache of arms, many modern and foreign made.[62]

Moving to Rabwah uprooted the Ahmadis from farmland and other sources of income. The community's internal structure changed in relation to the shift in national boundaries, and critics of the Ahmadiyya argue that Ahmadi leaders financed their activities and lavish lifestyle by "sale of title to burial in the 'heavenly graveyard' at Qadian".[63] Transnational connectivity became all the more important. With Partition, the Ahmadiyya Khalifatul Masih Bashiruddin Mahmud Ahmad emphasised the role of missions in the sect:

> At the present time Africa may be regarded in some respects the weakest, in other respects, the strongest part of the world. It is weak to outward appearance, but strong in its possibilities. Ahmadiyyat spotted this secret about 24 years ago and sent her missionaries to Africa. As a result of this timely action thousands of people abandoned Christianity and became Muslim. At present the best organisation of Muslims in Africa is the Ahmadiyya. Christian missionaries and workers now hesitate to confront Ahmadiyyat.[64]

Arguing that neither Arabs nor anyone else controlled Islam, he wrote that Ahmadiyyat, by its missionary expansion, had established a jamaat where none had existed. With Hindus having little idea of religious missions, the success of the Muslim missionaries could help India shape a pluralist outreach promising "goodwill to all religions" (*sarva dharma sambhava*). This was no natural outgrowth of Hinduism, but instead a carefully constructed practice that had an important root in Africa.

Fears of religious conflict and partition dividing Nigeria at the moment of its independence were also at work. Jugran had taken his cue from Nigerian statesman Chief Obafemi Awolowo, who had recently travelled to India and suspected the British of cultivating pro-Arab Islamic brotherhood sentiments in the North of Nigeria to force a difficult situation of separatism, while also degrading

Nehru and India as anti-Muslim to paint Nigerians who sym-
pathised with Nehru as troublemakers to the Muslim Nigerians:

> "It is amazing", said Awolowo, "that the British refuse to learn from
> their mistakes. They created Pakistan with the hope that Pakistan
> will remain in their pocket, but it has instead gone into a pocket
> which the British do not like. The same thing can happen to the
> North [of Nigeria]. The British are encouraging these tendencies.
> They are helping in the revival of Islam in the North. They are tell-
> ing them of Pakistan, of the advantages of having an Islamic State.
> The British are telling the Northerners that they were a people who
> had a background, unlike the Southerners who were 50 years ago
> bushmen". This, added Awolowo, pleased the Northerners. They saw
> themselves as Arabs, as members of a big Islamic brotherhood, as the
> people who created civilisations on [sic] the valley of the Nile. They
> now looked towards the Sudan, of living with the Sudanese than
> with the people who lived in Lagos.[65]

Ill feelings were being caused by the British in order to prevent
agreement on the path forward to independence.

Jugran highlighted other new factors, notably the competition
between Nigeria and Ghana. Nigerians like Nnamdi Azikiwe,
whom Jugran trusted, expressed annoyance that they had not
been invited to the Bandung meeting, to which the Indian
replied that they did not know which region's premier to invite.[66]
The Indian government vowed thereafter to include all three
regional premiers in international invitations. The location of the
Indian consulate in Accra also provoked Nigerian disagreement.
Perhaps most surprisingly, Jugran felt nothing but contempt for
the Indian businessmen, mostly Sindhis, who were popular with
West Africans for the varied goods they carried but an embar-
rassment to the Indian government:

> It is because the Indian businessman is so dishonest himself that he
> considers everybody in the world dishonest. He lives in West Africa,

he sells his goods and makes money from the people of West Africa ... but his ideas are ... treacherous ... Perhaps an Indian is the only man who openly addresses an African as a "Blackman"! Ironic it may appear to be a citizen of India in the Gold Coast and Nigeria considers himself "whiter" than the man who has actually passed as a "whiteman" for a century.[67]

In opening formal relations with West Africa, the Indian authorities learned they needed to tread carefully in religious politics and, besides presenting India as a tolerant and plural nation, also consider African complexity. Swami Nisreyasananda's visit suggested a way for Hindu missions to present themselves as non-proselytising and universalist. This idea, however, was quickly challenged within Indian government circles as idealistic and naive. One Indian officer in the Gold Coast reported that he had recently met an American visitor who mentioned groups of people in West Africa who were seriously interested in Vedanta and were taking correspondence courses from an American group called "The Self-Realization Fellowship", founded by the yogi and guru Paramahansa Yogananda in California:

> You will appreciate that it would be unwise to allow credulous Africans to be exploited by money-making centres, professing to teach Indian philosophy, especially of America and for that matter even of India. You will observe that there has been a great deal of exploitation of this credulity of the African by various societies and manufacturers in India professing to send out charms and medicines. Official action is being taken to stop this. However, intellectual hunger for metaphysical thought cannot be bottled up and, in any case, we cannot ban contact of people in West Africa with places in America or India.[68]

America had become a virtual mecca, as it were, for Hindu-inspired movements like Yogananda's Self-Realization Fellowship founded in 1920. That it had appeared in West Africa so quickly seemed to surprise the Indian government. Just as the Ahmadis had found a conduit to West Africa via the United States, Hindu "new religions" appeared to be doing the same. However, in the political circumstances of the time, with the Indian government worried about its reputation, the circulation of Hindu ideas from America implied an illegitimacy that the officer suggested his superiors should nip in the bud. He recommended that the government recognise and encourage respectable societies and individuals who could "make available true philosophic ideas of India" to Africans. This recommendation also contained the familiar suspicion of the Indian diaspora as rapacious entrepreneurs, this time peddling inauthentic Hinduism.

The idea did not generate immediate enthusiasm, and in fact led to an intense debate in India's Ministry of External Affairs over the idea of Indian religious missions. Should India send doctors with "missionary zeal" or a Hindu swami to talk about Vedanta philosophy and other non-controversial topics?[69] As one opponent lashed out:

> I am quite certain that our funds will be far better spent in starting libraries and in giving more scholarships to African students etc. I also fear that even "non-controversial religious" activity on the part of Indian religious Missions in Africa will be misunderstood and will lead to embarrassment rather than understanding and better relations.[70]

During the colonial era, Hindu Indians of the higher castes in particular had vociferously denounced Christian proselytism, and beginning in the twentieth century, became locked in a virtual war with Muslims over the issue of reportedly forced conversions. The word "missionary" held negative connotations for many Indians in the first Congress government, but it was of course historically powerful for Africans and could be malleable.

India's commercial diaspora created the impression of having a colonising agenda; Indians who had fiercely resisted European

Christian missions had to see the hypocrisy of Hindu missions. Yet African interest in Indian religions was undeniable. Thus the government of India began to regulate Hindu missions in particular, and sponsor some more directly such as the Ramakrishna Mission. The proliferation of Indian-made religious goods has been traced to this period in the Gold Coast and Nigeria, with items including Indian devotional literature, Hindu images, and other paraphernalia including beads, particular herbs, and statues.[71] Anthropologist Rosalind Hackett refers to the Hare Krishna "Bookmobiles" in Nigeria and Togo, which began to appear by the 1970s, if not earlier, probably from a US source.[72] The situation was different in Southern and Eastern Africa, argued Shri Apa Pant, independent India's first Commissioner to British East Africa, where

> if we desire that our Indian friends settled [there] to do their duty by their adopted mother country, we shall have to assure that emotionally and intellectually they get guidance that would enable them to act properly. The visits of people like Shri Swami Nisreyasananda to East Africa does indeed help the Indians chiefly.[73]

Whereas in those areas, Indian settlers' behaviour undid any good work of the Indian government, in Western Africa, the absence of Indians as well as the cultural independence of indigenous peoples was ideal. Pant saw this after transferring from Nairobi to Accra, and wrote:

> In Nigeria and Gold Coast they say that after attaining their freedom, the first monument they will erect would be to their greatest general—the Mosquito!! Right from the start, it was evident that white dominions or large scale European settlement would be impossible in this zone. Africa conquers the white man here ... Thus, though the West will take part in the developments here and exploit economically this Zone, build industries and run big business concerns, the West will not "influence" this part of Africa in the sense that West Africans

will never be subservient to the rule of the West or will ever become an imitation of the West. West Africa will remain West Africa after absorbing all that Western capitalism has to give.[74]

In celebrating West Africans' freedom, Pant seemed not only to be contrasting it with other parts of Africa but also with India, where the influence of the British ran so deep after hundreds of years of colonial rule. His comments reflected too the self-doubt of Indians about what being Indian meant in the modern world, an issue that also came to the fore in the debate about missions that persisted through to Ghanaian independence in 1957. Seeking to put a hold on the Ramakrishna Mission centre in Accra because of the impending changes, the Under-Secretary of India's Ministry of External Affairs asked about one of the stated aims of Indian policy in Africa:

> Namely, "to show to the people in this country something of our way of living and thinking, with special emphasis on our philosophy of life." Should this be one of our aims? If so, what exactly is meant by "our way of living." Are our people—particularly our own officers in East and Central Africa—living as the masses live in India? Perhaps, the answer is in the negative. European way of life is the order of the day in East Africa. It is no use making the already confused situation in Africa more so by introducing a new way of life there. As regards the propagation of our philosophy, it may [be] pointed out that the needs of Africa today are material, not spiritual. Let the metaphysical activities be put over to a later date [when] Africa will be materially well off.[75]

In other communications, notably with the representatives of India's Commonwealth partner Canada, officials expressed bitterness about the racial politics then prevailing in Africa, where Europeans, Indians, and Africans all seemed entirely self-interested and incapable of cooperation.[76]

The most hopeful outlook an Indian government officer could have at this time, it seemed, was to blame the West and blur its dichotomising and divisive racial hierarchies. Apa Pant, whose close relationship with Nehru and long experience in Africa gave him a lot of sway, refused the false choice between African or Western and placed India in the role of forging a third way:

> Was there a third alternative? Could one envisage a synthesis of all that was vital, satisfying, beautiful and energising from all the cults and cultures, backgrounds and histories, African, Indian, Islamic and Christian? ... It was a dream of some of us that a new identity, a new personality, should be developed: more mature and more versatile, a new man for the modern age, with the potential of a world citizen ...[77]

This third way fit with Nehru's idea of non-alignment that marked India's biggest contribution to foreign relations during this period. But the wrangling behind the scenes reveals how much this was merely aspirational.

Conclusion

As racial segregation was breaking down, tensions were rising about cultural exclusion and superiority. The government of India wanted to combat the Indian diaspora's exclusivity and arrogance by tapping into the cultural economy that had emerged in earlier decades; but they had to avoid creating a new problem of cultural imperialism. Playing directly with religious politics in Africa did not seem to be a good strategy for the new government in India to take. African challenges to the way India had decolonised was, in fact, a mirror held up to the idealists in Nehru's administration—India did not symbolise any kind of noble future to many Africans, even if they were willing to ally with Indians in their ongoing struggle to become independent of European rule. Moreover, Britain and India's own diasporas were active in undermining what goodwill Gandhi and Nehru had built with Africans.

If religious missions could not be the answer, Indians had to take the lead from Africans themselves to find bases of postcolonial commonality and solidarity. In this, West Africa continued to be the object of Indian admiration, a view that of course placed Africans in the kinds of racial hierarchy that the Europeans imperialists had. Yet, as the next chapter shows, Indians were themselves fractured, and understood racial differences in Africa through their own divisions and desires.

3

RACE AS POSTCOLONIAL STRATEGY

Introduction

The Asian-African Conference in Bandung, Indonesia, in 1955, and the first conference of the Non-Aligned Movement in Belgrade, Yugoslavia, in 1961, are held as signal events that sparked other organisations, meetings, and movements in the era of non-Western solidarity. Yet, as with many histories, they have generated myths and oversimplifications. Some notable corrections to fabulations that historians, journalists, and activists have repeated include: the selective invitations of non-Western leaders, the absence of Kwame Nkrumah at Bandung, and Nehru's insistence on putting Asia first, "because it is a smaller word, not because Asia is more important or less". In private, he objected that Afro-Asian "sounded like aphrodisiac", political scientist Robert Vitalis reminds us.[1] Racism as a tool of colonial oppression was not explicitly discussed by Nehru, Egypt's Gamal Abdel Nasser, Nkrumah's representative Kojo Botsio, nor by the Sudanese or Ethiopian delegates, but it was by the Filipino Carlos Romulo, who was a complex political figure but educated at Columbia University and reliably pro-Western.[2] Indeed, some non-Western political leaders worried that a unified "darker race" would threaten global stability, echoing the multiplying fears of the US and the British after Bandung. Race haunted Western minds especially, and it grew into a rallying cry for worldwide unity amongst Black people, especially for Malcolm X and other African-American leaders.[3]

In this shadow, a radical approach to race emerged. After French President Georges Pompidou died suddenly in 1974, his former schoolmate and close friend Léopold Senghor composed an elegy which began, "In a Tamil night". Senghor, as President of Senegal, had made an official visit to India that year, as well as to China—hence the closing words, "Pékin-Madras"—but India is more than mere setting. Present throughout the poem, India is the source of a "lexicon": Madras, jasmine, Taj Mahal, Shiva, Dravidian.[4] In a lamentation for a French leader, even considering Pompidou's reputation as sympathetic to new postcolonial nations, France's absence is conspicuous. Afro-India is the protagonist.

Senghor conjured India, especially the nation's South, as the bastion of "the Blacks of Asia" or, in Herodotus's view, "Oriental Ethiopians", in the spirit of négritude—"the self-affirmation of Black peoples or the affirmation of the values of the civilizations of the Black world"[5]—that he, Aimé Césaire, and Léon Damas developed during their time in France. In "Africanising" South India's Dravidians, Senghor mapped the planetary expanse of Blackness, but this was not simply a reaffirmation. It was an important move at this moment as a way to repudiate Jean-Paul Sartre's appraisal of négritude as "antiracist racism". The Indianisation of négritude denied its "ghettoisation" and its fate to "die" at what was an early postcolonial moment of Afro-pessimism and Indo-pessimism.[6]

Conflicts in different quarters had strained postcolonial unity—national and international. Nkrumah, one of India's stronger African allies, was toppled in a coup in 1966, the same year Nigeria had its first military takeover. The anti-apartheid movement in South Africa had brought together Black and Indian South Africans, but segregationist legislation and violence imposed isolation and criminalisation that aimed to prevent transnational solidarities. Many African countries never fully accepted India's stated motives for sending troops to join the United Nations Blue Helmets in Congo, which Nehru agreed to do with a sense of nationalist pride—an ethical commitment and political realism—about the visibility India would get by taking a leading role in the crucial African state. The failure of the UN mission plagued India's relations with Zaire and other countries, especially those that carried out indigenisation policies that negatively impacted Indian settlers in Africa.[7] Beyond this, India's border disputes with China and Pakistan dissipated African goodwill further, with only four African countries supporting India against China. Another disaster occurred with Idi Amin's expulsion of Asians from Uganda in 1972, which not only bedevilled the Organization of African Unity, but also India's relationships with many countries over the fate of refugees and lingering fears about Indian "colonisation" in Africa. Could Indian displacement from Uganda have a cascade effect around the continent?

Out of these challenges, because of Senghor, Black India, an idea with some older roots, gained new purchase and prestige, but most of all could perhaps help humanise India and Indians. Indians could be embraced within *négritude*, a global Blackness that was defined by many characteristics but most importantly the persistent struggle to overcome inferiority.[8] Whether Indians were Blacks, not just non-white allies with Blacks, was a question that Senghor was prepared to answer amid the political exigencies of the postcolonial predicament facing Africans and Indians.

Senghor's answer, through poetry, art, language, and higher education, was an altogether unique response amongst political leaders. He announced in Madras, during his 1974 trip, the establishment of a department of Indo-African Studies at Dakar University that became a collaboration between the Institut Fondamental d'Afrique Noire (IFAN), the Indian Council for Cultural Relations, and Annamalai University in Chidambaram, India, which had a notable centre of Dravidian linguistics and was in close proximity to Pondicherry, the former centre of France's colonial possessions in India.[9]

Indians responded in kind. During that 1974 trip to India, Senghor was inducted as an honorary fellow into the Indian National Academy of Letters, Sahitya Akademi, described by Suniti Chatterji, president of the Academy, in his welcome address, as a "séance of the intellect and spirit".[10] Chatterji described Africa's suffering during the slave trade, colonial era, and struggles for political freedom that had led to "a cry for elementary human rights" not just amongst Blacks but "all Lovers of Man", who "for self-purification and greater compe- tence to help through knowledge", "were eager to know what the Black Man ... really stood for". Léopold Senghor, "with his uncommon poetic vision and gifts, and his fellow-Africans, like Sheikh [sic] Anta Diop and Birago Diop, and his intimate friend, Aimé Cesaire from Martinique", set out to answer for the world:

> Is there a proper African mentality—an Africanism, as a Way of Thought and a Way of Life, which can be placed side by side with Hellenism and Hebraism, with Latinism, with Germanism and Celtism, with Slavism and Sinism, and in a broader way, with Europeanism? What are the mainsprings and expressions of this Africanism, in both thinking and living?

Chatterji believed that African intellectuals held the answers:

> Some of us have been groping to find this for ourselves, and in India too—to frame an Africanism, an African Personality, for our own satisfaction. With our want of positive knowledge and experience, it

has been just groping on the dark. The Black African has found out that Black Africa—its Mind and its Art of Life—through the Continents, is a one and single entity. The African intellectuals have exercised themselves to find out a single word describing or giving the basic character of this mentality and culture in a tabloid form. And to Léopold Sedar Senghor particularly, and his colleagues of West Africa, we are indebted for this Latin-French word—*Négritude*, as giving the working of the Black African spirit: it is the Essence or Quality of being Black, Blackness as the mental, spiritual and material Quality or Faculty.

Before continuing with a biography of Senghor and presenting the award, Chatterji recited a Hindu devotional song to the goddess Kali that *négritude* brought to mind:

I do not fear the Darkness—I do love the Dark.
When I see the Dark, I think of God, my Mother, who is
Black and Inscrutable like this Darkness.
When I see shapes of Fear and Darkness, I call upon my
Mother, the Black One.
In the midst of the Darkness, I can see the light of the rosy feet
of my Mother.

This cosmic connection between Africa and India explains Europe's absence from Senghor's "Elegy for Georges Pompidou". Chatterji translated *négritude* into reincarnation that befitted the occasion: for "his conviction of Life merging into Death and of Death being only a continuity and extension of life", "the Black Man" brought to the world his *Weltanschauung* and ethos and "a novel dimension and meaning for man's life".[11]

Senghor—with his artistry and political skill—established a racial religious connection with India. He achieved this through a dialectic of rootedness and opening, *enracinement et ouverture*. From the 1930s, he had knit Sub-Saharan and Arab-Berber Africa together through homage to the liaison between the Queen of

Sheba and Solomon—a myth central to the Ethiopian Solomonic empire—that unified African and Semite in "a more diversified concept of the continent" in *Africanité*.[12] Senghor's revisiting of these themes in his poetry paralleled his attempts to balance relations between Arab nations and Israel, but after 1973, his alliances moved in the direction of the former. With India, Senghor's visit was celebrated with Kali, the dark and arresting "goddess of India" whose boundaries are nearly impossible to discern—was she worshipped as an Aryan Vedic or Dravidian ("some may say pre-Aryan tantrik") divinity?[13] Senghor's Blackness was not just a reminder of the goddess Kali, but also an entrée into the ancient Indian history of Aryans, Dravidians, and other tribes, and the caste system that added to the groundwork of modern racial thought. Senghor became the first prominent African to enter this charged Indian fray and to bring India into Africa's racial humanism that undergirded Pan-Africanism and Afrocentrism.

This project, the brainchild of Senghor, highlighted a West African-South Indian nexus, bringing a new dimension to the "darker races" within the "darker nations". He opened new pathways in a complicated relationship with a direct engagement on the question of race in African-Indian discourse, bringing it out of the shadows and into exchange and negotiation. Senghor was driven by competition with Cheikh Anta Diop, the influential Senegalese scholar known for his pioneering Afrocentric studies, particularly of Ancient Egyptian civilisation as the cradle of human progress. Diop was highly critical of what he considered Senghor's epistemological compromises, namely *négritude*'s insistence on *métissage*, a cultural mixing that compared and connected African and European civilisations.

Senghor, for his part, did not give Diop any recognition and often repeated the racialised views of African societies of European social scientists like Leo Frobenius, whose writings about caste and culture groups in the ancient world had a significant but complicated impact on Senghor and other Black intellectuals.[14] Even with the flaws of his vision, for African-Indian relations, Senghor brought an uncommon visibility and specificity to the relationship, including with regard to what Blackness meant in aesthetic and artistic terms. In the words of Wole Soyinka, he established a framework to "map the geography of the Black race" as far as India, Papua New Guinea, the South Sea Islands, and East Timor at the time of its independence from Indonesia.[15] For India, Soyinka's summation of Senghor's two "gifts" to Africa make a great deal of sense: one, an ability for conciliation, and two, life after power. On this second point, though Soyinka meant Senghor's ability to step down from the presidency without conflict, for India, Senghor's methods helped to de-escalate Indian notions of superiority in Africa.

India's 'strange failure'

Even as the political rhetoric of Afro-Asian optimism was building from the 1955 conference in Bandung, India's position in Africa was in a difficult limbo. Africans' admiration for the Indian independence movement and Indian nationalists like Nehru began to wane. The Sino-Indian border war in 1962–63 and the Indo-Pakistan conflict in 1965 exposed India's potentially long-term weakness.[16] China's military defeat of India made some African leaders change their loyalties to the winning side. This switch seemed easier, given India's half-hearted support for violent independence struggles in colonies like Kenya and Algeria. The members of the Casablanca bloc—Algeria, Egypt, Ghana, Guinea, Libya, Mali, and Morocco— were amongst those who preferred China, along with Tanganyika. Only Congo-Léopoldville, Ethiopia, and Nigeria actively lent their support to India in its border claims, while many other countries refused to commit to one side or the other.[17]

One Indian politics observer wondered, in 1965, about "the strange failure of postwar Indian diplomacy to make any creative use of the vast reservoir of African good will built up in the 1940s".[18] The lack of a vision may have been behind the slow pace at which the Indian government debated how to make cultural alliances. Anirudha Gupta, an international relations scholar based in New Delhi, warned in 1970: "If India emphasized the commercial aspect too often, the African countries may start viewing the joint ventures as an expression rather of 'economic imperialism' than of enlightened friendship".[19] He cited several reasons why relying on the "initiative of the private sector" could spell trouble, including the nationalising policies of African countries and India that could scare off foreign private capital. He concluded that neither India nor any African country had chosen to prioritise their relationship, save for "mutual sharing of some vague sentiments".

India's strategy with its African allies had indeed been largely economic. For example, when formal relations between Ethiopia and India were established in 1948, military cooperation was the main focus; however, by the 1960s, private and public Indian capital was pouring into Ethiopia, notably into the textile industry, which, by 1974, was the third largest on the continent.[20] In Nigeria too, Indian investments in textiles and then increasingly in food and other industries were extensive, also through a combination of public and private capital. The growing branches of family businesses like that of Kishin Chand Chellaram, the Sindhi businessman who first came to Lagos in 1923, and eventually moved his family there following their expulsion from Pakistan upon Partition, illustrate Indian economic expansionism.[21] Chellaram was a textile merchant with retail shops that the family opened throughout West Africa; similar family-owned firms moved into chemicals, food packaging, and other industries. India valued its relationship with Nigeria to the extent that, despite continual fears about the tenuous political situation, it was Nehru's only stop in Africa in 1962.

Through the 1960s, Indian businesspeople in many parts of Africa received more sympathy from the Indian government than in previous years, perhaps out of a desire to appease the diaspora, even while publicly supporting African independence struggles that some Indian settlers found threatening. In Kenya, a decade after Mau Mau forced India and Indians to take sides, the Indian government encouraged private ventures, hoping the economic power of the diaspora could be harnessed to foster more anti-China sentiment and better cooperation with India.[22] Nehru's daughter, Indira Gandhi, during her goodwill mission to Eastern Africa in 1964, referred to the thousands of Indian settlers and businesspeople in Africa as "Ambassadors of India". From African perspectives, the nickname might have been an inopportune reminder of the inconsistency of Indian loyalties: India's prioritisation of Indians over all other non-whites in South Africa in its United Nations motion against the apartheid government, and Nehru's inconsistent messages to Indian settlers about their stance towards their adopted African homelands.[23] Nonetheless, his daughter remained popular throughout Africa during her tenure as Prime Minister, despite the harsh criticism she endured in India.

African countries with less direct history with India inspired hope in India's foreign officers. India's first embassy in French West Africa opened in Dakar in 1961, and from there also served Côte d'Ivoire, Niger, and Upper Volta. Ambassador Dr Nagoji Vasudev Rajkumar travelled through French West Africa soon after he took office, and wrote of his meetings with Upper Volta's Foreign Minister Lompolo Koné:

> he agrees with us so far as the policy of "non-alignment" or "non-engagement" goes. This is so because Africans are really not interested in world problems … and couldn't care less what happens in

Berlin or Geneva or Vienna. "Non-alignment" therefore is a convenient peg on which they can hang their political garments.

He gave two examples that could be called productive disengagement: first, the withdrawal of Indian troops from Congo, which both Koné and Upper Volta's President Maurice Yaméogo requested. Second, Rajkumar related an incident concerning the Egyptian ambassador's attempt to exacerbate discord between Muslim leaders and Yaméogo, a member of the Catholic minority. The Egyptian was asked to quit, which he did, and President Nasser closed the embassy. These tensions were no doubt heightened by the pressure Upper Volta was facing between two blocs in West Africa, split between the control of Ghana and Côte d'Ivoire.[24] Given the delicate nature of these negotiations, Rajkumar suggested to his superiors that economic and political involvements were not necessarily the best areas on which to focus its Africa policy:

> Everyone spoke in highest terms of India's past achievements in the realm of philosophy, metaphysics, art and architecture. They were impressed by my Doctorate in Philosophy, but when they learnt my subject was Political Science, they were distinctly disappointed. They would rather have Philosophy than anything else! I got further proof of this predilection and respect for "spirituality" when the President and the Foreign Minister asked me several questions about our University courses in Indian philosophy and metaphysics and about the Hindu religion.

> The longer I stay in Africa and come to know the simple and unsophisticated peoples of this vast continent, the more I am convinced that they are not so much inspired by our economic and industrial achievements as by our spiritual and philosophical attainments in the past. They know very little about modern India; but what captures their imagination is not the Bhakra Dam or the Damodar Valley Scheme or the Chittaranjan Factory or the Aarey

Milk Colony, but our ancient temples, our philosophy and rituals, our sculpture and our handicrafts. And, I almost forgot, the saree, of course. They think our women are very feminine and attractive. They like our cultural values and our indigenous customs which are so different than those of Europe which they know. They explain that a big factory or a big hydroelectric scheme is something which they can see anywhere in the world. It is common and means nothing to them. With French and American aid, they too can have these and will have these in due course. But what they cannot have, and never will have, are the cultural and spiritual values and the philosophy of India they have heard so much about.

I have written at length on this subject of the Indian picture in the African mind because it was brought home to me very strikingly while I was in Ouagadougou. I can only hope we shall bear this in mind when we think of publicity and cultural relations with African countries.[25]

Although Rajkumar underestimated the strength of commitment to non-alignment amongst some Africans and also revealed his ignorance of African cultural sophistication, he understood the limits of economic aid in addressing what Africans actually wanted. He also seemed to understand that India did not represent modernity to Africans. He even described technical development as ubiquitous. Africans' disinterest in acquiring it, at least to his mind, led to his recommendation for a cultural approach of the kind that had been under debate in Nehru's administration.

A few years later in Senegal, during the centenary celebration of Gandhi's birthday, Rajkumar's replacement, Indian ambassador G. J. Malik, noted that though Senegal was struggling with a number of important economic and political issues such as poverty, Senghor had accepted the chairmanship of the Gandhi Centenary Celebration Committee, thereby providing a new opportunity for India to promote Gandhi's legacy in Western Africa and the French-speaking world. He is a poet and "senior statesman of

Africa south of the Sahara", with "keen interest" in Tagore, Gandhi, and Nehru, wrote Malik. "The personal interest which he is taking in the celebration of the Gandhi centenary should help greatly to promote knowledge of the teachings of Mahatma Gandhi so essential in today's troubled conditions", he added.[26]

The Senegalese press covered the celebration by reflecting on the relevance of Gandhi for their people. "Senegal, land of culture and dialogue, isn't losing sight of the Mahatma's teachings in our age dominated by hotbeds of tension and fratricidal struggles", wrote a reporter in *Dakar Nation*. Next to the article appeared a biography of Gandhi:

> Gandhi does not resemble the mystic and superhuman personage as one has liked generally to describe him. Gandhi was a leader who refused violence not only because he morally judged it to be bad, but because he had understood that violence is in vain and condemned in the end to failure ... He was neither a conformist Hindu—he was for advancement of the untouchable caste—nor a conformist pacifist. He reserved to himself the right not to be in conformity with himself.[27]

The author's suggestion that Gandhi's greatest impact—his teaching of non-violence—was something worldly and pragmatic, reflects a Senegalese outlook conditioned by inherited modes of coexistence from older Sufi traditions, but also an important new priority on seeking a "nascent, more humane form of universalism" of the Black Atlantic.[28] This sensibility of Gandhi contained a critique of his martyrdom, and also acknowledged the very real disagreement over non-violence amongst African nationalists.[29] African disagreements about non-violence separated the different African political parties formed before independence and, in the postcolonial era, continued to create fractures over the best means of resistance in the era of apartheid, the Cold War, and other political issues facing new African nations.

African engagement with Gandhi as a pragmatic philosopher demonstrated the potential of African-Indian inquiry but did not solve the Indian government's African policy problem. Neither Indian businessmen nor Gandhi's symbolism could provide for India a deeper connection between Indians and Africans.

Humanising India

Senghor's ideas about African-Indian history first came to him during his "sixteen years of wandering" in France from 1928 to 1944, spent mostly as a student.[30] He trained in linguistics at the École Pratique des Hautes Études at the Sorbonne under the direction of Professor Lilias Homburger, a scholar of historical linguistics, whose research focused on African languages. She published articles on possible Dravidian-African connections, based on the theory that the Aryans had migrated into the Indian subcontinent and found flourishing Dravidian civilisations—the Mohenjo-daro, Harappa, and other Indus Valley sites were excavated in 1922 and were attributed to these autochthonous peoples. Homburger argued in 1955, based on this evidence, that "Les Aryens ont pu detruire des civilisations dans L'Inde, ils n'ont pas été des initiateurs" (The Aryans destroyed the civilisations in India; they were not initiators.)[31] She also hypothesised from putative Dravidian elements in the Peul (Fulani) language of West Africa a common origin to linguistic groups. She is known through her mentor, colonial official and ethnographer Maurice Delafosse, although she authored numerous publications herself, surveying the growing field of African linguistics, examining the languages classified as Bantu (a language family that was under intense debate at the time), and postulating theories about ancient Egyptian offshoots in Africa and Asia.

Her research into possible relationships between ancient Egypt and India, particularly those that predated the arrival of Indo-

European or Indo-Aryan languages, clearly shaped Senghor's interest in Afrocentric theories of Egyptian civilisation's primacy in the ancient world and its human and cultural diffusion throughout world cultures. Her Pan-Africanist linguistic thesis, that all modern African languages were related "genetically" and derived from ancient Egypt, was rejected by most linguists, but she was correct about a vexed question in African linguistics of the time—the classification of the Peul language. This Western African language was assumed by many scholars to be "Hamito-Semitic", referring at that time to a branch of the Indo-European language family. This assumption was based on the observed characteristics of physical racial differences of Peul speakers when compared to other Western Africans.[32] She connected Peul to Sereer and Wolof, languages of West Africa, before many scholars acknowledged this now widely accepted view.

Hamitic, Bantu, Dravidian, and Aryan—these were the linguistic classifications onto which racial constructions were grafted, not only by European intellectuals and colonialists but also indigenous thinkers themselves. The historian of ancient India Romila Thapar notes that the reading of biological racial characteristics, namely skin colour, in the Sanskrit terms *arya* and *dasa* is anachronistic, but the fallacy of an Aryan race persisted in the twentieth century and did not die out even amongst Indians.[33] Similarly, the Hamitic hypothesis that a branch of the Caucasian race originating from outside the continent built Africa's highest early civilisations constructed race from Abrahamic religious texts. It captured the thinking and practice of Europeans in Africa as well as Africans themselves, across the continent in Nigeria, Rwanda, and elsewhere, where their racial ideologies were not simply echoes of European hierarchies but efforts to grapple with indigeneity, genealogy, and exclusion.[34] Senghor was a student of the racial science of his time, and when he served in the French infantry in World War II and after his capture by German troops, he understood its fuel to violence. But he did not turn his back on race; he instead embraced it.

Archaeological discoveries of the era added fuel to the smouldering debates about race. In addition to the Indus Valley excavations, the search for the birthplace of humankind was reinvigorated by archaeological discoveries in Eastern and Southern Africa through the early twentieth century. Africa and India were connected by famed Bantu linguist Harry Johnston and others in the 1910s, who viewed Southwestern Asia as the birthplace of humankind; but a figure who changed his view of the Chinese origin of humanity to an African homeland was Pierre Teilhard de Chardin, a Jesuit theologian and paleontologist whom Senghor read closely.[35] Senghor was deeply affected by this view and that of his mentor Homburger, who believed that Africans originated in Asia, and remained fascinated by the possibility of Lemuria, the lost land bridge connecting Africa and India named by nineteenth-century European occultists. This "fabulous geography" of Lemuria was very much alive in the minds of African linguists, Tamil scholars, occultists like the Theosophical Society founders Colonel Henry Steel Olcott and Annie Besant, and others. Within this seemingly strange collection of parties, a real nexus between African and South Indian interests existed. For Tamils, a collective nostalgia over territorial loss inspired new literary, scholarly, and political interests.[36] For Africans, the "Dravidian problem", the mystery of the "origin and racial affinity of those Indian languages confined to the southern half of the subcontinent", was a challenge to "Aryan-centric Indian and world history".[37] Aligning Afrocentrism with Dravidian history was thus a rejoinder to white supremacy and high-caste Hindu dominance.

Senghor spoke of Lemuria in his speeches and writings in 1974, laying out the compelling reasons to pursue Afro-Dravidian studies with reference to archaeology, poetry, religion, and linguistics. He called on marine biologists to undertake dives in the Indian Ocean, following the leads of "Tamil legends", the sangams that "refer to the existence, from time immemorial of flourishing cities long since buried beneath the seas". He argued that the cradle of mankind, if reckoned by Lemuria's geography, included East Africa and Southern India, thus allowing India to share in Africa's archaeological riches. Further proof, Senghor proposed, could be found in the Islamic belief that after the fall, Adam appeared in India, perhaps Sri Lanka, and Hawa (Eve) in Southern Arabia, before their meeting in Arafat. He even proposed an unambiguous definition of race as skin colour, but with an insistence that no race is pure and hence all race is historical. The problem of Dravidian origins was still "unsolved", Senghor argued, but therefore more intriguing to consider for possible African ancestry, for he considered that "a civilization with no admixture is a cultural ghetto".[38]

Senghor understood the power of the Dravidian paradigm, as we might call it, for postcolonial Africa, but not as a naive "fabulist" who romanticised Lemuria and other myths in service of nationalist fervour in the interwar years. Senghor was certainly explicit in his rejection of racial purity—especially in Blackness—as an ideal. He recognised that Afro-Dravidian connections could be by ancestral kinship or a putative common geographical birthplace like ancient Egypt. He also recognised the borrowed similarities, for example the word for "key" in West Africa's Wolof and South India's Tamil. By the 1950s, he had formed a mature understanding of Dravidian cultural nationalism as a means of promoting educational development and autonomy, namely in matters of indigenous language instruction and preservation through his friend Malcolm Adiseshiah, an economist and educationalist from Tamil Nadu who held top positions at UNESCO from 1948 to 1970. Adiseshiah worked with René Maheu (a philosopher by training), who also served in various UNESCO leadership positions and made several visits to Senegal, including one in 1970 to open the Regional Bureau of Education for Africa in Dakar.[39]

From its foundation in 1945, UNESCO had a mission to combat racial inequality and racism through publications, education, and media campaigns, that constituted an enormous task for an international organisation in its infancy.[40] These efforts were managed through national commissions, but they also had an effect on getting to the grassroots to change social perceptions of difference. The Senegalese-Indian connection shows how UNESCO tapped into the already formed race consciousness of intellectual leaders. Adiseshiah was like Senghor in surprising ways. Both men belonged to the small Catholic minority in their countries of origin, but perhaps more significant to their connection was Adiseshiah's vision for international development work—such as UNESCO's higher education efforts—that he believed should proceed from the ground up, from local and regional cultural movements. For Adiseshiah, his formative scene was the former Madras Presidency, after independence the capital of Tamil Nadu state and of the wider Dravidian language community. He secured UNESCO support for Tamil language studies and cultural site preservation, while also securing French governmental support for the Third World Tamil Conference held in Paris in 1970. He was not seen as an ideologue of Tamil or Dravidian cultural nationalism, but the backdrop for much of his life and career was the Dravidian movement, which began in 1916 with the establishment of the South Indian Welfare Society, the first formal organisation to call for the promotion of the interests of "Dravidians".

The movement, despite many upheavals, including tensions between the elite upper-caste non-Brahmin leadership in politics and activists from the lower or oppressed castes and tribal minorities, articulated important goals, like equal access to jobs and education, recognition of "self-respect" for Dravidians, and,

at one point, independent statehood. Its methods, such as boy-
cotts of and demonstrations against the nationalisation of the
Hindi language and North Indian domination, transformed
South India, not least for its opposition to the dominant Indian
National Congress.[41] Through Adiseshiah, Senghor understood
India to be far more complicated than a nation unified and symbolised by the Congress, Gandhi, and Nehru. The Dravidian
movement challenged this narrative and featured an entirely different cast of characters: the Justice Party, Periyar E. V.
Ramasamy, C. N. Annadurai, and the Self-Respect Movement.[42]
Blackness, though not an explicit reference to skin colour in the
early Dravidian movement, was signified in its flag with black and
red rectangles, which was adopted in 1949, a time when splits
had led to a reformulation of Dravidian politics—the flag was
distinct from India's orange, white, and green. Senghor wrote
that Adiseshiah "revealed to me the realities of Dravidian life,
which ever since then [the 1950s] I have found to be very close
to the realities of life in Negro-Africa".[43] These realities were
cultural characteristics but also politics: the calls for an independent nation (Dravida Nadu), Periyar's denunciation of caste discrimination and the subjugation of women, and, in the very years
of Senghor's friendship with Adiseshiah, the burning of books in
Hindi, which the government of India wanted to nationalise.[44]

Senghor's friendship seemed also to confirm for Adiseshiah
the value of a cultural nationalist outlook that conflated
Blackness and "Third World". At a symposium on culture and
development hosted by Senghor's Foundation and UNESCO in
Dakar in October 1976, Adiseshiah delivered remarks to support
spiritual comradeship. Robert Cummings, historian and director
of African Studies at Howard University, the only American
institution represented at the symposium, recalled Adiseshiah's
agreement with his long-time friend Senghor that a "new cul-

tural world order" was inseparable from economic development. He quoted Adiseshiah as saying:

> We thank Léopold Senghor for calling us in the Third World ... back to our people and our people's culture, not simply as the ultimate end of development but as the immediate needs and the only viable instrument (where ends become means and means become ends).
>
> – to achieve political freedom internally and internationally
>
> – to fight neo-colonialism in the economic sphere
>
> – to establish the new international economic order and to this end we pledge: We who have liberated our countries shall now liberate ourselves.[45]

Adiseshiah helped make clear Senghor's position that local demands formed the Third World, not the other way around, and that the preservation of local cultural identity was the priority of international alliances. Cummings believed that "in defense against cultural imperialism", African-Americans needed to respond to Senghor's affirmation of "Black heritage" by "strengthen[ing] the relationships and the commitment to international cooperative development". The symposium "was the realization of our greater need for Africa" in the global imperative for racial humanism, for the African diaspora and all global citizens.[46]

India's need for Africa, or, to put it another way, political realignment in the postcolonial world, has already been discussed, but Adiseshiah understood the problems of postcolonial educational development from a different angle through his decades of work at UNESCO. India needed Africans. From the late 1940s, Adiseshiah reported that UNESCO scholarship programmes had exposed strong anti-Indian feelings, particularly amongst East Africans, who refused scholarships to study in

India.[47] Starting in the 1950s, the government of India had con-tributed hundreds of thousands of dollars under the Indian scholarship scheme,[48] but as the numbers of interested students slowly ticked up, the issue of race relations at universities came to a head with Idi Amin's coup in 1971. At first his posture seemed to be a welcome change to Asian Ugandans, as his pre-decessor, Milton Obote, had imposed economic restrictions on them. During his term as the first Chancellor of Makerere University (the "Harvard of Africa"), many Asian students and faculty had contributed to its growth and stellar reputation.[49] Yet within a matter of months, memoranda between the Indian community and Idi Amin showed that economic grievances against Indians not only included commercial malpractice, but also "disloyalty" to the state by those who were educated at the expense of the Ugandan government, but who either did not return to Uganda to work in public service, worked in private practice, or refused up-country government appointments.[50] Perhaps Idi Amin's most bitter grievance was with Indian non-integration. He wrote in his 1971 declaration:

> I am aware that one of the causes of the continuing distance in social relations between the Asians and the Africans in this country was the policy of the colonial government which ensured that the Africans, Asians and Europeans had entirely separate schools, hospi-tals, residential quarters, social and sports clubs, and even public toilets with the facilities reserved for Africans being of the poorest quality and hopelessly inadequate. We have, of course, changed all of this but there are Asians who still live in the past and consider, like the former colonialist government, that the Africans are below them. This living in the past cannot help Asians in any way, nor can it foster the desired harmony and unity among races in Uganda.[51]

Arguments to the contrary, that few Asians had received schol-arships and some never received offers of government employment, or that Indian conservatism was matched by African practices of endogamy, appeared to fall on deaf ears. Amin believed that Indians were overly conservative amongst themselves (they separated along caste and religious lines) and therefore incapable of mixing with Africans. The estimated 80,000 Asians in Uganda were expelled in 1972. Persecution against non-Muslims grew after Amin returned from hajj with a stronger connection to his political alliances in the Islamic world.[52]

Sana Aiyar describes how Kenyan writer Bahadur Tejani's novel, *Day After Tomorrow* (1971), picked up on the pulse of these themes, and criticised Indians for their failure to become one with Africans, not only in national unity but also in sexual unions. Tejani advocated for the eventual disappearance of Asians in Africa, into Black civilisations, as the only antidote for Indian supremacy. The attack of Amin and the awareness of Indians like Tejani that Indians maintained a sense of biological superiority to and incommensurability with Africans, made the naming of racial problems impossible to ignore. The Indian diaspora had to grapple with what was no longer hidden, and did so in "multiple sites of belonging" and difference, especially the younger generations.[53] Expulsion created distinct Indian idioms of rejection and return that reveal the intense emotional registers of African-Indian experiences.[54]

Senghor constructed a different sense of Indian belonging that addressed the lingering worries about African-Indian bloodlines, which had reappeared in various conflicts, through ancient genealogies. While Senghor's Afro-Indian studies initiative was explicitly integrationist, the Organization of African Unity, in which he was an elder statesman, "adopted a curious attitude of non-interference" in its immediate response to General Amin's anti-Indianism; most of the African press, with a few exceptions, did not join the outcry against his accusations and actions. Perhaps this reticence arose from what Mahmood Mamdani argues was Amin's complexity as a hero whose actions were celebrated by many Black nationalists but reviled by others.[55] The "economic patriotism" behind Amin's expulsion was also surely a shared priority of African leaders who did not object.[56]

Anirudha Gupta points out that around the same time that Ugandan Asians were expelled, the same fate met Nigerians in Ghana, Ghanaians in Sierra Leone and Liberia, and all non-local Africans in Mobutu's Zaire. Lebanese were also victims of discrimination in West Africa. Gupta could have looked back before the 1970s too, to when the Zanzibar Revolution produced racial violence against non-Africans. In his view, Indians, who were better off than most, actually hid behind a "conspiracy of silence" until Amin forced the issue of their presence into public view.[57] Senghor's project was profound for its insistence on questioning and calling for research on race, particularly racial ambiguities and mysteries that muddied rather than clarified Blackness and, with it, Afrocentricity and the bounds of Black nationalism and internationalism. Increasingly singular notions of Blackness and Indianness, in contradistinction to each other, no less, were being forcibly reconstructed with unrest around the continent, often requiring Indians, for one, to put aside their religious, caste, and occupational differences, and Africans to align behind one idea of Blackness. Senghor's strategy was to confuse the categories.

The birth of Afro-Dravidian studies

The year that Senghor travelled to India was momentous not only for the reasons outlined above but also for some at home in Senegal. Senghor had faced some years of political difficulty, including an attempted assassination in 1967 (and execution of his attacker, Moustapha Lô, for treason), student protests in 1968, and the revision of the constitution in 1970. He finally allowed the creation of new political parties in 1974. Clamping down on political parties such as the opposition Bloc des Masses Sénégalaises and Front National Sénégalais, founded by leading intellectual and fellow at the Institut Fondamental d'Afrique Noire, Cheikh Anta Diop, was crucial to what, until 1974, had been the political monopoly of Senghor and his Senegalese Progressive Union party. Diop, one of his rivals, spent one month in prison in 1962 for his opposition.[58] After 1974, Senghor's strategy was diluted with paternalism.[59] Any political parties formed after the new constitution was instituted had to be allied with one of three existing recognised ones. Two years later, Diop's Rassemblement National Démocratique party was found to have failed in this regard, and thus he was confined in a kind of intellectual, rather than an actual prison at IFAN, until Senghor stepped down in 1980. Those years allowed Senghor to actualise Diop's theory of the ancient Egyptian origin of Dravidian civilisation in ways that would render Senghor's own commitment to Afrocentricity unimpeachable, whilst also shoring up his international reputation, which had begun to suffer before 1974 with his one-party rule.

Diop was critical of Senghor in numerous ways. He denounced him as indifferent to the problems of the Senegalese masses and too complacent towards the French former colonialists. He also attacked Senghor's essentialism in characterising the Negro-African in the emotional and religious terms of European stereotypes. While Diop named Senghor in his attacks, Senghor never once referred to Diop, as if he had not bothered to read his work.[60] Yet, of course, he had, not least in order to emphasise the relatedness of Black civilisations to Dravidian South India through historical developments, giving a fuller sense to kinship—through history, poetry, and genealogy—than Diop's physical anthropological and archaeological approach did.

Senghor promoted this sense of historical discovery through his addresses in India and Senegal to introduce the transnational collaboration of the department of Indo-African Studies at Dakar University. The Senegalese Ministry of Culture helped identify three of their students to send to study at Annamalai in India. The first Senegalese scholar to arrive in Madras was the linguist Cheikh Tidiane N'Diaye in 1974; Souleymane Faye and Mamadou N'Diaye went as doctoral students in 1977. Three Indian faculty members, K. P. Aravanan, U. P. Upadhyaya, and his wife Susheela, took up residence at IFAN in 1973. According to Dr Upadhyaya, the Indian government had not originally planned to send his wife, but Senghor made her a fellow, which convinced her own government of her value to the mission.[61] Besides university exchanges, news of the Afro-Dravidian project was disseminated via radio messages.

The project's participants produced many publications in addition to Senghor's own writings in Indian journals. There were Aravanan's writings (in English) including *The Serpent Cult in Africa and Dravidian India* (1977), *Dravidians and Africans* (1979), and "Notable Negroid Elements in Dravidian India" (1980). The Upadhyayas also produced several articles, which not only covered African-Indian historical linguistics but also added to Dravidian language studies, particularly on minorities, which had received little intellectual interest in South India. Souleymane Faye's doctoral research on comparative Sereer and Tamil informed his research on tonality. The project's impact on how these scholars framed their research questions was described years later by Dr U. P. Upadhyaya. He wrote that evidence for Afro-Dravidian affinity, to his mind, came to him through fieldwork, not through any assumptions established by the project itself. He explained the evolution of his thinking from the time of his arrival in Senegal in 1973:

I started work in African villages with a clean slate without presumptions. But when the work started I was rather astonished to see many points of similarities between the languages and cultures of these two ancient communities of Africa and Asia. Even if we dismiss some of these correspondences by considering them as due to chance or ancient borrowings due to migrations and contact we are left with certain strong evidences which cannot be explained away so easily. The fundamental unity of ideas between these different groups diffused in this vast region could not have been the result of mere commerce during Neolithic and early metal ages but must be due to racial unity and migration of population in those days.[62]

It is not clear whether Upadhyaya accepted the basic premises of Diop's theory of African origins of Dravidian civilization, or if he subscribed to a view that African languages sprang from a Dravidian root, perhaps in a civilisation lost to great floods. But his avoidance of the debate illustrates his faith in the project aside from this single question—there were many others and more rich discoveries to be made. The careful means of generating research questions and the ethnographic methods of analysis shaped his later work within India. He remained a scholar of Dravidian languages, and in Karnataka his project on the Tulu language, spoken by nearly 2 million people, has helped the language-community's claim for a separatist movement seeking redress for historical injustices.[63] The Tulu movement for language autonomy and mother-tongue preservation, alongside the dominant Dravidian language Kannada, is historically complicated by factors like the oral and literary entanglements and rural-urban dynamics, factors that the Upadhyayas understood better because of their studies in Senegal, where Wolof has a complicated relationship to minority languages like Sereer—not a simple dominance, but instead by multilingual peoples' social uses in home, work, and government.[64]

Upadhyaya's efforts to develop Dravidian linguistics as a scholarly field was also haunted by the politics of the Senegalese project as he sought to disentangle himself from Aravanan, who mistranslated some of Upadhyaya's work in Tamil, creating a rift between the two.[65] Aravanan's politicisation of the project had also bothered Souleymane Faye, who echoed Upadhyaya's description of the challenges of Afro-Dravidian linguistics research and the need for specificity, careful comparison, and recognition of African-Indian differences that was missing in some of the work of the project and its afterlives. In one case, the elevation of the baobab to the status of deity in the West Atlantic African worldview betrayed Aravanan's tendency for overly simplistic conclusions on much of the data, but especially the West African side.[66] This oversimplification was interpreted as an intellectual affront by academic scholars, unsurprising, perhaps, since Aravanan went on to have a political career as a populist ideologue of the Dravidian movement and as a Tamil filmmaker.[67] His showy style of politics was a distinct contrast to Senghor's, and was perhaps the source of some opinions that a tension existed between the two men. Yet the quality of Aravanan's scholarly work should not distract from recognition of how he translated his work on African-Indian cultural nexus into the political movement for Dravidian autonomy that was pitted squarely against Aryanism.

Just as Cheikh Anta Diop accused Senghor of racial essentialism, so too did some of the Afro-Dravidian scholars make the same claim of Aravanan, warning against the dangers of sloppiness in racial studies. The reasons for their caution are clear. His arguments about similarities between Dravidian and "African" physical characteristics (without contextualisation that his evidence was drawn from Wolof or Pulaar in West Atlantic languages) play on references to debunked techniques of craniometrical measurement and sexualised representations of Indian and African women's bodies. He relied on the work of Leo Frobenius without caveat, opening himself to criticisms that Senghor also received for giving "a local turn to a grand European dance".[68] In laying out commonalities, he rarely moved beyond speculation as to how these might have arisen, through inheritance of specific words following lexical patterns within specific languages, as the other comparative linguists in his group did. He never sought to understand the cultural matrix that produced similarities but not sameness. Senghor's supporters refuted their colleague by insisting on *historical* evidence of *métissage*, or cultural mixing, that was active and ongoing, and they perceived an insult in Aravanan's failure to study Senghor's work more carefully. The Afro-Dravidian project put *négritude* to the test and confirmed, at the very least, that it "will not disappear", as Senghor himself believed.[69] Philosopher Souleymane Bachir Diagne writes that Senghor may as well have had "humanism of hybridity"[70] as one of his slogans. That Indian scholars like Upadhyaya came directly to work in and defend *négritude* studies, not as "outsiders", amidst contentious debates and dismissive attitudes about Afrocentrism, is remarkable. African-Indian racial and linguistic studies was becoming a legitimate scholarly field through the same kinds of academic and political wrangling that established any other intellectual discipline.

For Dr Upadhyaya and Susheela, their time in Senegal fundamentally shifted their worldviews. Dr Susheela's research on the Beary people in southern Karnataka, showing that men and women spoke different dialects of the same language because the men were descended from Arab sailors and the women from local communities, was unique in approaching the gendered dimensions of cultural transformations in language, religion, and lived practices. Indeed, even the couple's interest in Islam was unusual, given Dr Upadhyaya's traditional Brahmin (high-caste) background—he had Vedic education through primary school with the goal of becoming a priest but moved to secular studies from there. His views on ritual and caste purity, a central feature of Brahminism, were transformed by anthropological fieldwork and living in Senghor's Senegal. He recalled "no society is without mixture", echoing Senghor's words from 40 years earlier, but also to describe his time living with Senegalese, not apart from Africans. His statement denies a fundamental principle of high-caste Hindu purity—even if a high-caste community's or family's mixed heritage were known, it would not be acknowledged publicly out of concern to introduce any doubt into that privileged caste status. Moreover, his mode of living flew in the face of Idi Amin's rhetoric about Indian self-exclusion, which resonated quite strongly for many Africans.

As if to challenge Amin's complaints of Indian domination of Makerere, Senghor included the three Indian scholars amongst the Senegalese contingent at the Second World Black and African Festival of Arts and Culture (also known as FESTAC) in Lagos in 1977. Meanwhile, he opposed the full participation of Arab North Africans and argued that they should only be observers.[71] Indeed, Senghor clearly understood the politics of inclusion at FESTAC to be a political matter, as the presence of West Papuans there attests: Senegal was one of the few African countries to side with them instead of Indonesia; in historian Quito Swan's view, because of the fallout of Bandung loyalties.[72]

Souleymane Faye, professor of linguistics at Cheikh Anta Diop University, lived in India in the early 1970s, when few African students were willing to go. He described some threats against him and his Senegalese colleagues, but also Indians' lack of knowledge about Africa that direct contact between Africans and Indians exposed. "People were very curious and maybe dismissive at first, but after so open and accepting. Even my friends introduced me as Nigerian or South African—that's all they knew of Africa, even after I tried to show them on a map where

Senegal was"![73] He learned Tamil fluently for his work, which was important for his studies but also for social acceptance. He was adopted by a family, with whom he attended weddings and other social functions, giving him a chance to break down tendencies towards non-integration that existed. Mamadou N'Diaye remembered that Indians asked him about his caste, which he explained existed in Senegal but not in the same way as in India. He told them: "I am a Brahmin, so I am free to go anywhere"! It is possible such conversations about caste happened between Africans and Indians, who amongst themselves might not speak freely; certainly, to see caste differences in action was shocking to the Senegalese scholars. Exclusion negatively affected Cheikh Tidiane N'Diaye, the first Senegalese linguist who went to India for the project. He was not happy at Annamalai. It is said that Senghor was asked to send more students after his arrival so that he would have some company.[74]

Senghor's seemingly arcane and relatively small project had the fairly big consequence of expanding the pathway for more Senegalese students to study in India.[75] In spite of this, after Senghor left office, the Afro-Dravidian project became inactive, in part due to lack of funding.[76] His successor, Abdou Diouf, did not want to be in Senghor's shadow, but also Senegalese ideas about India were firmly planted amongst different social strata so that one singular agenda was no longer central (as Chapter 6 shows). Senghor's efforts also made India seem a viable option for higher studies for Africans from wider Francophone West Africa, with little previous exposure to India. In 2016, the Indian consulate reported sending 150 students annually to India from Senegal, Cape Verde, Burkina Faso, and Guinea, the countries all covered by the office in Dakar. The attaché noted: "their English is very rudimentary most often, but the purpose really [of the sponsorship] is for them to see Indian culture".[77] Senghor's lexicon has survived in Senegalese-Indian networks, even if the explicit focus on race has not.

Conclusion

Senghor's Afro-Dravidian project, undertaken in collaboration with the Indian Council for Cultural Relations in Indira Gandhi's time, presents a unique intellectual history in which the Black (Francophone) Atlantic and the Indian Ocean worlds converged. It did not begin with an Indian diaspora in Senegal or an economic connection between the two countries. It also seems unconnected to popular passions for Indian films and music, called *Indouphilie* by self-described Senegalese lovers of India. At least this is what dance scholar Gwenda Vander Steene concluded, using evidence from the Hindi-language Bollywood-centred focus of *Indouphilie* social clubs and dance troupes in the Pikine suburb of Dakar to argue that there is a divide between intellectual and popular African orientations to India. But is this division so stark? Could Senghor possibly have conceived the idea from the moviegoers and then nurtured his long-standing Afro-Dravidian interests?

A radio programme playing songs from Indian films began on Radio Sénégal in the 1960s, hosted from 1965 to 1970 by Baïdy Dia; the first student, according to the Indophile doyen Idi Sidibé, to receive a scholarship to go to India.[78] After studying cinema there, Dia returned to take over the programme from 1973 to 1978. India-focused radio programmes grew in number and in content, with one in French called "India: Country of 1,000 Faces" (*L'Inde: pays au 1000 visages*). The film connection between India and Senegal in Senghor's government, with at least one filmmaker in his Ministry of Culture, Mansour Sora Wade, going on to make a documentary about *Indouphilie*, suggests that film and radio could have been Senghor's inspiration for scholarly engagement. During her time at IFAN, Susheela Upadhyaya also taught Hindi classes, and the couple hosted cultural nights when Hindi films were screened.

India may have provided Senghor with a perfect means for navigating between the popular and the intellectual, with *négritude* an ideal vehicle through which to merge art, philosophy, and politics. If so, it was also a critical moment for bringing India into the racial politics of the Black world, given what was happening on the African continent and around the world—the expulsion of Asians from Uganda and Black nationalism standing apart from other civil rights protests. What was particularly significant about the Afro-Dravidian project between Senegal and India was the intellectual import for race studies originating *within Africa and Asia*, from reimagining the ancient world to reconstructing and preserving minority languages. Another Afro-Indian movement, the Dalit Panthers, was formed in 1972 in Maharashtra, and its mobilisation around Black Panther ideology to fight caste oppression was criticised by some for using race as a "bludgeon", when caste was very different.[79] Senghor managed to avoid this criticism, perhaps because his Indian collaborators were pleased that he focused on Dravidian culture rather than social commentary, that Indians felt often revolved on stereotypes of caste. Perhaps this was a strategic choice of a skilled cultural intermediary like Senghor.

There is no doubt that Senghor's efforts have left their mark in Senegal and in South India, where educationalists still connect African and Dravidian experiences. The ongoing articulation of Dravidian aspiration by Aravanan, the scholar-turned-politician, has included other figures like Dr K. Ponmudy, who studied at Annamalai and went into politics and outlined a comparative approach in *The Dravidian Movement and the Black Movement* (1998), which draws inspiration from his personal witness to the 1960s liberation movements, and notes the impossibility of ignoring white and Brahmin supremacy in religious-ethical as well as political arenas. Outside this movement, that has been predominant in Tamil Nadu, in other parts of South India Senghor's *négri-*

tude has remained a crucial paradigm for expanding Black arts, that is now encircled with Africa and the African diaspora in the US, notably through historically Black institutions of learning.[80] Scholars, including African diaspora intellectuals and Europeans, continue to add new methods, such as human genetic research, and new theories, to give new currency to the studies produced by scholars of Afro-Dravidianism.[81] The Afro-Indian research of the Slovak scholar Cyril Hromnik, in which he claimed Indian and Indonesian origin for some ancient African words, garnered intense criticism from historians of ancient Africa and the Indian Ocean, including an attack from one South Africanist researcher who also worked for the Mormon scholarly journal *Dialogue*.[82] The idea of ancient Afrasia has cut across seemingly different polemics, though they share an interest in human origins.

While not mainstream, the mythical side of Afro-Dravidian history cannot be disproven or proven. *Négritude* and Dravidianism both live on and indeed have their own hybrids. Science seems unable to diminish cultural enchantment but instead revives it, a reason why Africans and Indians continue to proffer their "cultural connections" as evidence of a bond that is unique.

4

THIRD WORLD SCIENCE

DIASPORIC DREAMS AND DISILLUSIONMENT

Introduction

The Cold War and non-alignment obscured a host of other struggles and alternative visions of transnational connectivity, as Senghor's project showed. Science, technology, and infrastructure represented crucial concerns as they were the most immediate measure of postcolonial progress, and ambivalence about them was often ignored or silenced. The heady celebrations of "dreams with no costs"[1] ignored how dams displaced millions, electrification overshadowed access to water and other basic necessities, and some public health projects exposed poor people to dangerous experiments. Transnational science and technology became a site of racial and cultural politics, including even dissent against the nationalism that postcolonial politics had fostered.

The Edward Bouchet Abdus Salam Institute (EBASI), founded as an outgrowth of the International Centre for Theoretical Physics (ICTP) established in Trieste, Italy, in 1964, embodied a constellation of these politics. Established in 1988 "to provide synergistic scientific and technical collaborations between African and American physical scientists, engineers, and technologists",[2] its name signalled an unlikely union: the first African-American to earn any kind of doctorate—Bouchet received his PhD from Yale in 1876 in the field of experimental physics—together with Mohammad Abdus Salam, a British Indian (later Pakistani) who gained his doctorate in physics at Cambridge and, in 1979, became the first Muslim to receive the Nobel Prize in Physics. In Bouchet's honour, Abdus Salam, together with the African-American physicist Joseph Andrew Johnson III, spearheaded the idea to found EBASI in "the quest for African peoples to achieve tremendous heights in scientific endeavors".[3] Ghanaian mathematician Francis K. A. Allotey, a founding fellow of the African Academy of Sciences, wrote about Abdus Salam's mentorship to him both personally and in science education in Ghana, elsewhere in Africa, and amongst Black scientists worldwide. Abdus Salam thought like a Pan-Africanist, in Allotey's view. Through the ICTP, he wrote, African scientists were able "to keep active in research while staying in their home countries".[4] Allotey estimated that 600 African scientists met in Trieste annually. Over two decades, the value of these Africans forming their own collective with African-American colleagues became clearer with the creation of their own arm, EBASI.

Bouchet's life in the late nineteenth century was not far removed from the experience of Black scientists even a century later, in America or in Africa. Growing up in antebellum New Haven, where Nat Turner's rebellion and the *Amistad* slave ship revolt had played out little more than a decade earlier, Bouchet's "cognitive maps were developed very early by way of support in his community and his family who held astute notions about the value of education", even at the cost of "great personal risk".[5] The sense of a "Black aristocracy", of which Bouchet was a member, may have destabilised white views of Black inferiority,[6] but the isolation and exceptionalism he experienced probably also denied him the recognition he deserved. For twentieth-century Black scientists, added to the racial inequality were the nationalist competitions. Black scientists were supposed to represent modern aspirations of America and African nations, but African and African diaspora contributions to science were often overlooked or diminished by their white colleagues who dominated the field. As a Pakistani scientist born before Partition, Abdus Salam experienced some of these same dilemmas—displacement, pride in Islam, but the excommunication by orthodox Muslims for belonging to a minority sect. Salam believed the importance of EBASI was to ease the difficult choices minority scientists often had to make: "the idea [of the ICTP, the umbrella organisation and its offshoots]... is to minimize brain drain while providing opportunity for collaboration and access to top facilities".[7] He may have underestimated the importance of the Pan-African unification that his Institute would engender.

The Pan-African scientific imperative that arose within ICTP, with a Pakistani Muslim scientist at its helm, reveals a unique modern utopianism at the intersection of Pan-African consciousness and the diaspora unleashed by South Asian disintegration and ongoing sectarian conflict. Postcolonial nations placed enormous burdens on their scientists. It is a story of the reunification of one diaspora in the impossibility of another's. It also reveals the cultural imperative to decentre Western knowledge and the migration patterns of a new intelligentsia.

Abdus Salam's West African tutelage

The fundamental focus on Africa in the Institute in Trieste is traceable to African-South Asian educational connections in the Ahmadiyya Muslim mission in West Africa. Fazlur Rahman Hakeem, Abdus Salam's uncle, lived in the Gold Coast and

Nigeria for four decades and stood out amongst other Indian and Pakistani missionaries who went to West Africa. Hakeem had a notable reputation for his aggressive style of preaching, challenging West African listeners using both the Qur'an and the Bible to question the teachings of Christian missionaries, who had begun many of the schools operating in coastal West Africa during the colonial period.[8] The Ahmadiyya opened many of their own primary and secondary schools by 1950, that were just one part of a larger project to engineer the creation of an entire alternative social and leadership structure, a "counter-society".[9] Heads of Ahmadiyya missions and schools acted as political agents outside of existing Muslim structures that had been built by immigrant traders, mostly of the Hausa ethnicity. The Ahmadiyya rejected the longstanding expectations of Muslim leaders for communal labour and control over religious spaces and prayers. Their order had effects beyond their relatively small following—it forced other Muslims to denounce the Ahmadiyya's claim that they were the only true Muslims. By creating competition, the Ahmadis also spurred greater social welfare and voluntarism amongst older Muslim communities to open new religious schools. Even as Ahmadiyya schools declined in popularity in some places, government schools in West Africa launched universal education and adopted the use of Ahmadiyya-authored books like *An Outline of Islam*, published in Lagos in 1955.[10]

Hakeem wrote letters from West Africa to his nephew, who lived in Cambridge and then moved to Princeton. Partition had dislocated the Ahmadiyya community to the extent that being a missionary or a scholar abroad was arguably better than remaining in Pakistan. When Abdus Salam returned to Pakistan in 1951, he found the country engulfed in major sectarian clashes. The death of Muhammad Ali Jinnah, the "father" of the Pakistani nation, in 1948, and the assassination of Prime Minister Liaquat Ali Khan in 1951, left a political vacuum that religious nationalists filled. Jinnah had offered protection and citizenship to the Ahmadiyya, who were instrumental in the establishment of the Muslim state. When the Ahrar Party agitated for the official declaration of Ahmadis as non-Muslims in Punjab province in 1949, the attempt was defeated and the rights of minorities reaffirmed.[11] Then, in 1953, Amal, the parent organisation of the *ulema* (religious scholars), renewed calls for the declaration of the Ahmadiyya as non-Muslims and sought the immediate dismissal of the Foreign Minister Zafrullah Khan, an Ahmadi, whom they accused of using his position to support overseas Ahmadiyya missions. Anti-Ahmadi riots escalated throughout the country. Khan's job was spared because Pakistan was in the midst of negotiations for millions of tons of wheat from the United States and other Western countries.[12] After that, the situation in Pakistan for the Ahmadiyya and other religious and ethnic minorities worsened.[13]

Abdus Salam left Pakistan for a post at Cambridge and later moved to Imperial College in London. In 1955, Zafrullah Khan recommended Salam be appointed scientific secretary to the United Nations Conference on Peaceful Uses of Atomic Energy in Geneva, and the following year he was appointed as the head of the Pakistani delegation to the International Atomic Energy Agency (IAEA).[14] The work required diplomacy and the ability to communicate nuclear reactor theory, an area that was not Salam's specialty. This work also introduced him to new professional circles in Sweden, where he came to the attention of the Nobel Institute, and to nuclear non-proliferation activists around the world. Despite being from a discriminated sect, in 1960 he accepted the invitation of the new Pakistani military ruler, General Ayub Khan, to become the country's top science adviser, a part-time post that allowed him to keep his position at Imperial College. He founded Pakistan's space programme and played an instrumental role in architecting its nuclear policy.[15]

Abdus Salam faced struggles in Britain, though probably not open discrimination or professional rivalry that would diminish his research. Colombian sociologist Alexis De Greiff observes that in the scientific world after the 1950s,

> overt racism was considered politically unacceptable and against the scientific internationalism western scientists wished to promote. In the Cold War logic, the "free world" should stimulate mutual respect especially between their elites. The kind of discrimination that third world scientists suffered in the postcolonial era is far subtler, as the forms of resistance are.[16]

Salam returned to Pakistan on a mission of faith. The nation's military ruler Ayub Khan used science as a "seduction" on his virtual crusade for modernisation.[17] For Khan, Salam's credentials and the relative ignorance about the Ahmadiyya outside South Asia were useful for a new kind of science diplomacy, particularly as he was "a Muslim born in poor Pakistan". His membership in the British academy and the Pakistani government made him particularly well suited for the United Nations and other inter-national bodies. Indeed, the Muslim missionary worldview of the Ahmadis was internationalist even before Pakistan existed. By promoting Abdus Salam as a representative of the Pakistani gov-ernment, Khan took advantage of a practised evangelical network and style in order to burnish the national image.

Abdus Salam's work on nuclear energy also made him turn his attention to the peace movement and anti-nuclear activism. After the French nuclear test in the Sahara in 1960, Ghana became a global centre for non-alignment and nuclear non-proliferation that brought together African and diaspora activists, including civil rights leaders like Bayard Rustin and Martinican political philosopher Frantz Fanon. Kwame Nkrumah supported their commitment to peaceful resistance even in the wake of the Sharpeville massacre in 1960, and other violence against peaceful protesters. He also appreciated that atomic energy could promote "science equity".[18] The Accra Assembly (The World Without the Bomb) in 1962 was an effort by the Ghanaian government to convene global activists against nuclear armament, and Abdus Salam, as a high-profile Third World physicist, was invited to their network. Like Nkrumah, he knew the benefit of having multiple engagements in international nuclear politics. Julie Medlock, on behalf of the Accra Assembly, wrote to Dr Salam in 1964, just as he was moving to Trieste to set up the ICTP, to update him on several matters:

> Every time I hear the word "particle" I think of you! So I wonder if you saw this *London Times* article "New Force of Nature" of October 4—copy enclosed? The world's mystics call it the Supramental Force or the Seventh Ray, if I recall correctly. It is nice to see that the scientists are catching up! ...
>
> It is heartening to find so many of the original proposals made at the 1962 Accra Assembly coming up officially—and indicates that our hard work behind-the-scenes over these last two and a half years has had some real impact ...
>
> How is Trieste and how is the new job? We are really very proud of you, you know, for all the good work you are doing.[19]

She described meetings attended by the Ghanaian ambassador to the United Nations Frank Boaten, and anticipated that the next Assembly meeting would be held in Kenya in July of the following year, pending sponsorship from the Organization of African Unity (OAU). The process was being slowed up, she observed, by the Guinean OAU leader, "Diallo Telli rushing around Africa while his mail stacks up in Addis Ababa! ... but we expect to land right side up in due time".[20] A letter she wrote to follow up in 1965 contained bad news of delays because of the Congo Crisis and obstruction from the Pugwash Conference organisers, an anti-nuclear group originally formed in Canada by Polish physicist Joseph Rotblat and Bertrand Russell in 1957. Medlock suspected the Pugwash group was deliberating acting against the Accra Assembly. She mused as to whether the publicity manager of Pugwash was sidelining the Accra Assembly because of his personal insult at not being on their board: "Or does it go deeper into some sort of racial feeling or enmity toward Ghana and Nkrumah along the lines of the British press, or because somebody doesn't approve of Boaten and me"?[21]

The Accra Assembly's work faltered, and, with the ousting of Nkrumah in 1966, the Assembly further dissipated. Yet the influence of Nkrumah did not wane. The Accra Assembly was part of a Pan-African peace effort that included a spectrum of political movements and organised actions.[22] Scientists like Francis Allotey and Abdus Salam were so inspired by the "possibilities and promise of African Revolution" of Nkrumah's politics that they continued his legacy in their own way.[23]

Sectarian conflict and South Asian diaspora

As African leaders began to make official visits to Pakistan, the Ahmadiyya were observing closely. In 1961, Sir Ahmadu Bello, the Northern Nigerian Premier, visited Pakistan after stopping in several Middle Eastern countries and reportedly announced in Karachi his interest in a Pan-Islamic commonwealth. India watched nervously, as Nehru's government had suspected a decade earlier that this important West African territory might not sympathise with India for religious reasons.[24] The head of Ahmadiyya foreign missions, Mirza Mubarak Ahmad, referred to Bello's visit in a pamphlet called "Islam in Africa" (1962), and highlighted that Bello was a great-great-grandson of Usman 'dan Fodio, "a great Muslim scholar and an active missionary of

Islam". The Ahmadi saw 'dan Fodio as their predecessor in spreading jihad of the pen, rather than the sword.[25] References to precolonial African history and leaders like 'dan Fodio show how the Ahmadiyya analysis of the Muslim position in Africa had certainly matured since the sect's early days. Citing the extensive presence of Christian missionaries on the African continent to illustrate his own mission's response, Ahmad quoted from a piece in *World Christian Digest* by Cecil Northcott, a Congregationalist and journalist-biographer of missionaries like David Livingstone and Albert Schweitzer:

> Islam's bid to win Africa is also aided by Pakistan's ablest leader, Chaudhry Mohammad Zafrullah Khan, now a justice of the World Court [and Pakistan's permanent secretary to the United Nations at the time]. He stated at an Ahmadiyya Conference held last year that while African political chains are falling off, its spiritual bondage is still largely untouched. He also stated that while Moslems lack the funds which are available to Christian missionaries they possess potent advantages in the simplicity of Islamic teaching and its practice of brotherhood.[26]

The crusade to Africa of Billy Graham in 1960, with many stops in West Africa, drew the attention of the Ahmadiyya journalist Naseem Saifi in Nigeria. He denounced Christianity, communism, and nationalism as divisive, and proclaimed Islam to be the only unifier.[27]

The role the Ahmadiyya played behind the scenes of Pakistan's foreign relations is significant because of the persecution they faced in public life in Pakistan. While the sect had considered its mission as a riposte to the Christian West, especially Britain and America, the mission also had a far better understanding of African affairs than most others in South Asia or even the West. In 1970, with Abdus Salam's visible role in government, the spiritual head of the Ahmadiyya, Hazrat Hafiz Mirza Nasir Ahmad, became the first head of the sect to make an extensive tour through West Africa, stopping in Nigeria, Ghana, Gambia, Côte d'Ivoire, Liberia, and Sierra Leone. The whirlwind tour was not unlike Billy Graham's a decade earlier. Since then, the heady days of independence had given way to the desperate realities of the civil war in Nigeria and the toppling of Nkrumah in a military coup. With the restoration of democracy under Dr Kofi Busia; with Liberia under President Tubman economically strong; and with Côte d'Ivoire, under President Houphouët-Boigny, friendly to foreigners, West Africa was restabilised. The Ahmadiyya tour was good publicity. West African nations were in the ascendant, but also, having experienced political turmoil, were ripe for the launching of the Ahmadiyya Nusrat Jehan (literally translated as "world aid", but in the Ahmadiyya organisation in 1970, called "Africa Leap Forward"), a charitable wing of the mission focused on educational and medical facilities for Africans.[28]

The Ahmadi spiritual head, Khalifatul Hazrat Hafiz Mirza Nasir Ahmad, in speeches at public events (transcribed and published alongside many images in a booklet called *Africa Speaks*), declared the mission to promote Islamic aid. At a public event in Ibadan, he first paid his respects:

> The accounts of your country and people we received and read in the 1920s fired our imagination and I for one have ever longed to see things for myself and meet the people whose hospitality and kindly interest we have enjoyed since those days. Finding myself here I find a dream fulfilled. I have become aware of your history, of your culturally rich past.[29]

He noted elsewhere that: "Ahmadiyya revere Dan Fodio as a reformer".[30] Africa's "even richer future", he continued, lay with young people:

> It may be natural science that you study. It may be social science. It may be history or literature. It may be some branch of applied or

professional science, or it may be, as I hope, theological science. The pursuit of knowledge is the special prerogative of the youth of the world. But what I wish to tell you is that Truth is knowledge and that there is an Islamic way to pursue it.[31]

Ahmad explained how religion shaped all scientists, since "the believer and unbeliever both turn to the Unseen for help". While the unbeliever does not acknowledge or understand how the unknown is revealed, the believer understands the divine is the source of knowledge. He introduced his vision for the expansion of religious education alongside "modern" (i.e., secular/Western) education, and said that the Ahmadis would build 16 secondary schools and four medical clinics around Nigeria.

The Khalifatul delivered similar messages in Ghana, where many Ahmadi mosques and schools already existed. He spoke at the Kumasi University of Science and Technology and the Pakistan High Commission in Accra. In Abidjan and Monrovia, where Ahmadi presence was small but growing, he laid out plans for schools and clinics. He presented to the Gambian Governor-General Farimang Mamadi Singhateh, a convert, a garment that had belonged to the Ahmadi founder.[32] This ceremony evoked the early twentieth-century Ottoman sultan's bestowal of recognition on African leaders such as Blyden and others.

The association of Ahmadiyya members with heterodoxy, and in some spheres with Shi'a, only intensified Sunni critics.[33] Reacting against Ahmadiyya representations of South Asia in global Islamic networks, Indian and Pakistani Sunni scholars and other intellectuals called international conferences, such as one at Punjab University in Lahore in 1957, that was dedicated to critically analysing the question of how the Ahmadis expanded their worldwide presence. Economist Muhammad Ilyas Burney at Osmania University in Hyderabad, India, devoted an entire book in Urdu to attacking the Qadiani Ahmadiyya on a number of familiar grounds. He cited the prominence of African and Malayan Ahmadis to warn about the growing influence of the sect.[34] Leading theologian Sheikh Sayyid Abul Hassan Ali Nadwi, who was educated at Deoband and helped establish the Oxford Centre for Islamic Studies, accused the head of the Ahmadiyya, Mirza Bashiruddin Mahmud Ahmad, of being "a religious dictator and despotic ruler".[35] This opposition in academic and religious institutions reveals the growing challenges for Ahmadiyya scholars in gaining employment.

Partly in response, the sect's activities in Africa became all the more significant for Ahmadiyya professionals in Pakistan. At a Friday *khutbah* (prayer) in Rabwah, the Ahmadiyya Pakistan headquarters, the Ahmadi leader recounted his days meeting with West African leaders during which he requested plots of land on which to open new schools and clinics. In Nigeria's North West state, for example, "where Usman bin Fodio" came to reform Muslims, the governor gifted many acres for the Ahmadi effort.[36] Certain Nigerian Ahmadis rebelled against the previous Khalifatul and took over schools to turn them into money mints,[37] but the governor may have entrusted land to the Pakistanis because the Ahmadi clinic in the city of Kano had, over several years, accumulated a balance of £15,000 to expand the clinic into a hospital. The Pakistani leader vowed that all profits accrued from schools and hospitals would be reinvested in more schools and hospitals in Africa.[38] The Khalifatul, after having secured acreage in every country he visited, travelled to London, where he asked the well-organised Ahmadi community to invest a minimum of £100,000 in the six African countries he had just visited. He laid out a scheme whereby 200 devotees donated £200 each, another 200 the amount of £100 pounds each, and the rest £36 each. He set up a bank account in the name of the relief unit Nusrat Jahan and returned to Pakistan, vowing to never be like "those who had gone before us with a message of love [and] bled the land dry".[39]

West African Ahmadiyya sites offered Abdus Salam a network into which he could place his students and colleagues who needed to escape persecution in Pakistan and India. For example, one of Salam's advanced students came to teach physics and mathematics in a Ghanaian secondary school before setting off for doctoral studies at Imperial College, London. Salam created pathways for Pakistanis around the world.[40] As a result, amongst the South Asian Ahmadiyya diaspora in wealthy countries like the United States and the United Kingdom, it is common to find professionals who have lived and worked in Africa.[41]

Further Africanisation policies in East Africa forced many Indians to relocate, and amongst them Ahmadis whose homeland in Pakistan was not now welcoming. The exiled Ahmadis from Uganda and Kenya arriving in London numbered 50 per week and were to be housed in dormitories.[42] The scale of the migration is uncertain. Outside Eastern and Southern Africa, the traditional areas Indians had migrated to over several centuries, the Indian government estimates that today there are thousands of Indians living in Nigeria and Ghana. According to these sources, generations of Africans now in their forties to sixties have been taught by Indians. Pakistan, which has seen major outmigration, is ranked by the World Bank sixth in the world for "human capital mobility", as a measure of the migration of highly skilled workers (with India being first).[43] Religious conflicts in Pakistan, the limited opportunities for scientists and other intellectuals, including humanities scholars, and persecution drove the migration, along with dislocation produced by the Indo-Pakistan War in 1965.

The arrival of more Ahmadis to West Africa garnered growing opposition there. Haji Salahuddin Tayo, a Ghanaian missionary who worked with two Saudi organisations, Darul Iftah and the

Muslim World League, recalled the assistance he gave to organise the trip of Pakistani Ahmadi missionaries sent by Ayub Khan. He had complied, knowing little about the sect, but within a few years, and with more input from his Saudi and Pakistani sources, he turned against the Ahmadiyya. He railed against what he called "religious slavery", into which "Indo-Pakistani Ahmadiyya missionaries" had lured Africans.[44]

The Pakistani legislature officially declared Ahmadis non-Muslims in 1974, and created enormous problems for the sect, not only in Pakistan but also in networks that connected Africa and the Middle East.[45] Abdus Salam left Pakistan in 1974 and took up permanent residence in Trieste at ICTP. In some sense, he was refashioning his family's older profession of missionary work in Africa into a kind of Third World science evangelism.

Founding the ICTP

After Salam proposed to the International Atomic Energy Agency (IAEA) that a group should consider the establishment of an international centre for theoretical physics for scientists from developing countries, the Italian physicist Paolo Budinich recommended Trieste as a suitable site. Allied troops had only left Trieste in 1954, when the city was partitioned between Italy and Yugoslavia. To prevent Yugoslavian influence over the border town, an international science centre with United Nations backing could help shore it up as both Italian and Western.[46] It was also a neutral ground for visiting scientists. As Gabrielle Hecht has shown, the early politics of the IAEA, one of the main supporters of the ICTP, grew more complicated as decolonisation and shifting definitions of nuclearity muddied the "noble" claims of "peaceful uses of atomic energy".[47]

The invocation of the discourse of Cold War politics did not defuse postcolonial anxieties about atomic energy, nor did it erase the problems surrounding apartheid-ruled South Africa. Similarly, the ICTP's mission of supporting scientific research and collaboration faced political problems from the outset, particularly Indo-Pakistani tensions. One major stumbling block was Abdus Salam's proposal for theoretical physics, which the Indian delegation wanted to block. Salam's reported "rhetoric and histrionics" finally swayed leaders of developing countries on the IAEA board:

> "The basic notion that atomic energy can be released in the service of man was the brainchild of two men: Bohr and Einstein," he told an audience primarily made up of politicians and diplomats. He contended that "The first nuclear reactor was assembled and actually constructed by a theoretical physicist—Enrico Fermi."[48]

He laid out the differences between places like CERN and Brookhaven which "produce data", and a theoretical institute for interpreting and correlating the data.[49] India, with the largest scientific community in the developing world, was influenced by the argument of Surjit Mansingh that such a centre would not benefit developing countries.[50] This pretextual objection was overcome by the overwhelming support from the rest of the developing countries involved in the debate, but the Centre never fully escaped these tensions. This was not a Cold War issue so much as an expression of South Asian regional conflict incubated in decolonisation.

Daniel Akyeampong, a Ghanaian student who studied at Imperial College, London, with Abdus Salam, described how he was handpicked as one of the first scientists to arrive at the ICTP. He learned about the Centre's founding in 1964, while he was still in the UK, and after visiting Trieste in 1966, and returning to Ghana, he was made an ICTP associate. The associateship scheme allowed him to undertake a regular rotation of teaching for nine months in Ghana followed by a three-month residency at the Centre. In February 1966, Kwame Nkrumah was overthrown in a coup led by Major A. A. Afrifa. Frank Boaten, the Ghanaian ambassador to the United Nations and General Secretary of the pacifist Accra Assembly, conveyed to Abdus Salam the delicate political situation and uncertainty for the organisation. He wrote, "Considering the state of finances of the OAU and the difficult situation caused by many African changes of government in these recent weeks, there is a question as to whether we can obtain sufficient financial backing to proceed".[51] Nigeria had just a few weeks earlier than Ghana been rocked by a coup, and Boaten saw how the domestic and regional political crises would endanger transnational activism in Africa and beyond. Again, these threats were immediate, material, and destabilising, like the Indo-Pakistani conflicts, while the Cold War was a more distant theoretical problem. Akyeampong observed:

> In its early operation, the number of African scientists at the Centre was low indeed. There were only two, Skyim-Kwandoh and myself, from Ghana. We were to be joined later by Taha and Ahmed from Sudan, and Maduemezia and Nwachuku from Nigeria and later still, when Condensed Matter Physics became one of the recognised programmes of the Centre, Allotey from Ghana and Williams from Nigeria. The Centre has helped sustain quite a sizeable number of African mathematicians and scientists, many of whom unfortunately are no longer at home to train the next generation as envisaged by Professor Salam. These have joined the infamous brain drain—the tide Salam strove so vigorously to stem—not because they wanted to, but because unfavourable socioeconomic conditions so familiar to Salam made it difficult, if not impossible for these scientists to be creatively productive in their own countries.[52]

Salam keenly understood how political instability, such as coups d'état, affected scientific investment and policy in developing countries. It was, after all, Ayub Khan's accession that inaugurated Pakistan's nuclear ambitions and gave Salam a prominent role, albeit one that stifled his personal research agenda. Scientists who fell foul of new regimes suffered outside Africa and Asia as well. Physicist J. C. Gallardo, who spent time in Trieste in 1971, was missing for weeks before his family found him in jail, accused by the Argentine government of "irregularities".[53] In 1976, a new junta in Argentina drove out about 200 physicists within a few months. "By and large the actions of the Argentinian government can be characterized as a sort of preemptive and arbitrary brutality aimed at eliminating any possibility of independent thought", the American Physical Society wrote.[54]

African leaders began to suggest to Salam that his vision of science did not necessarily match with those of his colleagues. In 1975, Chief Olu-Ibukun, the head of UNESCO's Regional Office of Science and Technology for Africa, complained about the title of the ICTP and about governments questioned giving it financial support:

> For the most part, these finance affairs do not see the bearing of "theoretical" studies in science on the development of their economies, and hence are very unlikely to assign high priority to funding one of their nationals to study at their Centre. We have tried, of course, to provide more information which tends to dispel such beliefs.[55]

He recommended cooperation of the ICTP with UNESCO and the OAU in the development of an African network of specialised institutes focused on three areas of applied science: earth sciences, food science and technology, and electronics sciences and technology.

The ICTP was similarly criticised in the 1960s by a Brazilian physicist about the soundness of the Centre's research.[56] Abdus Salam's stature and diplomatic skills effectively sidelined the criticism then, but by the time Olu-Ibukun took up the challenge, the Centre was embroiled in controversy over the Arab-Israeli or Yom Kippur War of 1973. Many developing countries severed their ties with Israel, including many African countries with whom Israel had been cultivating links through technical assistance. Ghana—where Israel had sought to make significant alliances following Ghanaian independence—Kenya, and Côte d'Ivoire allowed some "interest offices" to remain open.[57] Africans at the UN had helped shift the organisation's position towards the Arab side, and in 1974 the General Conference of UNESCO passed three resolutions that aimed to exclude Israel from participation in international research activities. In retaliation, American and Israeli scientists boycotted UNESCO and its satellite units, including the ICTP, claiming that UNESCO's action to drive Israel out of the international organisation was antithetical to its core founding principle.

The refusal of these scientists to attend ICTP courses disrupted much of the planned work for 1975. Abdus Salam never declared his support or rejection of the UNESCO resolutions, and did not want to enter into the discussion about which countries could or could not sponsor scientists' participation at the Centre. He learned from his colleagues that Israeli scientists opposed the Centre, in part, because Abdus Salam kept close ties to African countries who were blamed for removing Israel from UNESCO.[58] Facing economic shortfalls at the Centre because of the boycott, Salam approached Iran and sought to shore up alliances with Arab countries. This strategy appeared to mirror the turn of Pakistan, where Salam still held government positions, towards the Arab world, though Salam privately disagreed with Bhutto's anti-Western rhetoric. Salam's careful politicking kept the Centre financially secure throughout the boycott, which lasted until 1977, when Israel was reinstated, but "the ICTP was scapegoated for Salam's conflicting and ambiguous links with both a third world country striving to strengthen its ties with the Islamic world and a third world center seeking Western support".[59] The boycott illustrated how "politicization of science and scientific institutions is a free-floating boundary between knowledge and power that, during a controversy, every actor draws upon according to his or her own interests".[60] Third World nations exercised power through their collective objections in international organisations, but also suffered for the political positions they took when the United States and its allies withdrew financial support.[61]

Olu-Ibukun held the upper hand with Abdus Salam. Nigeria, which was then experiencing an enormous economic upsurge with its "oil boom", had the largest African contingent at the ICTP annually. Olu-Ibukun sought to capitalise on Salam's desire for more African scientists to secure a working relationship between the Nigerian National Research Council and the ICTP and, for the whole continent, to put applied sciences on the Centre's agenda.[62] Nigeria's ascendance on the continent—economically, scientifically, and academically—was not to be minimised.

African scientists were leaving their countries, but African nations were also destinations for South Asian diasporas. From the late 1960s through the 1970s, as African countries began sending larger contingents of scientists to the ICTP for short courses and other stints, a noticeable uptick in the numbers of South Asian scientists included as part of African participation is clear. In 1970, for instance, Uganda sent one scientist, A. A. Patani, who was of Indian origin, but in subsequent years, Nigeria surpassed countries from Eastern Africa and the Indian Ocean (like Mauritius) with large Indian diasporas, in sending South Asians—including Indians, Pakistanis, and Bangladeshis— to the ICTP. The South Asian scientists never outnumbered the Nigerians, but were notably recorded as expatriate scientists.[63] The only other expatriate scientists in Nigeria were from Benin,

Ghana, and Yugoslavia, and the South Asians outnumbered them. Sudan also sent Indian engineer Ariacutty Jayendran to the ICTP, but Sudan's representation was small compared to that of Nigeria.

Salam's response to Olu-Ibukun's critique was insufficient. While acknowledging the problem of the Centre's name, which he said he had been considering for a long time, Salam repeated to Olu-Ibukun the well-worn message:

> The basic philosophy of the Centre is that although there are many institutions in the world training young men from many countries for doctorate degrees, there are none which look after them for research at post-graduate level. The Centre is therefore at the highest scientific standard so as to be a place of inspiration for young scientists who will have an opportunity to be in active contact with others engaged in the same intellectual exercise. The existence of such an opportunity where scientists from the developing countries can visit and continue with their research work for short periods of time is a deterrent to the "brain drain" which has resulted in the movement of scientists from the developing to the developed countries.[64]

One problem, clearly, with this argument was that some of the brain drain from South Asia went to African countries, which Salam should have recognised. Nigeria had vast wealth, albeit misspent, and many African universities paid better than European ones in the 1960s and 1970s, thus attracting South Asian scholars. The work happening in postcolonial African universities also interested South Asian scientists. Babulal Saraf, a professor of physics education who was forced into early retirement from his university in Rajasthan in North India, worked in Senegal in the 1970s, then Nigeria in the 1980s, before he moved to Tanzania. He came with high recommendations to African governments from Abdus Salam himself:

he has made a specialty of producing cheap locally made apparatus for teaching purposes in schools and colleges for physics education. Equipment is one of the bottlenecks in all our countries and he is one of the few people who can help in this regard.[65]

The irony of this recommendation is that Saraf's expertise was in applied physics. Moreover, he gained it, apparently, through decades of experience in Africa. Olu-Ibukun's prodding of Salam helped spur thinking amongst African scientists who led a new charge at the ICTP.

Pan-African power

Olu-Ibukun was not the only African scientist to propose a more Africa-specific and Afrocentric approach to the activities being undertaken at the ICTP. In 1977, Ugandan mathematics professor P. E. Mugambi suggested to Paolo Budinich, Salam's close collaborator, that an autonomous African organisation be formed: "I would like to see an organization such as the African Mathematical Union set up by the physicists themselves under which regional activities such as the ones in Malaysia could be initiated with international backing".[66] The Union, which was formed in 1976 in Rabat at the first Pan African Congress of Mathematicians, was the outcome of meetings that African mathematicians had held themselves,[67] and Mugambi's suggestion for international backing seemed to imply that non-African scientists and international organisations should recognise the global relevance of such African organisations. He mentioned a Zairian physicist, Dr L. B. Lofo, who was prepared to move ahead with an Africa-wide cooperation in the discipline, showing that Africans had organised themselves across linguistic differences, which the ICTP had long had a difficult time doing due to its Anglophone bias. Into the early 1990s, Salam was fielding letters from scientists based in Zaire and Algeria asking for French-language conferences, "due to the quasi absence of scientists from this part of Africa in international centres and meetings".[68] Salam responded to Mbaro Saman Lubuma, a Zairois (Congolese) mathematician, making clear he had been chastened over the years: "Since African scientists are all very sensitive to outside bodies doing something for them, I am sending this request of yours to Prof. T. Odhiambo first of all. After hearing from him and the African Academy of Sciences, I shall then be able to take action, if action is warranted".[69]

This Pan-African science association was part of a wider movement of Black cultural consciousness in action at this time, around the continent and in the diaspora. Notable were the World Black and African Festivals of Arts and Culture held in Senegal (1966) and Nigeria (1977). After the African Mathematical Union founded in 1976 came the Society of African Physicists and Mathematicians (SAPAM) in 1983 (later the African Physical Society), started by Francis Allotey of Ghana and Charles Nwachuku of Nigeria. They asked Salam to be the society's patron. The founding group included 34 African scientists who were concerned about the state of their fields and the "lack of cohesion" amongst African scientists.[70] In 1985, the African Academy of Sciences was founded, brainchild of Kenyan scientist T. R. Odhiambo, who first raised the proposal two years earlier at the first meeting of the Third World Academy of Sciences. African scientists focused on drought, desertification, and food security. The inauguration of the African Academy of Sciences in Nairobi in early June 1986 was also the occasion for a symposium on "Utilization of Indigenous Scientists in National Development" which emphasised the problem with "already existing studies [that] put emphasis on outside assistance. In contrast, this team and African scientists plan to emphasize building up of local scientific leadership, management, and capabilities".[71]

Odhiambo, Allotey, and other African scientists who worked closely with Abdus Salam, followed his example but forged their own direction in a Pan-African and indigenous sciences movement that was well underway by the mid-1980s. Allotey noted Salam's cultural pride in Islam that, by his later years, far overshadowed his Pakistani identity. After Salam received the Nobel Prize, his acceptance speech in Stockholm was the first to include lines from the Qur'an. Salam began to emphasise much more publicly the theme of Islamic science. He began many of his public lectures, including his inauguration speech for the African Academy of Sciences, with a reference to Islamic history, to the famed physician of Bokhara Al-Asuli, or the thirteenth-century Scotsman Michael who studied in Toledo. These references came from the heart, and his colleagues noted that "all through the years, Salam ... nursed a passion for the rejuvenation of science in the Islamic world".[72] Yet he lamented the state of science in the Islamic world, with its divisions (which included the label of apostate hung upon his own sect), leaders who feared religious backlash against science, assaults on free thought in some quarters, and other problems. He appeared in many venues, such as a 1984 meeting in Paris of two representatives of Islam (himself and the former Saudi Minister of Health) and two from the West, where he declared: "I have myself never seen any dichotomy between my faith and my science—since faith was predicated for me by the timeless spiritual message of Islam, on matters on which physics is silent".[73]

Salam's colleague in Pakistan, Pervez Hoodbhoy, suggests that the Ahmadi "never accepted excommunication" and became "more religious ... regrettably so, in the opinion of some".[74] Few Africans seem to have commented on or corresponded with Salam about his religious reawakening, as it were; one who did was Sadiq al-Mahdi, a politician who was a great-grandson of Muhammad Ahmad, the Sudanese Mahdi and resistance leader against the

British, who wrote in support of Salam's efforts to spur Muslims' "scientific and technological awakening".[75] Salam acknowledged but did not seem to understand Black racial consciousness.

As Pan-African scientists were coalescing around Black networks, they worked in parallel with Salam's Pan-Islamism, thereby separating strands that had been woven together by the Ahmadiyya. Black scientists garnered more material resources for research and collaboration from the sympathetic but somewhat removed Salam. The availability of funding for collaborative projects through the ICTP sparked a renewed Pan-Africanist push. The US boycott with Israel of the ICTP after 1973 further circumscribed that network.

By 1988–89, the Black American Society of Friends of the ICTP was formed by Professor Joseph Andrew Johnson III. Johnson had organised Black physicists' meetings as early as 1972, with the first one held at Fisk University.[76] He worked with the ICTP to "quickly and efficiently identify Black American physicists who were genuinely interested, on short notice, in scientific interactions with African scientists".[77] The Bouchet Institute was founded at the ICTP entirely for this purpose—to facilitate connections between African and African-American scientists that would lead to funded non-permanent posts for Africans in the United States. It was also implicitly understood, in that moment of intense international anti-apartheid activism, that these opportunities to spend time in the US were for Black scientists, not whites, from the African continent.[78] Johnson, together with his wife, Dr Lynette E. Johnson, won a grant from the American National Science Foundation, with which they sponsored African scholars and students at different universities. Other collaborators included Ronald Mickens of Clark Atlanta, Carl Spight, and Anthony Johnson at University of Maryland, Baltimore.[79]

The programme built upon a history of African and other non-American faculty at historically Black colleges and universities that stretched back at least to the 1950s. Given the paucity of African-American doctorates in the sciences in the first half of the twentieth century, many HBCU professors were white, and, in the 1940s and 1950s, many Jewish professors fleeing discrimination found safe havens at Black institutions. In the 1970s and 1980s, more Asian and Middle Eastern faculty filled the ranks, and in the 2010s, slightly more than half of tenured faculty at HBCUs were Black.[80] The situation at places like Fisk made immigrants' integration easier than in other parts of American society, according to Ronald Mickens, who studied there in the early 1960s, because no factors like race, religion, or other cultural differences were impediments. "We even invited people who hated Blacks and Jews to Fisk", he recalled, to hear what they had to say. That kind of ecumenism of thought had a practical consequence of breaking down hierarchies, he argued, which was essential to knowledge-production. The Bouchet Institute was designed for that purpose.

After the first meeting of EBASI was held in Trieste in 1988, Abdus Salam could not attend the second, but sent a note saying he was "proud to be associated with this important initiative which will provide the opportunity for Black physicists from America and from African countries to meet and interact with each other for their mutual benefit".[81] He added, however, a discomfiting postscript: "PS I sincerely hope you will be able to change the word Black". Soon thereafter, an effort was undertaken by Salam's nephew studying at Stanford to start a Minority American Friends of ICTP Society, with the help of the (American) National Society of Black Physicists led by Dr Sekazi Mtingwa, a collaborator with Johnson at the Bouchet Institute. African-American scientists helped Abdus Salam and the ICTP, after the problems with the Israeli-American boycott, make new inroads into America's diverse but unequal academic landscape. Reports from Johnson suggested the collaboration was bearing fruit, with hundreds of participants at conferences from throughout the African continent and the United States, and with the support of a variety of organisations and industries, from energy and petroleum, telecommunications, to health.[82]

A surprising victory for indigenous knowledge

When Abdus Salam died in 1996, a great many African scientists remembered him as providing inspiration. Lydia Makhubu, a Swazi scientist with expertise in medicinal chemistry, recalled Salam's recounting of a personal experience in 1988, at a conference on the role of women in science and technology development in the Third World:

> His brilliant daughter, Dr. Aziza Rahman, obtained a Ph.D. degree in Biochemistry from the University of London and went on to do research at the Cancer Institute of Columbia University in New York. What began as a brilliant scientific career for Dr. Rahman was subsequently interrupted by marriage when she selected to raise her family rather than continue as a scientist. This, ladies and gentlemen, is a typical story for women in science and those in academia— women aspiring to intellectual leadership in the Third World and elsewhere in the world ... I do not regard this typical story as a sad story but rather as one which highlights the important role of women in human development, social stability and cohesion, without which societies would crumble.[83]

The Third World Organization for Women in Science was founded in 1989 (and the name changed to the Organization for Women in Science for the Developing World in 2010), and Makhubu played an instrumental role in setting its agenda to improve quality of life in developing countries, to "link high-level scientific activities to grassroots concerns" like environment, food, and population, over military superiority. Her areas of expertise—traditional medicinal plants, bioprospecting, and medical pluralism—have become an increasingly significant research area of African nations, from the perspective not only of biological and chemical sciences, but also economy, multinational business, and international law.

Africans accorded South Asian academics and researchers respect and acknowledged that African capacity for science education and development was behind that of India and Pakistan. But scientific collaboration and missions exposed limits in the flow of influence in one direction or another. African scientists were confident in their knowledge that environment, climate, food security, and health should be their foci, even though their governments did not necessarily give them needed support; Pan-African networks to the United States instead helped them sustain research for some time. At the same time, Abdus Salam did not appear to accord race—Black solidarity, more precisely—the same legitimacy as political ideologies like Pan-Islamism and "Third Worldism". Yet, in the end, all three, in their entanglement in a new way at the ICTP, were operationalised within a small but significant transnational intellectual community.

Awele Maduemezia, Nigerian physicist, environmentalist, and frequent collaborator with Salam and others at the ICTP, wrote that the best teachers of basic sciences in developing countries, in his experience, were those who had studied the esoteric. Although many people in developing countries harbour suspicions that scientists do nothing practical, he wrote, those persons with abstruse areas of modern theoretical physics have "an uncommon maturity in their understanding of the subject" that can be adapted to practical lessons in basic sciences.[84] African-Indian scientific encounters provoked fundamental questions about the mysteries of nature and metaphysics. More recent considerations have identified metaphysics and spirituality as vital distinguishing characteristics that are unique to African sciences, along with environment and peace—themes that Makhubu highlighted.[85]

Conclusion

Measuring South Asian migration to African countries is difficult, but hundreds if not thousands of academics hailing from South Asia have taught in Africa since the 1960s, suggesting the reworking of an older cultural reputation for expertise and authority.[86] The historical presence of the Ahmadiyya mission, the political use of it by Pakistan, and the success of Abdus Salam all converged in the 1970s. Unlike the shopkeepers and merchants, South Asian teachers commanded respect that bears resemblance to the older history of itinerant Muslim scholars as high-status people known for their modest lifestyle. The intellectual diaspora of South Asians into Africa helped dislodge the image of the Indian merchant.

Yet the Indian and Pakistani intellectuals were not completely absolved of the suspicion of neocolonialism, especially concerning the increasing religious fervency of Abdus Salam and the Ahmadiyya. African and African diaspora scientists in particular respected his achievements and his passion, but began to diverge from his mission. As Thandika Mkandawire writes, African intellectuals have had a fraught but productive relationship with Pan-Africanism and nationalism because of the ongoing search for an autonomous space, where they have sometimes had to self-impose marginality.[87] At the ICTP, African scientists agitated to stake out their own collective position, which Salam perceived as a kind of Black self-segregation. Yet they achieved from cooperation a critical divergence to disentangle Black struggles from the larger Third World. Moreover, race and religion were not the same mission. In the story of the Edward Bouchet Abdus Salam Institute, two distinct diasporic experiences converged and grew apart: on the one hand that of displaced Black peoples who were denied an equal place amongst whites in the scientific world, and on the other of the Ahmadis as outcasts of a religious state and of the Muslim world.

Black scientists understood before Salam did the need for critical distance from Western science and from the nation state. Dr Carl Spight, an African-American physicist who on occasion visited the ICTP, wrote in 1974: "in the process of fundamental mastery of science and technology, caution is imperative lest we aid inadvertently in our own destruction".[88] By many accounts, he challenged Salam, who listened to him without always understanding the position in which Black scientists in America found themselves. Salam did not seem to understand race as a positive principle, until Spight and others helped him see that one of their main responsibilities was "the systematic demystification of science and technology and the reformulation of it to the service of the struggle of Black people world-wide".[89] Though Black scientists recognised the influence of the Pakistani Nobel Laureate on them, the prescient words of Spight seem quite clear evidence that the influence went the other way. Afrocentric scientists influenced Salam to see the struggle of Muslims in a world increasingly hostile to them as like the struggles of Black peoples. He had maintained a feeling that scientific development could supersede cultural politics, until the persecution of his own people fostered a new nostalgia for the unity of the Muslim world.

After the ICTP had brought them together, Black scientists and Abdus Salam diverged in their aims. African technological and scientific development suffered not only because of the lack of resources but also from the lack of control Africans had in setting agendas in high-level organisations. The agendas of the

IAEA and even national leaders did not match the goals of many scientists, who were not motivated only by personal gain. Some believed strongly in Pan-Africanism, and their political orientation made them critical and careful about faith in science. This lesson was ultimately the one Salam learned from them. The EBASI Institute was a symbol of how scientists could use the power they have to stake moral positions. Postcolonial science was not, in this sense, a unified collective enterprise of non-white peoples. Many experts and teachers saw their work in terms of cultural imaginations beyond the nation. Africans and South Asians saw their diasporas through very different lenses, exposing how Pan-African and Pan-Islamic politics remained important and sometimes on different trajectories even in the era of African-Asian solidarity.

5

HINDUISM'S BLACK ATLANTIC ITINERARY

Introduction

In 1998, the magazine *Hinduism Today* featured a story titled "Africa is Ripe for a Strong Hindu Future". The author, Ghanaian monk Swami Ghanananda Saraswati, contrasted the short history of Hinduism on the African continent with the old strong roots of Islam and Christianity. Invoking stereotypes about the "dark continent", he mentioned also the "inward looking" Indian migrants, "purely interested in their businesses, not portraying Hindu lifestyle", and their disinterest in mingling with Africans. Hinduism could have played a positive role in Africa, but Indians had kept it for themselves. Ghanananda urged readers to consider this new possibility: "Hinduism, alongside other religions, must help in harmonizing the efforts of all religions to foster the needed peace for both material and spiritual development of the continent".[1]

The swami said very little about African Hindus, whom he described as "a few people ... [who] practice Hinduism under the cloak of secret societies". He knew of, but did not mention, other Black Hindus in West Africa, including members of the Hare Krishna movement—the International Society for Krishna Consciousness (ISKCON)—which had started a network between Africans and African-Americans through the efforts of disciples like Bhakti Tirtha Swami, originally from Cleveland, Ohio.² Drawing attention instead to how Africans connect their lives to a Hindu way of life, he explained some similarities between African indigenous religions and Hinduism: "only Africans who have been exposed to Hinduism can appreciate these similarities". Such people had remained invisible to Indians, "who mix little with Africans".

The purpose of the Ghanaian Swami's writing was different from the magazine's, which had doubtless featured the Black swami in a more self-serving way to celebrate the apparently nonracial character of Hindu *sanatan dharma*—the eternal law or duties of all humans. By then, *Hinduism Today* was nearly two decades old, and was produced at the Himalayan Academy of the Hindu Monastery located in Kauai, Hawaii, founded by Satguru Sivaya Subramuniyaswami. He was born in California and travelled in 1947 to India and Sri Lanka, where he was initiated after two years as a *sannyasin* (one who has renounced) or monk. For the magazine's intended audience, Hindus dispersed throughout 80 countries, journalist Lavina Melwani wrote about the history of the magazine's evolution from a simple newspaper, hand-set by monks, to a multimedia editorial suite including a glossy magazine along with websites. The transformation reveals a striking contrast that Hinduism allows: "In India the pandits still sit on the ghats in Haridwar—nothing ever changes. But *Hinduism Today* has embraced change with enthusiasm in full cooperation with some of these same wisdom-laden pandits".³ The Ghanaian swami's being "a Black African", a phrase used several times in the article about African Hindus, was meant to signal a part of this remarkable feature of Hinduism—how tradition worked in modern terms. The racial universalism of Hinduism showed its enduring truth of human sameness.

The African swami's appearance in this magazine can be read in three distinct frames. First, the magazine, clearly meant for Hindus outside India, oriented readers towards an American spiritualist perspective in which the Hindu belief in an ultimate reality was to be found with the all-important *guru*, or teacher, as a guide to seekers to that "far shore", as Hindu texts often referred to liberation from life's upheaval.[4] The guru tradition was extremely successful in the United States, particularly amongst whites. The second frame is the intricate strands of Hindutva, Hindu nationalism, that developed across long distances inside and outside the Indian diaspora to construct a political ideology of India as a Hindu state. Hindutva "political monotheism" in the *sanatan dharma* aided in this construction.[5] It also established a competition with Islam that was sometimes implicit but at other times explicit. The third frame is the African one, which exposes the exclusionary—racial, class, and philosophical—practice of Hindu Indians. Swami Ghanananda's critique of the materialism and racial segregation of Indians in Africa reflects longstanding grievances, articulated within a religious moralism. Yet, at the same time, his view about African indigenous religions' kinship with Hinduism—that sanatan dharma has been with Ghanaians since "creation"[6]—raises a crucial question: does African Hinduism support the Hindutva arguments about Hindu civilisation as the progenitor of human intellect and belief? A similar question had confronted Africans and South Asians in science research and education, and Africans asserted a strong critique through it.

In Swami Ghanananda's movement today, there is also no simple story of African conversion to Hinduism because of Indian cultural domination and evangelism, as Nehru's government debated decades earlier. Just as the histories of Christianity or

Islam in Africa reveal African agency, so too does West African
Hinduism. Swami Ghanananda and other African Hindus travelled to India. Diaspora Indians visited the African swami before
his death in 2016 to seek his teaching and blessings. Veena
Sharma, a Kenyan Indian scholar, wrote of her trip to Ghana
where she had gone to study Akan religion. But finding herself at
the Hindu Monastery of Africa, she had "seen a form of the non-
dual Vedanta being practised there".[7] She experienced a distinct
inversion of the typical African-Indian relationship. Swami
Ghanananda's initiation and revered status turned the teacher-
student or guru-disciple relationship on its head, and established
an African spiritual authority that offered Indians more than a
celebration of Hinduism's cross-cultural appeal. It forced a recognition of secular racial structures in historical and religious relations and opened up new possibilities, quite apart from the language of race. Sharma, in her book *Advaita Vedanta and Akan*,
connected African and South Asian philosophy at their roots,
and, in her other writings on religious tourism, she questioned
whether "in this postmodern age, tourism as an industry can
somehow play a role in reducing phobias and prejudices that arise
from within certain religious traditions preventing spiritual seekers from entering into and experiencing sacred sites that could
enhance understanding of traditions that appear to be exclusive".[8]
Sharma broadens the principle of non-division in spirituality to a
statement of social and racial integration, with an implicit critique
of religious exclusivity that has a clear connection to her own
experience as an Indian in different African locations, from Kenya,
the settler postcolony, to the Pan-African Ghanaian state, where
she understood her birth religion anew.

Sharma is not alone amongst Indians who come to Swami
Ghanananda's Hindu Monastery, which welcomes Indians from
different parts of the subcontinent, including South Indians from
Tamil Nadu, Andhra Pradesh, and Kerala. Newer or perhaps

invisible Indian diasporas, who do not fit into the earlier merchant migrant presence, find a home in the Monastery because
Hinduism in India is highly regionally and ethnically divergent.
Moreover, some South Indian Hindus reject high-caste control
and its gender conformity, and embrace more social and cultural
intercourse with Africans than Indians who arrived in Ghana and
elsewhere in Africa before them. For several years, the Hindu
Monastery has hosted South Indians to perform the festival of
Makaravilakku, which celebrates the celibate god Lord Ayyappa,
and Ghanaians join Indians in performing *bhajans* (popular devotional songs) in Tamil, Telugu, and Malayalam. The festival in
India brings together Hindus from different castes, as well as
Muslims and Christians, and it is a scene of intense protest over
high-caste domination and the banning of women. In Ghana,
Swami Ghananandaʼs nonconformity beyond the strict Brahmin
(upper-caste) interpretation of the Divine Life Society where he
studied has rendered the Monastery a sacred space known to
Indians throughout the world.[9] African devotional practice has
produced a critical consciousness that even Western fascination
with and appropriation of Hinduism has not, especially on the
question of racial difference and distancing.

Miracles of survival: tales of slaves and soldiers

Well before Swami Ghanan, found his way to India, Africans
had been a part of pilgrimage in the subcontinent. The Habshis
or Siddis, the African-Indians who arrived in India as slaves, soldiers, and sailors as early as the thirteenth century, if not before,
have a special association with certain religious rituals, festivals,
and Muslim saintsʼ tombs. Many fakirs, for example, are Habshis
who organise cults for their own communities and for visitors in
regions of Southern Gujarat on the west coast of India, where

many African-descended communities settled over centuries. This is the location of the tomb, or *dargah*, of Bava Ghor, an East African saint who died in India probably before the sixteenth century. Close by is the tomb of his sister Mai Mishra.[10] Their tombs are sites of pilgrimage for Muslims, Hindus, Sikhs, Parsis (Zoroastrians), and Bhil (Adivasi), an aboriginal people classified by the Indian government as a so-called Scheduled Tribe.

Much further to the north and west, in the Sindh region, a few miles outside the (now) Pakistani city of Karachi, another shrine features a Habshi presence, there known as Sheedis (or Siddis in India), in this case for the saint (Pir) Mangho, who came from Iraq in the thirteenth century to what was then a cluster of fishing villages. Drums accompanied by songs in Kiswahili are played for a week, while a sacrifice of meat is made to crocodiles, who are believed to be manifestations of the Sufi saint.[11] The ritual expertise of Siddis today has made their music and dance known throughout much of South Asia, particularly on the western coasts, and in world music, but it could have also been a mechanism for manumission of slaves. The British declared slavery illegal in India in 1843, and slaves were designated to the lower strata, but not the lowest, in the caste system, which existed in both the Hindu and Muslim social orders, despite Islamic tenets against such hierarchies. Being ritual experts offered a special place for the non-elite African-Indians, most of whom were not agriculturalists but rather military slaves, domestic servants, and otherwise working in urban sites.[12] Musical castes have allowed space, albeit amongst the lower ranks, for Muslims living amongst Hindus. Some other groups, including the intersex/trans/non-binary *Hijra* and *devadasi* temple priestesses, occupy a place outside the caste system as travelling entertainers. Siddis in some regions were not cast out, but instead absorbed into the social order as Sufi musicians.

Muslim Siddis in Gujarat created an alternative kinship based on spiritual bonds, known locally as *jamaat*, legitimised through public rituals. Their unknown or remote origins, physical differences, and servile ancestry mark the Siddis as different. Some researchers have focused on their darker skin, but that is not an immediate marker of lower social status where many people, particularly the vast agriculturalist majority, are dark. Layered upon Siddi genealogy is the "thermodynamic theory" that governs classifications in Indian cosmology across religious communities—hot and cold designations attached to foods, medicines, moral dispositions, body constitutions, and spirits.[13] The Siddi are seen by their neighbours as hot-blooded, hot-tempered, and fiery, but these are valued qualities in the veneration of the saint Bava Ghor. Dark skin has been associated with dancing, clowning, and performing, and many Siddi jesters appeared in royal courts in earlier times. In today's religious festivals, Siddis are known for their dancing as "mad fakirs" who become possessed by the spirit of the saint. The performance re-enacts how Bava Ghor and Mai Mishra became saints through their miraculous acts to slay demons and bring sustenance to the villagers.

This Black presence in Indian public spaces puts into relief the contrast with the experiences of newly arrived Africans and African-Americans in India. The first publicised trip of an African-American group to India was the 1935 "Pilgrimage of Friendship". The civil rights leader Howard Thurman, together with his wife and another couple, travelled to Sri Lanka and India to be the first African-Americans to meet Gandhi and other Indian nationalists. Their trip was a highly staged event across the Atlantic and Indian Ocean. The event aimed to symbolise that Christianity belonged to the non-whites of the world. It was conceived by the Student Christian Movement in the United States, which was an alliance of the YMCA and YWCA, and its Indian counterpart, represented by Augustine Ralla Ram, the head of a student Christian movement for Ceylon, India, and Burma. Ram had experienced a profound conversion that pushed him closer to the African-American struggle against oppression. A North Indian Brahmin convert to Christianity, Ram earned a reputation as an outspoken critic of British rule in India, which irritated the British YMCA leadership, who discouraged political activists amongst Indian converts.[14] He worked throughout his life to fight the image in India that Christianity was necessarily tethered to the West and that the Indian church had to bear the "unwanted imposition of the West".[15] He hoped that the African-American Christian delegation, as "representatives of another oppressed group, [could] speak on the validity of the contribution of Christianity".[16]

Thurman was as an ordained minister and professor of religion at Howard University. He gave many public lectures in India. He visited Rabindranath Tagore and Gandhi, amongst other Indian nationalists, who asked him questions about African-American history that tended to centre around leaders like Booker T. Washington and George Washington Carver. Perhaps these African-Americans were known to Indians through the filter of British and American media. Thurman's most intense conversation was reportedly with a Ceylonese lawyer, who questioned him about Blacks' reception of Christianity in light of Christian apologies for slavery. He answered by noting that Jesus's teachings could be separated from Christianity.[17] The discussions brought out a mystical and spiritual side of Thurman that lasted well beyond his sojourn in India, where he regretted that he was mostly met with questions from his hosts about being Black in America. Upon his return to America, Thurman became a spiritual adviser to many African-Americans, who considered him to be a moral leader. He understood the contradictions of being a Black activist believer in non-violent resistance. In this he was considered an important influence on Martin Luther King Jr., who made his own trip to India in 1959. Thurman's biographer,

Walter Fluker, called him "a holy man for the new millennium" because of his focus on a person's higher purpose, which proved enigmatic and sometimes overly vague to pragmatic observers like W. E. B. Du Bois. But Martin Luther King Jr., Jesse Jackson, and other religious leaders valued his spiritual and intellectual teaching. It could contain and give expression to the contradictions and ambivalence that Black leaders felt.[18] Benjamin Mays, the president of Morehouse College, travelled to India a short time after Thurman in 1937, and learned from a different kind of experience: being classified by Indians as an untouchable.[19]

A short time after these African-American visitors travelled to India, tens of thousands of African soldiers arrived to support the British Army in World War II. Amongst them, nearly 74,000 men hailed from West Africa, some of whom made publicised trips to sites like the Taj Mahal.[20] In the 1940s, the *Royal West African Frontier Force News* featured photographs of African soldiers and former soldiers in military and civilian clothes, including some dressed in the *babbar riga*, or traditional long gowns worn by Muslim men in Northern Nigeria. The photos show Africans as tourists in India, although some Africans also wanted to be photographed as proof of their survival during the war. As Oliver Coates discovered,

> Two military clergymen, the Reverend Hunter of the Gambia and the Reverend Solarin from Ijebu Ode in southwestern Nigeria, were so frustrated by repeated rumors that they had died during their service in Burma that they had photographic portraits taken to prove to relatives back in Africa that they were still alive.[21]

The miracles of African survival are embedded in old rituals, while newer Black pilgrimages attest to the Black struggles for rights and African bravery in war. This spirituality associated with India, explained to Swami Ghanananda by an ex-soldier, was the catalyst for his conversion.

Modern mysticism

Swami Ghanananda was born Kwesi Essel in 1937, in Senya Beraku, in what is today the Central Region of Ghana. Described as a small fishing village by European travellers and slave traders, Kwesi's birthplace was the site of Fort Good Hope, one of the slave "castles" built by the Dutch in the early eighteenth century. The village had an intimate link with the sea, both in terms of its livelihood and its loss, of humans sold into the slave trade over hundreds of years and then more recent precarious migrations in search of work in Europe.[22] Kwesi's family members occupied important positions as healers and ritual specialists—his father was a herbalist and his mother a "traditional princess and a priestess".[23] She was the more powerful one, he remembered, as "the spirit would possess her and she would tell [the people] what they wanted to know".[24] She served as a priest to the Chief of Senya Beraku until her death in 1945. Kwesi then began to work with his father as an herbalist, but longed to understand better his mother's spirit trances, which he tried to achieve through prayer. Meditation led him to a man whom he described as a traveller from Ghana to India and Burma, who told Kwesi he might be able to access more Hindu esoteric objects if he could get in contact with Indians in India.

Kwesi began collecting whatever Indian talismans and pictures he could find, which he said were available and fairly sought after in Ghana. Wanting more, he later told biographers, he wrote to "someone in India" and began receiving pamphlets that were written in unknown languages but had pictures of goddesses and gods to which he was immediately drawn.[25] They reminded him of his mother, he noted, and also Mamme, or Mami Wata, in whom his father believed. Taking what appears to be a new direction in Mamme practices along the Atlantic coast, Kwesi began more intense fasting because it helped him reach the spiritual state. Fasting was an indigenous practice amongst the Ga, in which priests endured ascetic hardships for the purificatory benefit of the entire community.[26]

Kwesi moved away from his village to Accra, where he gathered a circle of followers who were attracted to his supernatural abilities and teachings. His move coincided with the appointment of one Opanin Kow Essel, aged 32, as chief herbalist of Senya Beraku in 1952, as reported in *The Daily Graphic* newspaper.[27] Possibly the brother of Kwesi Essel, this man rose to serve the then paramount chief of the village, Odefey Kweku Issiw IV. This appointment might have displaced Kwesi, who did not really return to his birthplace until more than 50 years later as Swami Ghanananda, to negotiate with the heir of the chief to rent land upon which to build a new branch of the Hindu Monastery.[28] In Accra, he used the personal powers endowed to him by his parents—the special ability to communicate between humans and spirits—to venture beyond ritual specialty on behalf of the village chief, to offer services for ordinary people. He provided not only herbal remedies but also meditation, spiritual intercession, and the exploration of foreign metaphysical practices, such as the chanting of Sanskrit mantras and the adornment of the body with the bindi on the centre of the forehead.

He described how, during his search in Accra for incense and other goods for a prayer session, he learned of the Divine Life Society in Rishikesh on the Ganges River in the Himalayas, where he eventually went. "A young man at the door of the shop", he recalled, presumably an Indian shop, "asked what I wanted. I said I want India books. He gave me a Divine Life Society pamphlet".[29] His mentor, who had been in India as a soldier with the British Army, told Kwesi that India was the best place for spiritual education.

Hindu images from "India books" had come to Ghana decades ago, but the soldiers had produced their own images of India in the army newspaper and in an oral culture about the war. Even though the vast majority of the nearly 69,000 Gold Coast men who served in the forces from India through to Burma were not literate, publications were a medium of exchange between soldiers. They also relayed personal experiences through spoken interviews given to literate Africans which were published in military gazettes like *Kintampo Camp Weekly*. The literate Gold Coast soldiers, like their peers from throughout the continent, had more interaction with Indians that gave rise to a "new sense of values".[30] Some educated soldiers went with Indian servicemen to visit their families, drinking spots, and other entertainment venues. The military authorities prohibited drinking on bases, and despite films and debates on politics hosted at army locations, experiencing Indian life was a kind of freedom. Though religion was significant in the military, as the British were concerned to provide appropriate meals for Muslims and Hindus after the 1857 mutiny,[31] little research on African soldiers' experiences in this regard exists. John Baku, a soldier who became a political activist upon his return to Ghana, had learned of Gandhi from an Indian on a train—described as "Jesus in India"—and got a glimpse of him from a rooftop in Bombay—"an old man with glasses".[32] Such "sightings" provided authenticity and cultural translation. Some evidence suggests African soldiers discussed and engaged in religious practices during their tours in Asia, perhaps to defend themselves against the insults of "cannibals" and "monkeys" they endured. African soldiers returned to their countries with a better sense of how to defend themselves against claims that they were culturally inferior and not yet ready for independence. Through knowledge—gained by travel in India and its traditional and modern spaces—they gained an important sense of pride in African indigeneity.

Including the former African soldier in India who advised Kwesi about the Divine Life Society, soldiers who made it safely back to West Africa were seen as survivors who had harnessed spiritual protection and power in India.[33] Some African ex-servicemen kept track of happenings in India even after they left. The Divine Life Society had only recently been founded in 1936 by Dr Kuppuswami, a Tamil doctor in Malaya who returned to India to Rishikesh in 1924, the year of the first strike by Tamil labourers in Malaya.[34] Kuppuswami became politicised like other Tamil activists who, in a letter to Reverend C. F. Andrews, a confidant of Gandhi and campaigner for the rights of overseas Indians, bemoaned the loss of the moral training of their people, who had become a nation of "coolies", living and working wherever they could for money. The Self-Respect or Dravidian movement founded around this time had an impact on Kuppuswami's renunciation of materialism and his old life once he arrived in Rishikesh, where he was initiated as Swami Sivananda. His ashram really only gained a more public presence during the World War II period. Within a crowded and competitive field, the ashram was tiny, relying on publications to get across its particular messages, focused on healing. In 1945, the ashram added an Ayurvedic pharmacy, and three years later, the Forest Academy, where disciples could study with the guru. Thereafter he instructed far-flung followers to form branches, with the South African one becoming the first in 1949. Given the importance of ex-soldiers' political activism into the 1950s, it is possible that Kwesi's mentor also knew about the Divine Life Society through Pan-African networks arising from anti-apartheid resistance.

The Divine Life Society pamphlets provided good reading material, suited especially to Kwesi's interests. The major focus of *Health and Long Life*, the monthly magazine published during these years, was the Ayurveda school of Indian medicine— including varieties of tonics, powders, oils, and other medicaments—and spiritual discussions about meditation, the Bhagavad Gita, and asceticism. Articles on topics like hygiene, "home physic" for common ailments, and Indian surgery offered both theoretical and practical information in clear prose that made the texts seem authoritative, approachable, and commonsensical. Cover photos showed Swami Sivananda, clothed in a simple waistcloth with a towel over his shoulder, sitting cross-legged by the Ganges or standing near a tree; or, as a young professional with a Western-style suit, shirt, and polka dot bow tie, his dark hair parted down the centre and combed carefully, both of his ears pierced, and a dark bindi or spot between his brows (when worn by men, signifying consciousness or healing and clarity). The back cover contained advertisements for special products, like Sivananda tooth powder, Brahmi Amla Medicated Oil, and Chyawanaprash, all produced in the ashram's pharmaceutical works. The benefits of these products included curing oral diseases, removal of "brain-fag", strengthening memory-power, longevity, vim, vitality, tuberculosis-prevention, and enhanced concentration, memory, and energy.

Health and Long Life reminded Kwesi of the spiritual work his father and mother had taught him in Senya Beraku. The December 1956 issue of the journal explained the reasons for understanding Ayurveda:

> During the British Rule in India, we were hypnotised by the glamour of the western civilisation. We have imbibed a few of their good but many of their bad habits. Some habits, perfectly suitable for a cold country like England, become meaningless even harmful when adopted thoughtlessly in a tropical country like ours.
>
> With the regaining of political independence, we should also shake off the mental slavishness and turn once more with pride to our ancient customs, based on an accurate and intimate knowledge of the country and people for whom they were framed.[35]

These were not new sentiments in Ghana, where traditional healers had been engaged in reclaiming and reasserting their medical authority for decades, to better compete with and defend against the oppression of biomedical practitioners during the era of British rule.[36] Literacy, and the related practice of numeracy, was one strategy for increasing public trust in healers in the colonial Gold Coast, where successful biomedical campaigns and the active destruction by British authorities of important sites of indigenous expertise had damaged faith in indigenous medicines. "Healer literacy" might have been a wider phenomenon around the African continent in the first half of the twentieth century. In the same era, from the interwar years, the Divine Life Society engaged in efforts to standardise Ayurvedic practices, offer education and training, and generate consumer interest by a pharmaceutical works. The Society of African Healers in the Gold Coast was engaged in similar efforts. In 1934, Joseph Ankonam Kwesi Aaba, a leader of the healer literacy movement in the coastal Gold Coast city of Sekondi, laid out a vision of the nation as embedded in indigenous knowledge: "a country that does not develop its own crafts, arts and industries should be likened to a vessel without a compass".[37] The swami's vision in *Health and Long Life* suggested another spatial element to distinguish indigenous medicine—the tropics—and its peoples as having a particular constitution.

Imagining an environmental basis for the bodily difference of non-white peoples surely reproduced some of the racial typology that underpinned European biological science and eugenics. Yet, for the swami, it also re-authenticated traditional medicine as a part of racial nationalism or even a sort of racial transnationalism. Its physical location in the tropics enhanced the Divine Life Society's status—sitting on the banks of the Ganges, at Rishikesh—as a pilgrimage site, "the place of the sages".

Kwesi eventually responded to the invitation that appeared in *Health and Long Life*, usually in its final pages:

> The ashram has now grown into a worldwide organization of dynamic spiritual activities, with numerous departments and residen-

> tial quarters, where students of Yoga from parts of India and the world at large pursue their respective paths of evolution under expert guidance, and live in the saintly company of Sri Swami Sivanandaji Maharaj ... Anyone is welcome to construct here their rooms (a single room costs Rs.2,500) and extend their home into the spiritual abode of Sri Gurudev.[38]

He received a personal invitation and gathered funds to make his way to India in 1969.

Kwesi could not have gone unnoticed when he arrived in Rishikesh. He remembered feeling utterly lost and inadequate, filled by a sense of shame that "the colonial masters had not taught them (the Africans) anything but Christianity, and now at the Ashrama in India he could not understand anything either, the language was foreign and he could understand nothing of all that was chanted".[39] Several of the renunciates notified Swami Krishnananda Saraswati, the general secretary of the Divine Life Society, who later became the Ghanaian's guru. Swami Krishnananda was known as a worldly man. After his own renunciation and initiation in 1937, he worked with Gandhi's campaign to promote Hindi as India's national language, and during the Mau Mau crisis, travelled to Kenya to offer spiritual counsel to the Indian diaspora and later to Congo and other African countries. Swami Krishnananda's greater commitment to service (*seva*) over religious teachings led him to begin a charitable organisation in Mauritius in 1967. He was known to have experience with Africans. He counselled Kwesi to "listen to the noise from their mouths" of those whom he did not understand, "and understanding will come". "You had no money, yet you came. You made the journey. It is God who made you come".[40] The Ghanaian disciple was accepted into the Society "for something more" than a casual visitor pilgrimage.

Swami Krishnananda travelled to Ghana in 1975 to visit the Indian diaspora, several years after Kwesi had returned home, and found the Ghanaian guru had formed a following of Africans and

Indians. The resident Indians recognised Kwesi's skilful conduct of prayers in which he recited Sanskrit verses. Swami Ghanananda explained the ritual of the offering of the sacred light to the deities (*aarti* or *arathi*) in one of his books, *Some Basic Ideas about Hinduism*: "Arathi is a ceremonial offering of love and devotion to the Lord. This is also welcoming prayer to the Lord. The symbols used represent the five primeval elements of creation—Earth, Water, fire [sic], Air and Ether".[41] After speaking with Indians about the Ghanaian, Swami Krishnananda, who seemed not to remember his former student, asked him why he had been in India before, a question to which Kwesi answered: "To know God".[42] After this and more trials through which the Indian seemed to be testing the Ghanaian, the guru and disciple sealed their connection. That year, the Hindu Monastery of Africa became the ashram under the direction of the new monk Swami Ghanananda, initiated by Swami Krishnananda of the Divine Life Society and the Human Service Trust charitable organisation.

Africans recognised Swami Ghanananda's religious authority in many attributes that Indians also revered. His travel to India and initiation by an Indian swami of course set him apart, but Swami Ghanananda had also honed a power of orality—chants, verses, *mantras*. These were used less for the transmitting of information and more for their quality of repetition, concentration, and steadfast recitation. When the Ghanaian had not understood the words he had heard in Rishikesh, he listened and learned to use sounds, rather than the meaning of words, as the focal point of worship—the power of mantras was the power of thinking of divinity, as taught by the Divine Life Society in Japa yoga.[43] Swami Ghanananda practised a new kind of religious experience focused on the body that merged the familiar elements of traditional healing with a foreign Hindu logic that affirmed some of these elements.[44]

Disciples and casual visitors to the Monastery were initiated into Hindu sounds—bells rung at specific times, silence at others, mantras and *bhajans* performed communally. The Hindu gods and goddesses are kept in their sanctums, to which the doors remain closed except on a regular schedule for their waking, dressing, feeding, and *darshan*—or seeing. Thus, Swami Ghanananda reoriented the most apparently aberrant aspects of Hinduism, especially the worship of multiple deities, as compared to Christian or Muslim worship, with a unique kind of popular devotion that was accessible to people of any background.[45] He added new layers to the process already underway with Mami Wata worship, absorbing elements from the human and natural world over decades.

Swami Ghanananda wrote numerous pamphlets and books laying out the methods and mechanics of Hindu practice. The guidance was practical and presented as tools—how to meditate, breathe, light lamps, and fold one's hands. The books were free to visitors at the Monastery and served to attract people who wanted to read about religion and the relationships between different religions, especially Hinduism and Christianity.

His writings describe similarities between some elements in Abrahamic religions on the one hand, and Mami Wata, other indigenous belief systems, and Hinduism on the other, including spiritual protection from the temptations of the material world and affective belonging based on individual or personal attachment rather than a communal bond. Yet the embodied focus on physical bodies in Hinduism and indigenous religions is striking and common to these cosmologies, with roots in very different traditions that today may be classified as "traditional non-Western religions", but that share modern and changing characteristics. Modern Mami Wata cosmology holds that humans may be deities or kinfolk to them, living amongst other humans and inhabiting worlds that look a lot like ours—there are old, young, men, women, and babies, Black, white, and brown, in the Atlantic and Indian Oceans.[46] Every body and every space could have sacred power, a possibility that transnational Ghanaian-Indian Hinduism realised. Swami Ghanananda helped make Ghana a site of Hindu pilgrimage.

Ghanaian guru gone global

Along with Swami Ghanananda's Hindu Monastery of Africa, other Hindu-based movements also gained adherents in Ghana and other parts of West Africa in roughly the same era. The International Society for Krishna Consciousness (ISKCON) was established in the United States in 1966 by Srila Prabhupada, a Bengali claimed to be an incarnation of Chaitanya, the fifteenth-century mystic who preached of Krishna's supremacy. The movement is said to have formally come to West Africa under the aegis of Swami Prabhupada's disciple Brahmananda Das, in 1979.[47] Born Bruce Scharf, Brahmananda was one of Srila Prabhupada's first disciples in New York and the first president of the city's temple. He retold the history of ISKCON's beginnings in Africa in a 1975 article in *Back to Godhead* magazine. His journey began after he received an order from Swami Prabhupada for him to go immediately to West Pakistan to preach. He left his teaching at Florida State University in Tallahassee for New York in order to fly to London. From there, he went to Paris and then by train through Turkey, Iran, Afghanistan, and finally to Pakistan. He began to preach to students—following the common practice of ISKCON members who were known for singing, dancing, and serving food on college campuses. Following anti-Indian unrest and the reported killing of four American Hare Krishna missionaries by Pakistani soldiers, Swami Prabhupada called him to Bombay, where the swami himself was. Brahmananda then sailed to Kenya, where he remained for a long time under government surveillance for failing to produce an outbound ticket. Surprised to see white people dressed as *sadhus*, in saffron robes, crowds gawked at them in Mombasa. Swami Prabhupada eventually joined Brahmananda in Kenya to recuperate from illness and to preach. ISKCON members preached to Indians and African students, travelling to Kenya, Zambia, Rhodesia (Zimbabwe), and then further afield to West Africa. Brahmananda wrote that upon their return to Kenya from travels to other countries, they were greeted with "Hare Krishna" everywhere. "Previously I had written a letter to Srila Prabhupada expressing how much I appreciated Vrndavana [Brindavan, Krishna's birthplace on the Ganges River] ... Now it appeared to me that, by his grace, Nairobi had become a Black Vrndavana".[48]

The arrival in West Africa of ISKCON had a clear root in Black communities. Brahmananda's entrée in 1979 into Lagos, according to ISKCON history, was facilitated by Bhakti Tirtha Swami, an African-American devotee, born John Favors, who was a prominent activist, scholar, and educationalist. He was founder of the Third World Center (since renamed) at his alma mater, Princeton, in 1971.[49] The timing of Bhakti Tirtha's conversion is not clear, nor is the history of his career in West Africa. When Brahmananda faced challenges finding housing in Lagos, which ISKCON missionaries had usually found in the homes of expatriate Indians, Bhakti Tirtha convinced an Indian hospital owner to open up rooms in which to lodge the two missionaries and eventually to rent space for their mission.[50] The story implies that there was some resistance by Indians to ISKCON. It was only some decades later that more Indians began to accept the American-origin sect as legitimate. Scholarly accounts suggest that Bhakti Tirtha came with other African-American ISKCON members.[51] The "Friends of Krishna" community grew into the thousands in Ghana and Nigeria, and in other regions of Africa, but remained under American leadership. Bhakti Tirtha oversaw the African region and the Governing Body Council, the central body for the worldwide organisation.

In Ghana, their "stubborn" use of Sanskrit, strict controls on devotees' vegetarian diet, and other behaviours that detached devotees from local culture have kept the ISKCON Ghanaians "alien". ISKCON even prized this separation by highlighting an Indianness in its Chaitanya Vaishnavite roots.[52] While a similar detachment and exoticisation of Krishna worship occurs in the US, the land of ISKCON's birth, the movement's separation from local Ghanaian society came against the specific backdrop of Ghanaians' connections to India and Indians, including the Hindu Monastery where Indians and Africans worshipped together.

The disciples and other regular visitors to the Hindu Monastery included well-educated professionals and also working people who were comfortable and mobile.[53] The earliest members of Swami Ghanananda's community included university science professors, musicians, and civil servants, including many women. Traders and other businesspeople who had connections to Indians, particularly the Sindhi shopowners, as well as aficionados of Indian cinema, were also attracted to Hinduism, though less so to the Monastery and instead to the more youth-oriented movement of ISKCON.

ISKCON's membership and reputation worldwide, on the other hand, was mostly young and white, with some presence of other races at first.[54] Its values were ascetic, preaching non-materialism, and had associations with counter-cultural social life, like drug use. ISKCON's reputation changed in the decades after the death of Srila Prabhupada in 1977, following numerous scandals surrounding purported criminal behaviours, including accusations of murder and extortion. This change came after an increasing number of Indian immigrants arrived in the United States and began to see ISKCON as useful for inculcating their children in Hindu learning. At the time of its entry into Ghana, ISKCON repre-sented a youth fringe for Ghanaians and Indians, with religious leaders based in America who enacted controlling and strict teach-ings through a Black American representative. In America, it took "micro-interactions" of Westerners and Indians to bring legitimacy to ISKCON and erase the stain of it seeming to be a cult.[55]

ISKCON and the Hindu Monastery share common features of Krishna consciousness and Vedanta—Vedic teachings and focus on texts like the Ramayana, meditation, and *satsang* (communal devotional singing). However, the two sects practised distinctly different bodily cultures. Swami Ghanananda, raised in the Mami Wata worldview and a student of the Divine Life Society, founded by a once-practising physician, emphasised that care for the physical body was indivisible from metaphysics. A written plea for help amongst the swami's papers, dated from 1999, is revealing. The writer is a man who is worried that his brothers and sisters remain childless, except for a half-brother who does not share the same father with them. He explains that his family has also suffered a number of deaths in recent years. He reports having a dream just before writing to the swami, in which his family's clan, the Asakyire, symbolised by the vulture, met at his house and would not tell him what they discussed. He then noticed a black mark on his arm.[56] He begs the swami, as all-seeing, to touch and breathe on him for purification and protec-tion. For ISKCON, the second core principle of the movement states: "We are not our bodies but eternal spirit souls, parts and parcels of God (Krsna [Krishna]). As such, we are all brothers, and Krsna is ultimately our common father".[57] ISKCON uses the language of "bodied-ness" to describe difference—"Black-bod-ied", "brown-bodied", or female.[58] As an anti-materialist and devotional culture inflected by a discourse of anti-difference with roots in the American youth revolution, Krishna consciousness sought to deny the significance of difference.

There has been an understandable tendency to locate Ghanaian Hindu currents by reference to Christian and Muslim religious transformations, where modernisation has tended to intensify, not diminish, religious experiences in personal and public spheres. New religious movements like ISKCON and the Hindu Monastery fit within the themes of globalisation of local cosmologies and the competition for converts. Ghanaian Hindus explain their attraction in terms of indigenous and original beliefs and practices that run between Africa and Asia. This is also reflected in the cultural and political priorities of the postcolonial era; Jerry Rawlings, who launched the first of several coups in 1979, was especially committed to indigenous identification and Afrocentrism. He took an explicitly Pan-African approach to economic reforms, notably in the realm of tourism.[59] Ghana's "structural advantages in cornering the Diaspora tourism marketplace are many".[60] Hinduism likewise benefited from the time and place.

The basis of Ghanaian Hinduism lay in an invigorated sense of biological and spiritual rationalism. The Hindu Monastery acknowledged the cultural inheritance of human reason and experience in the deep past, passed through the ages via teachers to disciples. Africa, as the origin of humanity, was the birthplace of reason. This mirrored the work of Third World science, and in particular, provided an allied metaphysics to the indigenous science and healing movement that found new life under political regimes like Rawlings's administration.

Swami Ghanananda studied the work of Dr Anthony Kweku Andoh, a Ghanaian immigrant to the United States who established the North Scale Education and Research Institute (NSERI) in 1982, together with his American-born wife Kali Sichen-Andoh. Andoh's father, Dr Joseph Emmanuel Andoh, was born in 1907, had worked in the British Gold Coast Forest service and then in the Forest Herbarium in Kumasi as a botanist. He identified many tropical plant species for Western researchers.[61] Anthony Andoh then received advanced education in Britain at the Royal Botanical Gardens at Kew and worked in Southern Africa on botanical and horticultural projects before moving to the United States, where he met his wife, who was a pioneer of what today would be called integrative medicine. After earning a degree in nutrition from California State University, Chico, where she developed the first government-approved nutritional programme to treat attention disorders, she studied "oriental medicine". The couple moved to San Francisco and grew African plants in their garden, which they sold and used in research published in their many books on herbal medicine, ethnobotany, African religions, and healing. When their daughters decided to attend historically Black higher education institutions in Atlanta, the couple moved there and established NSERI, which sat on five acres of land. Their business operated between the US and Ghana, and promoted NSERI's home-study course, "to prepare student neophytes to enter into an advanced program of understanding the health and well being, physical, emotional and spiritual, of the whole person from the African perspective".[62]

The Andohs brought indigenous belief and science to the business of botany, specifically in plants like *Moringa oleifera*, known commonly as moringa, a word originating in the Tamil language for the tree and its edible tuber, the drumstick. Moringa has become a popular natural medicine sold all over the world in different forms since the early 2000s. Its most popular species originated in the Himalayan region, while nine others occur in the Horn of Africa and Kenya.[63] Anthony Andoh was no doubt one of the earliest researchers to consider commercial farming of moringa in West Africa. In 1990, he studied the prospects for moringa in Senegal for Church World Service, an interdenominational Christian relief organisation established in 1946 to focus on food and agricultural development.[64] The dissemination of moringa via this organisation occurred in East Africa too. Church World Service distributed 20,000 moringa seeds in Tanzania along the routes taken by European explorers in the nineteenth century.[65] Tanzanian farmers saw the value of the plant for its hardiness during rain shortages and other difficult conditions, but the Andohs realised another enormous potential of a larger-scale production. The couple established farms in Elmina, Dr Andoh's birthplace, on a 20-acre plot of land.[66] Produce from the port at Tema was shipped to NSERI in Atlanta, packaged, and sold under the label of Harbinger Herbal Nutrients. Mama Kali, as Andoh's wife is known, notes that while the vast majority of customers are African-Americans, they distributed through the All African Healing Arts Society in Europe, Asia, and the Caribbean to customers of all backgrounds.[67]

The Andohs were innovators of a kind of Africana herbal renaissance and entrepreneurship. Later projects like Nebedaye Farms in Charlotte, North Carolina, also started moringa farms as the basis of mutual aid by Black farmers. In 2014, Bernard Singleton began Nebedaye Farms in abandoned urban lots. The farms have been used to grow healthy food for local residents and to teach horticulture to at-risk young people. Singleton, an African-American horticulturalist, chose to study and plant moringa as an African origin crop, and has since become one of just two certified moringa producers on the US East Coast. His farms supply Asian restaurants, which had long been using the drumstick.[68]

Amongst Africans and the diaspora, moringa has been rechristened "nebedaye", a pidgin word from the English "never die" for its hardiness in any growing conditions.[69] Its historical global circulations have been to some extent "forgotten", as a plant taken from India by the British to African colonies for ornamental uses and then, in the postcolonial era, distributed by missionaries and aid workers as a self-help tool for poor communities.[70] This forgetting is important and significant for a postcolonial enchantment with the "traditional"— foods, medicines, healing, and religions. It also engenders entrepreneurship and knowledge-preservation and production amongst diasporic communities who develop commercial networks across the Atlantic.

The view of the body in an "African perspective" is a conceptualisation that has been shaped by Pan-Africanism, not only in a cultural sense, but also a commercial one. This holistic healing operates on a racial basis, in which tropical plants such as moringa, originating in the African-Asian Old World, are promoted to have a healing power for diasporic peoples in America. Thus, environmental determinism in racialisation is a current of thought, particular in shaping an idea of the indigenous which is "in a continuous existence",[71] not broken by the slave trade, European colonisation, or migration. Race consciousness is alive in the biosciences as well, in which there is an apparent dichotomy of race as real "at the molecular level", but socially constructed in the everyday. New biocitizens must navigate this dichotomy, argues sociologist Dorothy Roberts, as they face a welter of medical therapies and activist calls for the better use of science on behalf of peoples who have been abused and neglected in medical history.[72] The biopolitics of race is global in phenomena such as the commercialisation of plants in a historically dense cultural economy. Even though moringa use is hardly restricted by race, its legitimacy as a "traditional" therapeutic certainly stems from its racialisation as an African-Asian species that is ambiguous in its precise origin.

Dr Lydia Makhubu, the Swazi professor of chemistry installed by Abdus Salam as president of the Third World Organization of Women in Science, wrote:

> As the world has moved into a scientific and technological age, the origin of herbal medicine in many countries remains shrouded in mystery and often sounds fantastic to those trained in modern sci-

ence. Traditional bioprospecting requires no scientific training but is directed by ancestral spirits and revealed to those who are spiritually endowed by their ancestors and thus selected to become traditional medical practitioners (TMPs). How, then, do traditional medical practitioners acquire the vast knowledge of medicinal plants that enable them to go into the wild to identify plants with healing power and prepare life-giving potions to heal the sick and the dying?[73]

In the borderland between science and belief, Swami Ghanananda, Anthony Andoh, and many Ghanaian Hindus felt they could create a legitimate modern basis for indigenous cultural paradigms. Ghana, India, and other African and Asian nations have established major industries based on this cultural logic. This cultural economy has expanded because of the physical migration within Pan-African and Pan-Indian networks. These have intersected now, allowing for potent material bases of support for nonconformist communities.

Ghana and India embarked on integrated approaches to traditional medicine simultaneously. The attempts to manage them by their governments go back many decades. In Ghana, the Centre for Scientific Research into Plant Medicine (now the Centre for Plant Medicine Research, CPMR) was established in 1975, through the work of Dr Oku Ampofo, who studied medicine at the University of Edinburgh and Liverpool School of Tropical Medicine. More recently, the Ministry of Health established an Expert Committee on Traditional Medicine that works with an advocacy group of traditional healers, supported by the Business Advocacy Fund.[74] In 1995, the Indian government established the Department of Indian Systems of Medicine and Homeopathy, since renamed the Department of Ayurveda, Yoga and Naturopathy, Unani, Siddhi and Homeopathy (AYUSH). In 2014, the Modi government elevated AYUSH to a Ministry. Ayurveda, seen by Hindutva ideologues as an authentically "indigenous" system, gets the most support.[75]

These parallel currents intersect through Ghanaian Hinduism. While traditional medicine has its own history apart from this new religious movement, the cultural logic that supports it has produced a new kind of African-Indian convergence and potential competition.

Conclusion

Mathematician Dr Ravindra Kumar taught at the University of Port Harcourt, in southeastern Nigeria, from 1981 to 1986. In his book, *How to Be One with God: An Autobiography of a Scientist Yogi*, Dr Kumar, now Swami Ravindranand, recalls that his family left Nigeria after staying one year with him. He was alone, except for a domestic servant named Elizabeth, and began intensive meditation. He writes: "there was a beautiful Krishna temple run by the ISKCON ... in Port Harcourt where they had regular services and discourses. I attended quite regularly and generally I was engrossed in devotional songs and many a time I would go into ecstasy with tears flowing from my eyes".[76] He became a life member of the Hare Krishnas, but did not confine himself to any single faith. His meditation practice grew, and on one occasion he experienced an intense light that seemed to come from nowhere, without generating any heat, which he believed to be a physical manifestation of the Hindu Brahman or transcendent reality; he likened it to Carl Jung's High Self and the Polynesian Huna sense of the body, or white light. He reports an encounter with a black cobra, which he describes as the fulfilment of dreams and premonitions involving serpents and as a moment when his fear gave way to oneness with the snake. This was a turning point—he left for Zimbabwe shortly after, where he began to write his spiritual diary, studied serpent cults, and continued on his path to becoming a swami.

In Port Harcourt, Kumar met another Indian mathematics professor, S. D. Bajpai, who gave him a book by a swami that explained the principles of cosmic energy and Siddha yoga, a school of yoga founded just a few years earlier. Bajpai's experience in Nigeria led him to write an article, "Patterns of Mathematical Thinking are Much the Same as the Fundamental Patterns of Life", which addresses what he considered then to be the great challenge for men in his profession: to find "a philosophy of teaching mathematics".[77] His proposal to teach mathematics as part of the everyday was supported by Hindu teaching about infinity, lessons on zero as more powerful than the atom bomb, and the resulting decrease of fractions multiplied by themselves: "this process is similar to the process of capitalistic society. In the capitalistic society, the rich become richer, and the poor poorer".[78]

For Indians of the twenty-first century, "science and religion have ... in recent times been mobilized to together form a political Hindu nationalist vision"[79] of the kind wielded by Prime Minister Narendra Modi. "Science and religion are syncretic collaborators" in India's rise as a global power. The Indian diaspora has played a crucial role in this "archaic modernity", which has an appeal in nonconformist subcultures all over the world. Ancient history was a means of constructing the world as India. Vinayak Damodar Savarkar (1883–1966), who was the principle architect of Hindutva, in 1937 offered a message of "sympathy and loving remembrances to those of our co-religionists and countrymen abroad who have been building a greater Hindustan without the noise of drums and trumpets in Africa, America, Mauritius and such other parts of the world ... holding out as remnants of the ancient world empire of our Hindu race".[80] It remains to be seen how Hindu and cultural chauvinism affects Indian relations with Africans, at the grassroots and in multilateral relations. Renu Modi and Ian Taylor have shown how, from the 1970s, the Indian government created policies and cultural logics to define overseas Indians as perpetually belonging to India, which means an extension of the Indian nation to "wherever the Indian diaspora exists".[81] Even as the spatial imagination of India has grown, however, the identity of the Indian as a Hindu has grown narrower.

As with the ICTP and Black scientists, the aims of Black Hindus and Indian Hindu nationalists might be divergent. Swami Ghanananda's critique of the Hindu diaspora signals that the Hindu Monastery of Ghana can survive as an autonomous African religious community, one that Indian Hindus might increasingly look to as a refuge from the rightwing religious nationalism gripping India today.

6

NÉGRITUDE BEATS BOLLYWOOD

Introduction

What made two men in their early twenties set off from Calcutta on a bike tour of the world in 1982 is still unclear. One of them, Ram Chandra Biswas, has been interviewed for numerous media outlets across the world. In 1991, he told *The Oklahoman* that he dedicated his effort to peace: "against nuclear war, against drugs, against divorce".[1] He renounced sex and drugs, and his personal habits drew attention from Western audiences in particular, who wondered how this pair intended to save the world. His partner Somnath Mukherjee offered his own explanation for their trip: "I believe that people are alone when they are born. Only the Supreme One/Unique One guides each person. Like your bag [he pointed to my purse], there is a bag with things inside that you have put there. The Supreme One has done the same, for each of us".[2] Both men felt a calling, but, after setting off together, first for East Africa, and making it across the continent, their fates diverged. Somnath stayed in Senegal while Biswas continued, making it to the Americas and eventually back to India. Somnath remained in Senegal for more than three decades.

175

Both men came from modest backgrounds, and yet their trip garnered interest and support from the Indian government. The government secured free passage for the men out of India, and photographs show the then Minister of Finance, Pranab Mukherjee, presenting them with flower garlands and Prime Minister Indira Gandhi sending them off.[3] Biswas recalled her words to them: "Gandhi cautioned us never to beg for money and portray India in a poor light. We started with a dollar in our pocket ... the plan was to begin in Africa as it would be the most difficult terrain".[4] It may have been physically arduous, but Biswas reported that Africans treated them more kindly than any others in the world: "I have never received more hospitality than in Africa. In a poor country you will find humanity, hospitality, love, peace ... In a rich country you'll find anger, jealousy, fear and selfishness".[5] Somnath experienced the generosity of the Senegalese (*teranga*) at a time of desperation—his bike and other belongings were stolen—and while at the Indian embassy in Dakar, a man who had lived for two years in India invited him to teach Indian dance to his family. "My reason for staying began with a lot of problems", he remembers.[6] He continued to teach dance and Hindi language classes and organise occasional events for the Indian embassy for over 30 years. His former travelling companion, Ram Chandra Biswas, performed magic and gymnastics to support his travels. Apparently, they were not the first globetrotting Bengalis; decades earlier, the revolutionary Ramnath Biswas had travelled around the world, including through much of Asia and in East and Central Africa, and published travelogues that opened Indians' eyes to many insights, particularly into how other peoples saw them.[7] It was perhaps through his writings that Indians learned that in Burma they were called "kala", the name "Black" that Africans in India were called. Interestingly, Biswas's acquaintance, when directly questioned about it, defined "kala" as "foreigner".

For a simple young man like Somnath, living as an Indian expatriate in Dakar showed him a side of his countrymen he came to dislike. There were few Indians residing in the city when he arrived, mostly Gujarati speakers with French citizenship, and as their numbers increased over his 28 years living there, they were friendly though curious as to why he remained there, with no car and no real house. They invited him to stay with them in their large bungalows and offered him jobs at their companies, on the condition that he gave up his Hindi language and dance teaching in the suburb of Pikine, a working-class neighbourhood. This was what he really enjoyed, learning Wolof to be able to better explain concepts like *mudras* (gestures) in Indian dance that his rudimentary French did not allow. But they did not appreciate his classes, which he could not do while working for their businesses: "I would have to start work at 7 in the morning and work until late hours". He was dismissive of many of them, arguing that "the Indians are very materialistic and also racist. Their purpose here is to make money. I have had a lot of problems doing what I do. It is something they don't understand or appreciate".[8]

Somnath's misgivings about India's globalisation grew as Indians continued to migrate, as they had done for centuries, into new lands like Francophone West Africa, fuelled by India's economic liberalisation a decade after Somnath and Biswas had left. These wayfarers, making a point of travelling poor, and acting, in the words of one journalist, as "self-appointed messenger[s] of peace",[9] seem to have discovered that their own dim view of the African continent, perhaps influenced by Afropessimism in the media, was misplaced. They came to believe that it was economic development—not African traditionalism, civil wars, or military rule—that demonstrated the dangers of humanity's darker side. The apparent conflict between India as an economic power and its cultural chauvinism amongst its diaspora bothered Somnath. Though Somnath and Biswas may have represented a type of alternative youth, Third World hippies of sorts, many Indian novelists and other artists on the left express similar views.

Somnath credited his own views to his communist education, unique in India to Bengal and Kerala in the Southeast. But in retrospect, this was nostalgia for an India he only remembered, because after nearly three decades, it was life in Senegal that had nurtured his love of cultural pursuits over material prosperity, and the desire to pass on his culture to Africans.

What Somnath stumbled on in Dakar was entirely unexpected. The year before he left India, Senghor had resigned and his protégé Abdou Diouf had become president. Senghor's Afro-Dravidian exchange continued but ultimately petered out without much investment, according to Vidya Diaité, who met and married her husband, Cherif Diaité, when he was serving as ambassador to India under Senghor in 1978. When she moved to Senegal, she worked as a translator for Diouf, which she continued through the subsequent presidency of Abdoulaye Wade. There was an *Indouphilie* fad in Senegal, she recalled, with women wearing saris sewn with pleats, and talk of Dravidians common. The Senegalese-Dravidian connection was uncanny, Diaité, a Telugu, remarked—right down to the level of superstitions like avoidance of buying salt and thread after dark, which Tamils also did. Her husband helped process the visas for the Indian professors going to L'Institut Fondamental d'Afrique Noire (IFAN), so she knew about their work on folklore and other topics, but the connection was not easily explained in academic terms.[10] She felt a bond that Somnath too began to feel.

A familiarity made them both feel at home—Diaité was accepted into the highest levels of Senegalese society (her husband was an important political figure; Senghor called her his Dravidian) as well as amongst lovers of popular culture caught up in the *Indouphilie* fads that Vidya herself had little interest in, such as the soap opera "Vaidehi". She was a Francophone, having grown up in France where her father was stationed with the Indian Army. She enjoyed working as a professional translator for international organisations. In Senegal she lived a cosmopolitan life, whereas in India many Indians held a "narrow view of foreigners" which she blamed for their racism. This was on full display when she returned to India to visit family during the 2014 Ebola outbreak in West Africa, which saw negligible cases in Senegal. Nonetheless, the Indian authorities at the airport gave her a difficult time. In stereotyping about Africa, India seemed to be no different than the Western-controlled international agencies that had put on hold her translation work, citing Ebola concerns.

Somnath and Vidya came from very different backgrounds, and lived in Dakar neighbourhoods and social circles that might not often meet, given the vast class divides. Yet both have found home—they share a sense that being in Senegal allowed them a freedom and openness impossible to find, they say, in India. But this is only part of the story, because Senegal itself has created their desire to stay and be surrounded by cultural tolerance and the work in cultural translation that they prize.

Work in cultural industries, particularly African-Indian enterprise, had, of course, a high profile in the form of President Senghor's Afro-Indian studies going back to the early 1970s. And Senegalese popular cultural interests also included *Indouphilie* of different sorts—Bollywood, dance troupes, and Hindi language classes designed for everyday use. A small country with a vibrant and varied cultural economy presented Indians with a picture of cosmopolitanism, indeed even a contrast with India, which despite its vastness and cultural output nevertheless harboured ignorance and suspicion of difference and a parochialism seemingly heightened amongst its expatriates. Many saw teaching Africans Hindi language and dance as worthless. As Swami Ghanananda had noted, Hinduism too would not be shared by some in the Indian diaspora in Africa. Culture was jealously guarded by the Indian diaspora, but Somnath used it to develop a network in a new land. Somnath's Senegalese friends valued his work, life story, and his humility in sharing his cultural inheritance.

Quite apart from Senghor and Indira Gandhi, an African-Indian cultural economy continued to grow in different directions, especially through music, dance, film, and fashion. The flow of commodities was largely one way, from India to Senegal, but a small and growing Senegalese movement eastwards can be discerned. Following the arrival of the first scholars to Annamalai University in the 1970s, connections between Senegal and India which had begun with a love of Indian films grew into a wider media explosion of *Indouphilie*. While the trend grew in local organisations of cinema societies, dance clubs, and arts schools, African global cultures came into their own, intersecting with and growing in directions diverse from and diametrically opposed to Bollywood and *Bharatanatyam* (Indian classical dance). There was Senegalese stardom in the world music scene, with griots like Thione Seck, whose 2006 record, "Orientissime Touba-Madras-Paris", charted a geography akin to Senghor's poetic place-making that laid out his Afro-Dravidian vision. Seck's Sufi-inspired music reveals "the remarkable capacity of Senegalese Islam to adapt to the aesthetics of everyday life" and bring India into these rhythms,[11] but other West African performers like Germaine Acogny and Nollywood filmmakers have become highly critical of obsession with India, instead seeing Africa as a cultural mecca. With African ascendency, the modern identity of the Indian nation is on display for the world, including consumerism, beauty defined by fair skin, and, at times, apparent mimicry of the West.

Indouphilie, *an entertainment industry*

In 1970, a young man named Amadou Khalil Rassoul Badiane hosted a weekly radio show called "Echoes of the Orient" on the Senegalese national station. An aficionado of Indian films, he had years earlier started a club called "Amis des Inde" with other young men and women who shared his passion.[12] According to one of the original members, Adja Coumba Diop, who performed Indian dances with a troupe—including folk circle dances with sticks, pots, and other accoutrements—the club had actually begun meeting years earlier, around 1960, after they started going to the movies. They were school-age youngsters, whose parents forbade them to go to the El Mansour cinema, opened in 1954, near where they lived. The theatre first opened with French films, but popular demand made them switch to Arabic and Hindi films. The Indian films usually came on last in the evening, and the children stole out of their houses to see them. They began a new ritual—to meet after each movie to discuss the dances, study the dialogue, decipher the language, and develop profiles of each actor. The club's members christened each other with nicknames, like Raaj Kumar, whose fame grew for his roles in major films like *Mother India* (1957) and *Waqt* (1965), and Hema Malini, beloved for her appearances in *Abhinetri* (1970) and *Andaz* (1971). The club brought young lovers together, their children bearing the names of Bollywood stars and carrying on the tradition of Indian dance and dress, and some long-lasting friendships. Yet the Friends of India also experienced break-ups, due to their growing responsibilities as adults and the rapid urbanisation that changed the lives of working-class and poorer Dakarois.

After World War II, the population of Dakar grew quickly and Medina, the African neighbourhood during colonial times, began to see an influx of migrants from rural areas. To manage the inflow of people, the authorities created the planned suburb of Pikine in 1952. Groups of residents from each quarter of Medina were moved into the provisional camp-like new area, which ended up as a mixed enclave of the descendants of the indigenous Lebou fishing community that had predated the arrival of Europeans; urban dwellers, including migrants from Mali and other neighbouring territories; and Senegalese newcomers from outside

Dakar. With independence in 1960, and rising political tensions with Mali, many migrants in Pikine scattered and the government seized their plots to establish more resettlements. Pikine was a constellation of both spontaneous and planned flows of people.[13] Within this social fabric, the cinema houses became centres of entertainment and camaraderie. Dakar's suburbs, which came to have the largest population centres in the city, kept moviegoing alive during the economic collapse in the 1980s that led to hard times for theatre owners. Digital technology that enabled home-viewing and the popularity of series also reduced the number of moviegoers at cinemas. But theatres in Dakar offer a peek into "an in-the-know clientele".[14] The original Friends of India disappeared because of the closure of movie theatres and instead splintered into *Indouphilie* groups spread throughout the suburbs. Clubs in other cities like Rufisque were growing too.

These neighbourhood cultural groups came to life on their own largely through the women and children who were committed to studying and teaching dance and developing their own lineages of transmitting *Indouphilie* knowledge. At least one of these Friends of India, Amadou Badiane, benefited from high-level Senegalese-Indian relations by securing a scholarship to undertake cultural studies in India from 1975 to 1978. He studied Indian classical music, Hindi and Dravidian languages, English language, batik cloth-making techniques, and Rabindra Sangeet or "Tagore songs", the corpus of music by Indian polymath Rabindranath Tagore.[15] Badiane's musical and language abilities were so remarkable that he became the first Black person to sing in Hindi in India at a public performance with the renowned playback singer Mohammed Rafi. The two performed before thousands in Calcutta. Before Rafi died in 1980, he had sung nearly 30,000 songs, many with the renowned female playback singer Lata Mangeshkar. Badiane returned to Senegal an expert in all things Indian.

Badiane was an internationalist par excellence. Frustrated by bickering and competition between various neighbourhood associations, he aimed to create lasting and meaningful connections between Senegal and India. He claims to have initiated, in 1985, the idea that UNESCO should establish the Mahatma Gandhi prize, which was finally realised in 1995, the United Nations Year for Tolerance and the 125th anniversary of Gandhi's birth. Badiane had directed his proposal to UNESCO to the then Director General, Amadou-Mahtar M'Bow, a fellow Senegalese citizen who had served in Senghor's administration as Minister of Education and Minister of Culture and Youth. Badiane was also a key confidante of Somnath Mukherjee—he had hired him as artistic director—which brought Badiane's dance troupe a special cachet and provided Somnath with the impetus to start Bharat-Pehchane, "Knowing India", the cultural organisation through which his different classes were offered.

Knowing India meant, in Badiane's view, the ability to appreciate the diversity of Indian film, music, and dance. For example, enthusiasts like him knew that besides Bollywood were the Tolly- and Mollywood offerings, that is, the Tamil, Telugu, and Malayalam films. Besides the different languages, films could also be classified as "jinn films", those that had ghosts, demons, gods, and other supernatural beings. "The pantheon is so rich", Badiane noted, and films with fire worship and other ceremonies reminded him of the Mande epic, *Sundiata*, that his grandfather had told him. He could hear and read how devotional registers differentiated Indian music, including film songs; he had studied and sung classical *ragas* (melodic frames) in India.

Many Senegalese came to understand the magic behind playback music, a staple of Indian films that was misunderstood at first by Senegalese until Badiane corrected them. Film numbers recorded by songsters like Rafi and Mangeshkar were lip-synced by Bollywood actors, a realisation that transformed how Senegalese

Indouphilie saw acting and singing and understood their own mimetic performance—*Indouphilie* artistry was mastery in mimicry. Crucially, Indian actors and actresses themselves had to grapple with the question of difference—of class, caste, religion, region, dialect, and so on—in becoming film characters, when sound entered films in the 1930s.[16] Affect, tone, accent, volume, and other features of the human voice were now as important as the character's physical appearance. *Indouphilie* performers implicitly understood that inhabiting a Bollywood character was a complex exercise.[17] An underappreciated aspect of African interest in Indian films is the diversity of India on display. This was a familiar sight from their own cultural milieu, whereas Western films that depicted white actors seemed homogeneous and monocultural.

Mamadou Pam, of the younger *Indouphilie* generation than Badiane, recognised that love of India transcended film-watching and could be expanded into new ventures. His own initiation into Indian films came when his uncle took him to see *Farishta Ya Qatil* in 1977, about a murderer who saves survivors of a train accident in the desert from marauders—"angel or devil?", Pam mused. Challenged by his uncle asking him if he felt ignorant knowing nothing about Indian languages and cultures, Pam obsessively studied Hindi by watching and collecting Bollywood films. He opened a video rental shop, and, when Indian and Pakistani customers came, he quizzed them about words and their subtleties in songs and film dialogue. Pam became the host of the Radio Dunya programme and in 1998, seized upon a new idea with the release of the box office romance *Kuch Kuch Hota Hai* starring Shahrukh Khan and Kajol: he would stage a Miss Kajol contest. It began with a taunt to women listeners to hear who could best deliver lines. Next came a beauty contest, where Kajols from many Dakar neighbourhoods and cities—Sicap, Thies, Rufisque—came to compete, and viewers had to pay an entrance fee to be able to vote. Seeing the competition, a young woman named Diwo Diallo, who had come at first as a joke, put in a serious performance and took first prize. The feedback between media and club culture has kept the radio shows of Pam and another *Indouphilie* host, Mamadou Kane, popular. In the 2000s, new spaces of *Indouphilie* innovation opened up with Senegal's television explosion, and Kane and Pam began to host "Allo Bombay" and "L'Inde au Sénégal" respectively, the most popular shows in the country.[18] These men broadcast in Hindi, and when they eventually visited India, they could easily navigate the big cities from what they had learned through Indian films.

The multigenerational and multimedia development of *Indouphilie* in Senegalese Indian popular culture defies easy characterisation. Some have cited a notion of "parallelism" of African and Indian cultural experiences of negotiation between tradition and modernity, especially in the realms of the family and romantic relations.[19] Yet there were many kinds of attractions involved in the Senegalese love of India. New relationships and kinships were created in the chains of transmission of knowledge about India that ran between teachers and students, ideologues to whom younger generations paid homage, and the fan clubs of local Senegalese performers of Indian music and dance which sprang up around Dakar and other cities. A sense of personal attainment also grew through contests and performances at parties, where a performer's status in their community was ranked according to their prowess in performing India. Senegalese spectatorship of Indian films was a popular art form with its own economy of exchanges and meaning.

Négritude's *critical gaze*

This movement caught the eye of the documentarian Mansour Sora Wade, a renowned filmmaker who had been intimately involved in creating Senegal's international reputation for moving pictures. Wade's roots were in Ouakam, a fishing village lying a few kilometres from Dakar. He has maintained a strong identification with his ethnic community, the Lebou, who are known for their cultural autonomy even with their proximity to the city, which has continued to grow. As the Lebou enclaves are threatened by the encroaching sprawl, their presence, way of using language, and spatial organisation as "villages" demarcates a border between Lebou "tradition" and Dakar's modernity, or, in other terms, between "dormitory suburbs" and "motorway".[20]

Wade attended Cheikh Anta Diop University in Dakar and then the University of Paris VIII for cinema studies. He was drawn to Japanese and Indian films because the practices of daily life—such as sitting on the floor—that were pictured appeared similar to Senegalese ways of life. His interest was in the fact that Asian traditions were distinct, and in how the positioning of the camera captured these "habitudes". Cinema could express cultural difference. The films made by Satyajit Ray and Masaki Kobayashi were amongst his favourites for their study of characters and their relationships. After his return to Senegal, he began working in television in 1976 and focused on adapting these techniques of telecasting a specific Senegalese everyday practice—the telling of tales, indeed, "everything that had a relation to African mythology".[21]

All of his broadcasts were previewed in the Ministry of Culture, and, after seeing them, a woman working in the Ministry's Centre for the Study of Civilizations approached him to work in the Senegalese cultural archives division. He accepted the invitation, and for eight years focused on organising the audiovisual holdings, especially recordings of oral traditions, including myths, folktales, songs, and epics. Selected footage made it into his earliest films, *Fary, l'anesse* (1988), *Aida Souka* (1992), and *Picc Mi* (1992). The first two focus on women and their power—sometimes mystical—while the third follows the travails of two poor young boys who meet and navigate together the streets of Dakar, their grim and precarious existence forgotten temporarily in the warmth of their companionship. He set the boys' story to the music of Youssou N'Dour, a musical master whose adaptability in his artistry and in his entrepreneurship in television, entertainment, and even politics is unparalleled.

Wade's most famous film, *Ndeysaan* ("The Price of Forgiveness", 2001), based on the novel by Mbissane Ngom, brings together many of the elements that shaped the filmmaker's life, from his Lebou ancestry to the reverence for and reclamation of history and tradition for one's present circumstances. Launching him into international recognition, this film also placed Wade within the overlap of two world-renowned Senegalese cultural phenomena: *négritude* and filmmaking, with the likes of Ousmane Sembène and Djibril Diop Mambéty. Yet his success also brought the kind of criticism that Third World artists on the global scene garner in relation to their politics. As Samba Gadjigo shows in his biography of Sembène, the lack of recognition given to this iconic Senegalese artist is perhaps because he was an artist-activist who eventually de-emphasised his Marxist humanism to focus on literary and film pursuits.[22] Film scholar Manthia Diawara sees Wade's *Ndeysaan* as a revival of *négritude*, celebrating African values. Particular to *négritude* philosophy and the film's story is the habitation and convergence of multiple realities—the village present, the world of the ancestors, even the space between the film's actors and the audience.[23] But as criticisms of *négritude* grew, with economic development in most African countries faltering in the 1980s, and denunciations of celebrations of essentialism that centred on the romanticisation of tradition and non-modernity, Wade's film was critiqued for affirming Western gazes on Africa. He was accused of making the Global South into a tourist site for the Global North, for those in search of an unchanged, simple, and "traditional" other.[24] The focus on *Africanité* in Wade's artistry, like that of others working in Senghor's vein, also bothered "critics and curators [who since the 1990s] sought to nurture a colorblind globalism that focuses on shared experiences of transnationalism and world citizenship, as well as technological and political interconnectedness".[25] Wade's film was too African.

Yet there is another way to read the movie, as an opening of "the African mind to certain dimensions of its own world which Western influence has obscured", writes renowned literary studies scholar Abiola Irele.[26] He argues against other scholars that *négritude* was irrelevant, or, worse, a repository for fantastical cultural nationalisms. Confirming Irele's view of *Ndeysaan*, Wade's later project *Dakar-Bombay* (2011), a still uncut documentary tracing *Indouphilie*'s socially intricate and embedded evolution, reveals other African worlds and worldliness that is transnational yet non-Western—a balancing act that "national" cinemas of developing countries have had to navigate differently, and with an arguably greater burden to address questions about relevance, relatability, and resources compared to Hollywood films or European ones. As such, Senegalese documentary realism about Indo-Senegalese art-worlds operates outside the "dialectic between difference and sameness" that Brian Larkin argues to explain the popularity of Indian film outside India, particularly in Nigeria and other countries living between modernity and tradition.[27] Such readings miss the longer history of Africa-India cultural connections, and in those, a sustained study and celebration of Blackness.

While Bollywood has been harshly criticised for prizing whiteness, particularly in its figuring of light skin as the ideal for feminine beauty, Wade's documentary is remarkable for the camera's focus on Senegalese women and men, their bodies, facial expressions, styles, and differences amongst themselves, as well as the different kinds of Indian forms and figures. The aesthetics of Wade's film are tuned to Africans seeing Africans and the African gaze on African-Indian relationships within a *négritude* frame. African film is performative, not passive viewing. Just as diasporic Indian filmgoers, to take one group, have heterogeneous and complex viewing practices, not all tied to nostalgia, spectating and performing film may be a means of revering and identifying with a "national culture", or "disidentification" that de-emphasises or demotes national identification to place greater emphasis on ethnic-linguistic, gender, racial, and/or place (rural vs. urban) affiliations.[28] In the telling of Badiane and other interlocutors in *Dakar-Bombay*, Indian cinema allows Senegalese identities of playback artistry that are split persons—Hema Malini/Emma Malini Sy, Diwo Diallo/Kajor, Abdou Fediore/ Mahendra Kapoor ("The King of Breath"). Without this duality, Bollywood would mean much less to the Senegalese. As Badiane says, "Après Bombay, c'est Sénégal". The connection is unthinkable: "Who would have thought: a small country in West Africa, 10,000 kilometers as the crow flies from India".[29]

Wade's documentary about *Indouphilie* is ultimately a celebration of Senegalese beauty as much as, or perhaps more than, a homage to India. It is African creativity that the viewer sees in the Senegalese performance of the Indian "classics". *Dakar-Bombay* also decentres India and destabilises the use of film as a nationalistic enterprise. The Senegalese are shown many Indias, not just a single nation projected into the world. Senegal is the stage where Indians and Senegalese perform. Wade's film confirms the brilliance of Senghor's Pan-African arts patronage as continually reborn, the "changing same" discussed by Paul Gilroy in *The Black Atlantic*—that touched other major figures in the globalisation of Black arts.[30]

Codifying African classics: the move away from Indian aesthetics

A more direct move away from Indian aesthetics has occurred in the post-Senghorian dance world. Mudra Afrique was a dance centre in Dakar formed and run by Maurice Béjart from 1977–82. No other dance project in Francophone Africa could compete with it, and its central place in the modernisation of African dance placed it at the centre of critical issues of the politics of cultural creation and consumption. The formal name of Mudra Afrique was the "African Centre of Research and Interpretive Development". Béjart was the director, while Léopold Senghor supported the Centre financially and Germaine Acogny was the manager.[31]

Béjart, born in 1927 in Marseille, was the great-grandson of a Senegalese *signare*, mixed-race women in France's urban Senegalese colonial outposts, and the son of French philosopher Gaston Berger. Through their shared love of Senegal and intellectual affinity, he and Senghor found their common outlook for the establishment of Mudra Afrique. Béjart founded the Ballet of the 20th Century dance school in Brussels in 1960, and, influenced by the poetry of Tagore and a visit to India, choreographed *Cygne* (1965) to Hindu devotional music, and *Bhakti* (1968) showing dancers meditating to Krishna, Shiva, Shakti, and other gods.[32] The name "Mudra", meaning hand gestures in Sanskrit, came from his reverence for Hindu spirituality and especially its embodied forms in vocal music and dance. The change in his orientation, coming in the cataclysm of 1968, was meant to signify a revolutionary challenge, as it were, to Western classical dance. Whereas students were previously steeped in ballet, Mudra forced ballet to change by thrusting it into the current century by globalisation, and parallel schools were established outside Europe, with Dakar being its home in Africa.

Germaine Acogny was born in 1944 in Porto-Novo, in what was then the French colony of Dahomey. Her mother died when she was five years old, and she and her father, Togoun Servais, who worked in the French colonial administration and also composed original poetry, moved to Senegal. She left for France after secondary school to study physical education and sports, and in Brussels she met Béjart. She returned to Senegal first, and began to teach at the Institute of Art. After her promotion to the position of director of African dance there in 1972, Senghor came to see her personality and work as definitive of *négritude*. Perhaps most attractive to Senghor was that Acogny had "classical" training in ballet and in the Yoruba arts—dance and spiritual practices—through her grandmother, whom Acogny celebrates in her writings and choreographies. She saw her dance as contemporary African dance, and what contemporary in Dakar meant in cultural terms in the late 1970s was experimentation with Blackness and its boundaries—mapping the edges of difference, where Africa and Asia were conjoined, and Africa and Europe too. It also meant testing European epistemological hegemony in which Africa was perpetually traditional. Critics of *négritude* felt African traditionalism was reified in the politics of Senghor. Yet Acogny was one artist who helped convince him and the world of *négritude*'s contemporary and modern significance. In an interview she gave many years after she had worked between West Africa and Europe, and before she opened the centre for traditional and contemporary dance, L'École des Sables, in Toubab Dialaw, a coastal village south of Dakar, in 1998, she explained:

> I learned classical dance and created a connection to African dances using my body. I integrated classical dance steps into my technique just like the Europeans ... But Picasso did not admit his "Demoiselles d'Avignon" are completely African. Europeans often do not want to admit what they have absorbed from Africans. They prefer to say what they have learned from Asians, from Indians, from Hindus. But they do not easily say what they have absorbed from Africa. And that is offensive and insulting. I say I am from Benin, I have an instinct from Benin and Senegalese gestures. I was also lucky enough to be

able to unite these two cultures, as well as the French one, and I have not denied my identities in the process.[33]

Significantly, Acogny's *négritude*, while emphasising the process and anti-purity of *métissage* that Senghor valorised, also challenges her mentors—both Béjart's and Senghor's virtual obsession with Eastern, particularly Indian, cultural forms. She saw instead that Europeans obscured Africa and refused recognition of Black contributions by ignoring them or valorising Asian, and more specifically Indian, sources above all others.

Acogny's critique coming from the world of dance is important for several reasons. First, European balletic tradition had assimilated Indian *Bharatanatyam* and epics for centuries with dancers adopting Indian names and personas, costumes, and gestures. Further, even allowing for the orientalist and fantastical other that India represented for some European artists, European artists had long recognised Indian and other Asian traditions as "classical". Through her choreography, Acogny forced European artists to recognise the classical in Black dance. She performed "the mother of African dance" that she had developed from dance and music as well as Yoruba history and indigenous cosmology.[34] Dance was a means of communicating with the divine in the Yoruba worldview. She codified this system in movement for audiences who held assumptions about African "traditional" dance as unchoreographed and without symbolism. On top of this structural core—the grammar—African dances "translated" into live performances.

Contemporary African dance, with leading figures like Acogny, "interrupted the white gaze".[35] She challenged white audiences, as the main consumers of African and Asian dance, to rethink their conceptions of a formal canon and their comparisons of non-Western art. It is perhaps a critical spirit that has made Pan-Africanism survive, even as fads including Bollywood have faded. *Négritude* in Acogny's conceptualisation went beyond Black character to develop cultural theory. The new formulations of *négritude* have diminished the significance of Bollywood in West Africa because Black cultural autonomy and critique grew stronger in India's shadow.

Projections of pride

It is not difficult to imagine why African critics of Bollywood would become amongst the most vocal—they know these films intimately and from a distance. Staple elements of Bollywood films include: an abstract national community represented through traditions, especially epics and myths that many people know from oral story-telling, folksongs, and images; codes of *dharma* (duty), and renunciation; the central figure of the mother; lush jewellery and dress, when appropriate to the character's status, in the style of painting traditions like Raja Ravi Varma's in calendars and posters; and, with some safe success, transgressions that do not overturn the traditional order. In this mix (*masala*), "modernity is incorporated, but order is upheld".[36] Melodrama serves to envelop viewers in a collective emotional universe. Fantasy and detachment from reality enable Bollywood to rally diverse viewers, often with the mother-figure as the bearer of the weight of emotion, symbolism, and social life. Women characters are loaded with social expectations, dilemmas, and power. Yet Bollywood has increasingly struggled to calibrate tradition, with women actors perhaps being the most obvious bearers of changing cultural norms about dress, demeanour, and values.

Critics of Indian film, including those involved in filmmaking, have commented on its detachment from reality, trafficking in stereotypes, lack of representation of India's diversity, and thoroughgoing shallowness. In parts of Africa without large Indian diasporas, Bollywood's success has been uneven and not lasting, from a fad to a "divorce" and even to just one amongst many possibilities now available with television shows. Outsiders, struck by the apparent passions of African filmgoers, especially girls and women, have not appreciated the dynamic responses amongst Africans to Indian films as they treat African viewers with "condescension" as "backward".[37] While Bollywood films used to display a mastery of tools and techniques of aesthetic representation with high production values, their stories no longer stand up to competition from American and Nigerian films, and even Mexican telenovelas, today. Some West African viewers no longer have a continuous relationship or affection for Indian films and, since the 2010s, increasingly television shows, with their episodic reconnections, are highly sensitive to the changing look of Indian outputs.[38]

For instance, in Côte d'Ivoire, Bollywood films cannot even be found in shops of pirated videos, although musicians often play Hindi songs in a nostalgic kind of way. According to one social commentator, "The zouglou singers Yodé and Siro revisit the same tear-jerkers as Bollywood ... placing lovers at the mercy of the religious, which here has the power to undo the strongest of bonds. People feel more concerned by this social reality that affects them directly, sung in French and in Dioula". Meanwhile Ivorian television broadcasts endless telenovelas with "less and less explosive sighing"![39] In Mali, with the collapse of cinema houses have come new fashions amongst the women and girls who in the past may have watched Indian films. Bamako's main cinema no longer shows any Bollywood films. Only the Office de Radio et Télévision du Mali (ORTM) programmes a late-night "Hindu" feature on the first Wednesday of the month for the women and girls who still enjoy Indian music. As the journalist Moussa Bolly says, "it must be stressed that this fringe now prefers African sitcoms and Brazilian or Mexican soap operas".[40]

Even in Senegal, with its deeper *Indouphilie* roots, the weekly programme by Mamadou Pam was not always popular. "That kept a large audience glued to the TV screen. But it only lasted three years", notes the journalist Aboubacar Demba Cissokho. "It is still true that for the dozen or so popular cinemas still functional in Dakar and the rest of the country, the films screened are those that give a large place to music. Audiences are no longer only made up of women, however, as they have found other slots on the private TV channels".[41] In the few remaining movie theatres, there is a rotation of films including Bollywood and American films, crime dramas, and karate movies. Efforts to keep cinema popular have included mobile screenings in rural areas. Film, even as a vital staple of Senegalese international reputation, has not had substantial government support since the 1980s, when the economic crisis hit.

Journalist Hector Todouvossi from Benin, where the history of visual Indian iconography may go back a hundred years to Mami Wata, explains one reason for the fall in popularity of Indian films: "the actors are no longer the same and the new actors are rarely at the level of the elders".[42] Even popular Indian films amongst pirated videos now have to compete with kung fu, Hollywood, and Nollywood industries. Film piracy has brought more viewers but fewer committed fans because it enables more choices and affordability.

In the early 2000s, it became clear to Indian filmmakers that bigger returns on their investments were in sales of international rights as opposed to domestic sales. Countries like South Africa and Mauritius, alongside the UK and the US, have large Indian diasporas and a situation where filmgoers go to malls instead of cinema houses, providing important new markets.[43] In these two African countries, where nostalgia and yearning for cultural connection to India are strong, filmgoers have a lively tradition of dressing up as their favourite film stars, flocking to see stars visiting from India, and attending Bollywood concerts. Indian diasporas in Kenya and Tanzania consume Bollywood films in the same way. In South Africa, Bollywood is racialised, unlike in other African countries. Going to Indian films is largely an Indian affair and seen even in post-apartheid South Africa as a "cultural activity" that is "good clean fun" and acceptable to all generations. Black people found the spectacle of Indian fans dressed up as their favourite actors and actresses "crude and silly".[44] Diasporic nostalgia in a racially segregated society sharply divides and politicises films that in another context might have uneven social relevance.

In many West African countries, the popularity of Indian films has been sustained by predominantly Muslim areas. In Northern Cameroon, Central Togo, and Northern Nigeria, Bollywood still commands largely female audiences. There again, the closure of cinemas as well as the growing similarity of Indian films to Western ones—in terms of the dances, costumes, hairstyles, and themes— has contributed to some decline; but perhaps more important are competitors such as Mexican and Peruvian soap operas. African shows made by Nigerians, Beninois, Burkinabe, and Malians are better at providing what Indian films used to offer.

In Senegal, Indian serials have also replaced films in popularity to some extent. In 2010, the visit of the leading television actress of the show "Vaidehi", Pallavi Kulkarni, to Senegal was arranged by Mamadou Pam, the media personality.[45] The screaming crowds who greeted the actress, who was not well known in India, revealed that participation in public spectacles and performances sustains the popularity of Indian films and serials.

There are several reasons for the waning interest in Indian film amongst African audiences. African films have overshadowed Indian ones, while competition between Bollywood and Nollywood, as the two largest film industries based on output, has split viewership. Scholars of film in Nigeria have probably underestimated the popularity of Indian films in the South in a certain era (and perhaps overestimated their appeal in the North), but it is clear that the indigenous film scene in the South—known globally as Nollywood—has caused the decline of interest in Bollywood films in Nigeria and around Africa. The two are similar in their appearance of non- or anti-Hollywood or Western positionality. They also have some interplay between them that provides the foreign one historical legitimacy and the indigenous one a modernising authority. Bollywood films, like the Tamil-language *Singam*, have been shot in locations in South Africa. According to media journalist Tony Rajkumar, "Bollywood wants to get its hands on Nollywood". He notes Indian efforts to partner with the Nigerian film industry, with the aim of developing distribution networks. Bollywood investors planned to solicit the Commonwealth Business Council (CBC) to create a film fund worth $100 million. The Indian government has also tried to use Bollywood as a form of Indian soft power in Nigeria by proposing, for example, to work with the Export-Import Bank of India to underwrite the creation of a film city near Kano, in the North of the country, in 2013.[46]

Such plans have turned out to be almost entirely aspirational rather than real. When Africans have studied filmmaking or made films in India, they have largely done so only by private means. Niji Akanni was one of the first Nigerians to study film in India at the state Film and Television Institute of India in Pune between 1995 and 1998. Others like Chukwuma Osakwe went to India because it was easier to get a visa than to the United States. Osakwe went to India in 2009 and made what is considered the first Nollywood-Bollywood collaboration, *J.U.D.E.*, with Parveen Kurma as the assistant director, in 2012. The film contained many autobiographical elements about a young Nigerian professional trying to make it, first in Lagos before setting off for India, where he faces racism and bigotry.[47] In 2016, rom-com *Love is in the Hair*, written and directed by two women, was released in theatres. The story begins with a man trying to seduce a woman using *juju* on a piece of her hair, which turns out to be an extension made with Indian hair.[48] Rita

Onwurah, the writer, is a successful businesswoman whose career straddles a number of fields. Many Nollywood filmmakers who find success in a multimillion-dollar industry realise they do not need the kinds of training programmes held in New Delhi in 2014 for producers and directors from Kano. Seeing first hand the rhetoric of Indian-African partnership being contradicted by the exclusion of Nigerian students from employment in film in Bollywood, as well as other kinds of racism, the independence of Nigerian filmmakers has been a point of pride. Some Indian filmmakers, including Narender Yadav, have criticised Bollywood for many reasons and have tried to address racism in the industry. He argues that the Nollywood-Bollywood nexus should be considered the avant-garde of filmmaking. Yet the overwhelming tendency of Bollywood to ignore reality and refuse partnerships with African film industries has led critics to assail the film industry (and by extension, India) for its political failures in the Third World, echoing Arundhati Roy's argument that the gains of the Non-Aligned Movement have been squandered by nationalism and neoliberal corporatisation.[49]

The 2020 release of *Namaste Wahala*, a film billed as a partnership between Bollywood and Nollywood, tried to respond to the critics. A love story between an Indian man and a Nigerian woman set in Lagos treats all the familiar themes—family disapproval, jealous spies, and secret trysts. The harshest critics of the film are Nigerian reviewers, who find the quality lacking and the story "too Bollywood", not enough Nigerian. Reviewing for *Pulse Nigeria*, Precious "Mamazeus" Nwogu pans the quality of the directing, sound, and editing.[50] Anthropologist Girish Daswani, whose family has roots in West Africa like that of the producer and director, Indian-Nigerian Hamisha Daryani Ahuja, argues that the film misses a rare chance to introduce the longer history of Indians in West Africa, which includes real-life African-Indian couples who were rejected by the Desi (Indian) community.[51]

Bollywood has forgotten history, and with it its former colonial and postcolonial political spirit. While Indian avant-garde films are coming into their own, the Bollywood mega-industry has lost its art for picking actors with staying power. As with *Namaste Wahala*, major backing from the Coca-Cola Company and other products means films are vehicles for advertisements on Netflix and other services. Perhaps most significant of all, Bollywood has muddled "its conception of the hero and destiny", that once seemed to emanate from the soul of India itself. Africans now choose African-made films that speak to forces of good and evil (including supernatural powers of spirits, churches, and *juju*, as well as human relationships), justice, and power in the world around them. To stereotype or uncritically characterise African filmgoers' habits is to ignore that "it is on the ideological terrain and in the autonomy of imaginations that competition lies ... If Bollywood wants to strike up a chord in African hearts again, it no doubt needs to think less of markets and more of its own society's relation to the world".[52]

Many Africans increasingly reject Bollywood's pursuit of whiteness, reflected in the appearance of its stars. In India, skin-lightening creams are used by the masses of women and men. Fair & Lovely, a lightening cream made by Unilever, has annual sales of more than $500 million. The product first became available in India in 1971, and soon after in Sri Lanka and Thailand.[53] While products for whitening the skin may have been present before this time in African countries, their popularity is a more recent phenomenon associated with urban women. Economic deregulation has also caused the proliferation in the number of lightening products on the market and their marketing.[54] A boom seen in the sale of Fair & Lovely in the 1990s has been tied to the growing employment of young women in retail and sales.[55] The increasing circulation of Bollywood films and serials in African communities and throughout the world, after satellite television first came out of Hong Kong's STAR TV, led to more consumption of lightening creams.[56] Fair & Lovely was endorsed by major Bollywood stars including Shah Rukh Khan and Aishwarya Rai Bachchan.[57] Ideas about the superiority of lighter skin, which probably long existed in Asian or African societies, have been intensified by mass media and communication technologies.[58]

White or fair skin brings racial capital in many countries of the Global South—not simply because of legacies of colonialism or social hierarchies, but due to the commodification of the body in widely circulated images. Shehzad Nadeem argues that "the desire for fair skin is ultimately a desire for distinction and self-control".[59] A Senegalese woman told an American reporter that "women bleach their skin to come across as modern women who can modify their skin tone as they wish". It is a matter of choice and of bending the boundaries of possibility—after all, Black and brown women do not want to be white women but lighter women.[60] Some middle-class educated women deny they bleach their skin and blame poorer women, but the fact that lighter skin is associated with better incomes, "endogamy" in marriage and relationships, and beauty in advertising suggests the opposite—lighter skin in Africa, Asia, and even the West means refinement and greater wealth.[61]

Skin lightening has, however, been confronted by defenders of Blackness. In Côte d'Ivoire, activists created a beauty pageant called "Miss Authentica" that only allows competitors with non-bleached skin. In 2016, the Ghanaian government imposed restrictions on skin-lightening products by banning the sale of cosmetics that contained hydroquinone.[62] While estimates suggested that the prevalence of skin lightening in Ghana, used by about one third of adult women, was far lower than in Nigeria (77%) and Senegal (52–67%), many Ghanaians reported that lighter skin made finding a partner, getting promotions, and gaining respect easier.[63] Few Ghanaians felt the ban would work. Black Lives Matter demonstrations that followed the murder of

George Floyd in the United States in May 2020 had many consequences, but perhaps one of the most unforeseen was the outcry against skin-lightening creams in Africa and India. Although Ghana, Rwanda, Senegal, and Uganda already had unenforced bans on these creams, Indians turned new attention to their country's own backwardness in this regard.[64] Following a pressure campaign, Unilever changed the name of its product to "Glow & Lovely" in India in June 2020. The campaign targeted Bollywood stars who used their social media to denounce racism, all while they were profiting from skin lighteners and their fairness on screen. Inspired by Black activists, India's "Dark is Beautiful" campaign, led by organisations like Women of Worth, founded by Kavitha Emmanuel, have found support amongst African and African diaspora activists.[65] The African critique of Bollywood has translated into an influence on Indian women.

Racial ideals also fuel the hair industry. In this lucrative industry, one major production site is India, where women "produce" hair in Indian temples. The largest producer is the Tirumala Sri Venkateswara Temple in Andhra Pradesh in South India. Processed hair is sold across vast networks, from Hindu to African and African-American women. African women's ability to purchase natural hair from other women means still being natural, in a context where "natural" is politicised and directed against the use of products like skin lighteners and false hair.[66] In a major boost to Indian involvement in this industry, the Indian company Godrej has purchased the Lebanese-owned Darling Ltd., a synthetic hair manufacturer, distributor, and retailer with production and retail sites throughout the African continent.[67] The company was established in Senegal in the 1970s, and then expanded throughout West Africa before moving into East African markets in the 1980s. Today, Darling being the leader in sales of wigs, hair extensions, and braids in Africa, means that Indians have acquired a major part of the African beauty industry.

Under apartheid in South Africa, hair was made an official indicator of race by the Population Registration Act of 1950, but the end of white rule only created a more complicated commercialisation of hair:

> An essentializing discourse [about hair] concealed the homogenizing practices that were pervasive throughout the exchange of hair, and drew attention away from the politics that motivated its circulation. Overall, it distracted from the economy of otherness, where the production, distribution, and consumption of Indian hair served to reinforce racial and gendered hierarchies.[68]

Hair extensions and weaves, like skin lightening, represent body modifications that are not individual projects but rather "a mode of enacting a group identity" and exclusion by aesthetics.[69] Pan-African and African cultural nationalists' opposition also necessarily essentialises Black womanhood in defending and honouring it. Yet Black women, especially the younger generations who celebrate and embrace untreated hair and skin, have also influenced Indian women by giving them a model and language of protest they seemingly lacked until recently. Pakistani writer Mehreen Kasana explains that blogging has brought about platforms for African-Americans, Arabs, and South Asians to create feminist solidarities around resistance to discriminatory popular culture and other kinds of political issues.[70] These examples make clear that whereas Bollywood once presented an ideal of feminine beauty, for the moment it has become a centrepiece of cultural and even anti-racist protest.

Conclusion

Senegal maintains its identity as a source of *négritude* inspiration and a location where both Africans and Indians have reimagined themselves. In a vein similar to Senghor's Afro-Dravidian project,

Senegalese film has brought Asia into *Africanité*. Dak'Art, the Dakar Biennale, is the only international forum dedicated to contemporary art by Africans and African diasporic artists hosted on the continent, occurring every two years since it consolidated earlier exhibitions and received formal support from the Senegalese government in 2000. As a Pan-African collective, it is a recommitment to Senghor's *négritude* vision. The structure has been to emphasise and retain African initiative, while also cultivating an international presence and market for African art, though in 2014, the Biennale organisers began to invite non-African artists.[71] Many came as a part of this new direction with a Global South focus. Sumesh Sharma curated "'India's Search for Power, 1966–1982' (Indira Gandhi's Foreign Policy)" with support from Clark House Initiative, a gallery in Mumbai. The artists' guiding vision is that:

> The assertion of the Global South can only arise if we imagine Pan-Africanism as a spiritual point of departure for culture, literature, music and the visual arts in Latin America, Southern Arabia, South Asia and South East Asia. African Diasporas have existed here for centuries apart from the historic waves of human migration. To inhabit a radical contemporaneity we need to inherit a radical history ... All totalitarian regimes have addressed their existences to authenticity and purity, which are inherent falsehoods. Artists are thus invited to participate in a biennale project that inspires them in situationist histories that arise by chance and are not scripted. India today grapples with the unfortunate burden of determining its idea of nationhood, its diversity does not allow narrow European definitions that the regime in power enforces upon the republic's citizens. The anti-national is the writer, the artist, the intellectual, the musician, the religious minority, the untouchable and all those who do not conform to some manifestation of the author.[72]

The collective included artists from India, Senegal, Tunisia, the US, Switzerland, Ireland, France, the UK, Pakistan, West Bengal,

Poland, and Burma. Somnath Mukherjee, working with French photographer Aurélien Froment, brought his Senegalese dance troupe to the festival.[73] Also honoured was Geoffrey Mukasa (1954–2009), a Ugandan who had studied art in Lucknow and had a stand at Art Dubai, who was one of the few Africans featured in the modern section.

The Indian government and businesses may see in Africa only markets for profit-making, or a missionary field for Hinduism. But disillusioned Indians, fearing what their nation is becoming, have been inspired by African humanism, philosophy, and art. Pan-Africanism and Black women's activism, in particular, have provided Indians with a cosmopolitanism that has translated into dissent against cultural homogenisation and discrimination in India and the Indian diaspora that has been fuelled by rightwing xenophobic nationalism and neoliberal economic growth. A small West African country's cultural pride and wider Pan-Africanism have inspired surprising critical reflection for citizens of one of the world's emerging powers.

CONCLUSION

Africans and Indians have grown together and apart in a process that has produced distinctly different identities of Black and Brown. The British mediated between them, and African-Indian histories generated from English-language sources bear the legacy of an Indian Ocean world inhabited by Arab Muslim seafarers, Indian merchants, and African peasants. But this world is geographically larger and includes also Hindu missionaries, French-speaking poets, African pilgrims, women teachers and translators, and dancers, singers, and filmmakers. The Indian Ocean may offer a unique method in the study of global contradictions and complications, as Isabel Hofmeyr proposes, but its comparison to the Atlantic has imposed tropes of aberration and absence—of modern racialism, for instance.[1] This book shows the connectivity and co-constitution of the Atlantic and Indian Ocean worlds since the turn of the twentieth century.

A Pan-African or Afrocentric reading of these stories reveals Africa as critical in Indian imaginations. Indeed, Black cultural consciousness has been vital to Indians and India and has salvaged postcolonial possibilities for the Indian diaspora in Africa. Although underappreciated in Indian public and intellectual discourse, modern India's status as a cultural mecca was made possible, in part, through its relations with Africans and Africa. African nations offered Indians and Pakistanis opportunities and religious and cultural refuge to escape the turmoil in South Asia. For several decades after the 1960s, negotiation and exchange made Afro-Indian solidarity a thing of substance.

Since Narendra Modi inaugurated the first India-Africa Forum Summit in 2008, which is held every three years, "shared history" has tried to put a romantic gloss on expanding trade and investment in African countries.[2] Yet India has no genuine identification with any single African nation, except perhaps South Africa, as argued by Alexander Davis. He suggests that India's relationship to African countries has changed from shared resistance to domination to a relationship that "reflects or even creates" hierarchy.[3]

This shift has been abetted by history—told in the most self-serving ways—pulled over the ugly present. When Dr Sylviane Diouf and Kenneth Robbins brought the New York Public Library exhibit "Africans in India" to the Indira Gandhi National Centre for the Arts in New Delhi in 2014, African immigrants had just recently been victims of attacks in the capital.[4] In contrast to the grainy video captured in a Delhi metro station of a mob beating three African students, the exhibit featured images from Deccani and Mughal art and other genres depicting African slaves' attainment of "the pinnacle of military and political authority" in a relatively "open-minded" Indian society that tolerated religious and ethnic minorities.[5] Rather than useful reflection, however, the exhibit reaffirmed for many Indians their superiority. For example, Harshini Vakkalanka quoted the Programme Director of the Indira Gandhi National Centre, Dr Mangalam Swaminathan, in her review in *The Hindu*:

> The major aspect that one can take away: India was a flourishing nation, where people came seeking employment, as far back as fourth century. Indian culture assimilated them into the society, as it had done with several other faiths, cultures and lifestyles. There was

CONCLUSION

mutual give and take culturally, part of the broadminded tolerance of India. Africans in India are an indelible part of Indian history and heritage. We need to do more research and come up with exhibitions, research papers and publications.[6]

On the other side, writing in *The Times of India*, Siddharth Varadarajan urged "Indian politicians and civic leaders ... to address racism toward Africans—and northeastern Indians".[7] He demanded that universities "who court African students", Bollywood, and the Indian government at the highest levels, should intervene, lest India be called out for its hypocrisy—"when Indians are attacked abroad", he noted, the outcry is "in overdrive". Yet some defences only deepened the divides within India. Al-Jazeera reported the clumsy response of the MP Tarun Vijay, that the British introduced racism and the Indians could not be racist because they "live with the south" and "have Black people around".[8] He later apologised to those who did not feel the same as him, saying Indians were often the first to condemn racism.

Modi hoped to assuage African governments' justified remonstrations against the treatment of their citizens in India at the India-Africa Summit in 2015. His address sketched a historical narrative of oppression and redemption reminiscent of the Garveyite and Ahmadi discourses of the past. Welcoming his African guests, he described Africa as "the land where history began, humanity grew and new hope rises".[9] Africa's Atlantic shores were once "history's tragic crossroads", but now "at the frontiers of many successes". With ancient civilisations, young populations, and rapid economic growth, the future lay with African countries and India. Of course, he did not address African-Indian entanglements in the religious and intellectual realm, or the question of descendants of African slaves in India. Modi would rather forget the Indian diaspora's ambivalent role in Eastern and Southern Africa, in favour of cheap developmentalist

propaganda that surely draws the ire of the left in India and
African nations. While Nehru's diplomats worried about how
Indian merchants in Africa made the Indian government's gestures of goodwill appear hollow, Modi's government today seems
satisfied with hollowing out historical knowledge entirely.[10]

Knowledge is at the centre of Africa-Indian conflicts. As the
African protests against Gandhi garnered curiosity, criticism, and
anger around the world, Zimbabwean political scientist Chipo
Dendere observed of the #GandhiMustFall movement:

> We should not put [up] statues of people we are not clearly under-
> standing. We need open conversation about our history and the
> contributions of Black people. We are going to be disappointed by
> most people. Our few resources may not be best used for pulling
> down statues but rather to debate history.[11]

But debating history may be far costlier than pulling down
statues.

India's higher education network is the largest in the world,
and African foreign students are critical to its international
reputation:

> Of those foreign students who do come to India, African students are
> the most numerous. In fact India is the topmost non-African devel-
> oping country destination among African students for higher educa-
> tion. According to . . . AISHE [All India Survey on Higher
> Education], Sudan and Nigeria are the third and fifth biggest source
> countries for foreign students in India. African students coming in
> to India take up courses as diverse as engineering, medicine, phar-
> macy, management, or even those that help them secure a career in
> the services sector.[12]

This factor of young, educated, mobile migrants coming to India
is often missed in analyses that do not delve into deeper intersectional factors—such as class, gender, and age—in rising racism
in India. While India competes economically with China and

other BRICS countries, weaknesses persist in India's growth. As political scientist Zachariah Mampilly argues, because India and African nations are still relatively weak states in the global system, non-state actors are vital intermediaries in and about India and the Global South more broadly.[13]

Within higher education, the growing population of qualified students and rising incomes of African and Indian families is driving demand for seats at Indian and other universities around the world. The competitive state of higher education and the stakes for Black-Indian relationships are played out particularly in South African universities, with their system of reservations intended for Black people who were shut out of white universities during the apartheid era. Many Indians feel entitled to some reservations and "see affirmative action as reverse racism".[14] While "race boundaries are being reinforced in South Africa" in an era of scarcity, these claims of Indians about exclusion in education are not unfamiliar. They echo those of higher-caste families in India, who complain that their deserving children are denied seats at universities because of the reservations for Scheduled Castes and Scheduled Tribes. In Tamil Nadu, for instance, where reservations are amongst the oldest in India, the Brahmins have long had a "supranational" identity as a professional diaspora, and amongst them graduates of the Indian Institute of Technology have used their cultural capital abroad, claiming even that they represent "Brand India" in Silicon Valley.[15]

Of course, the language of race does not necessarily apply in all histories and needs careful consideration. But race, caste, and other logics of exclusion intertwine in complicated ways in different spaces and moments of African-Indian entanglements and migrations. As Suraj Yengde has argued about how caste works in the Indian diaspora, it moves and "feeds on native practices, like a parasite".[16]

Past ideologies of Pan-Africanism and Afrocentrism marked Indians in different ways, from Idi Amin's brand of Afrocentrism which exiled Indians as vestiges of colonialism, to Black Consciousness in South Africa and "political Blackness" in Britain, in which Blackness was a strategy of solidarity. Reflecting on political Blackness, philosopher Kwame Anthony Appiah writes that categories of identities are "expansive ... multiple, interactive and, yes, subject to revision".[17] Perhaps no meaningful revision will be possible whilst the self-segregation and endogamy, against which both Du Bois and Idi Amin chafed, continues.

Literature, art, film, and soap operas perhaps better convey African-Indian desires and disillusionment. Many novelists come to mind: W. E. B. Du Bois, Ngugi Wa Thiong'o, M. G. Vassanji, and V. S. Naipaul. Younger generations include Amitav Ghosh, Tahir Shah, and Mukoma wa Ngugi. Since the 2000s, conferences have been convened to revive the Afro-Asian Writers' Association, and, as Frank Schulze-Engler argues, "it is necessary to break away from the idea of Afro-Asian literature being mainly or even entirely predicated on a common history of colonial victimhood and anti-colonialist resistance".[18] Even literary explorations of race need not be narrowly conceived in anti-Western frames. Senghor understood that the arts captured the gendered, mythic, and supernatural aspects ignored in formal African-Indian histories. Women film-makers have been especially good at representing the unspoken. Mira Nair's *Mississippi Masala* was better received than Ahuja's *Namaste Wahala*, but both are unmistakably challenging. Before them, at the turn of the twentieth century, Pauline Hopkins, author of *Of One Blood: Or, The Hidden Self* and many other works, created an essential connection between Africans and Indians through their ability to perceive the supernatural.[19] This idea was linked to the romantic and racist notion of Black emotional intelligence, discredited later by critics of intellectuals like Senghor who continued to espouse it, but it captures an ineffability. The Igbo-Tamil writer Akwaeke Emezi, author of the novel *Freshwater*, described it differently through their own personal story of *ogbanje*, an Igbo spirit born into a human body, a kind of malevolent trickster, whose goal is to torment the human mother by dying unexpectedly only to return in the next child and do it all over again.[20]

> If *ogbanje* represent an overlapping of realities—a spirit who looks incredibly convincing as a human, then what does it look like for one to experience gender dysphoria and take surgical steps to resolve that? Our language around gender identity is often so Western, how can we intersect that with non-Western realities? For example, is there a term for the dysphoria experienced by spirits who find themselves embodied in human form? It was inevitable that I'd be drawn to these overlaps, since I live there, inhabiting simultaneous realities that are usually considered mutually exclusive.[21]

Ekwezi reveals uncomfortable new idioms—spiritual, bodily, racial—of multiplicities and hybridities. *Freshwater*, told through the spirit-possessed child of a Tamilian mother and Igbo father, unsettles cultural paradigms that have little to do with anticolonial nostalgia and solidarity. Nonconforming, lived African-Indian experiences told in memoirs, films, paintings, dance, and other forms, are constituting "fledgling genres" of writing from "contact zones".[22]

Kamala Harris, elected as Vice President of the United States in 2020, recounts the meeting and marriage of her parents—her Jamaican father and her Indian mother—as uniquely forged by the civil rights movement. They were students at the University of California in Berkeley in the early 1960s, and met in Oakland at a march. They later divorced, and both of their daughters pursued equal rights as lawyers. Her mother's "marriage was as much an act of rebellion as an act of love", Kamala Harris writes. "Explaining it to her parents had been hard enough. Explaining the divorce, I imagine, was even harder".[23] What her mother's family, Tamilians who Harris says were part of the Indian independence movement and then worked in Zambia in refugee resettlement, actually thought, may be taboo for a carefully crafted political biography.

But history can fill in her silence. Also filling it are Indian politicians who are flummoxed by the "Kamala Conundrum": the possibility that she might take the side of India's minorities over the Hindu majority and the ruling BJP party.[24] Some Indians were quick to point out publicly that Harris calls herself Black, not Indian, and is a Christian, not a Hindu.

Few believe the myth of Indian anti-Blackness. Yet disbelief need not be translated into anti-Indian racism, but should rather be turned towards the project of excavating attempted and unfinished projects of non-Western universalism and humanism and histories of their failure, amidst the peril of neoliberalisation and exclusionary nationalisms. Political leaders aside, peoples' histories present African-Indian alternatives.

Indians should take African challenges seriously. While the Indian government believes it is treading lightly with its multicultural exhibitions and the curtailment of permanent Indian settlers in Africa in preference for "floating diasporas" who mingle and go,[25] disembodied interactions of Africans and Indians, distant and devoid of human contact, are dangerous. This was precisely the problem with the doomed Gandhi statue in Ghana—a looming silent Mahatma. This kind of claim on African space, in the guise of gift-giving, was not the strategy of Nehru or Indira Gandhi. Given that the Mahatma still inspires critical reflection and will not be forgotten even without continuous adulation, we may turn our attention to the many other African-Indian stories that wait to be told.

NOTES

INTRODUCTION

1. Mungai 2015.
2. Ngugi wa Thiong'o 2012.
3. Ibid.
4. Adibe 2017; "India Failed to Deter Xenophobic, Racist Attacks: African Envoys", *Times of India*, 3 April 2017; https://timeso-findia.indiatimes.com/india/india-failed-to-deter-xenophobic-racist-attacks-on-africans-envoys/articleshow/57989227.cms (accessed 4 April 2021).
5. Mahajan 2019. See also Desai and Vahed 2019; Myburgh 2017.
6. Kwoba, Chantiluke and Nkopo, eds. 2018.
7. Rawat 2020.
8. Guha 2018; Hall 2011.
9. Robb, ed. 1995, p. 1.
10. Yengde 2019; Wilkerson 2020.
11. Mullen and Watson, eds. 2005.
12. Goyal 2014; Hofmeyr 2007; Balachandran 2014.
13. The scholarship on the Siddis, or Sheedis in Pakistan and Kaffirs in Sri Lanka, has grown quite large and intersects many disciplines. In addition to the scholarship of Edward Alpers, Helene Basu, Renu Modi, and others, see also Obeng 2003; Obeng 2007; Jayawardene 2013; Das and Upadhyai 2017; Prestholdt 2020.
14. Alpers and Goswami, eds. 2019.

15. Ali 2016; Alpers 2017; Jayasuriya and Pankhurst, eds. 2003.
16. Alpers 2000; Chatterji and Eaton 2006. Habshi and Siddi are sometimes used interchangeably, but differences of migration and settlement circumstances distinguish these groups.
17. Quirin 1998.
18. Tamari 1991; Irvine 2017; Ware 2014, p. 167.
19. Hall 2011, pp. 72–3; Mamdani 2009; Tamari 1991.
20. Barnes 2003, p. 63.
21. Sanders 1969; Eltringham 2006; Thapar 1996; Zia-Ebrahimi 2011.
22. Hall 2020; Glassman 2021.
23. Soske 2017, pp. 40–5.
24. Aiyar 2015, pp. 31, 56, 58, 66.
25. Ibid., p. 31.
26. Van Stipriaan 2003; Rush 2008.
27. Peterson 2017; Atiemo 2017.
28. Brennan 1998.
29. Yengde 2015.
30. Bhatt 2019.
31. Desai and Vahed 2015, pp. 44–5.
32. Shepherd 1988, p. 109.
33. Appadurai 1990.
34. McCann 2013.
35. Lee, ed. 2010, p. 4.
36. Davis and Thakur 2016; Thakur 2018.
37. Uche 2012.
38. Frenz 2019; Frenz 2014.
39. McCann 2019a.
40. McCann 2019b, p. 369.
41. Horne 2009.
42. Contursi 1993; Slate 2012a.
43. Diop 1987, p. 16.
44. Howe 1998.
45. Aydin 2017, p. 5.

46. Rush 2008.
47. Davis 2018, p. 243.
48. Robb, ed. 1995, p. 20.
49. Hall 2020; Pierre 2012, pp. 2–3.
50. *The Economist* 2019.
51. Mills, Obasanjo, Desalegn, and van der Merwe 2020.
52. Vittorini and Harris 2011; Aiyar 2015; Mawdsley and McCann, eds. 2011.
53. Pierre 2012.
54. Menon 2017.
55. Dalit Camera 2020.
56. Gandhi 2015, p. 38.
57. Bora 2019.
58. Kooria 2020, p. 353.
59. McCann 2019a; Burton 2012; Davis 2018; Thakur 2014.
60. El Nabolsy 2020.
61. Hodgson and Byfield, eds. 2017, p. 6.
62. Ndlovu-Gatsheni 2015.
63. Lee 2021, p. 3.
64. Moyn and Sartori, eds. 2013.
65. McCann 2019a.
66. Hofmeyr 2015.
67. Howe 1998.

1. A CULTURAL ECONOMY BETWEEN THE BLACK ATLANTIC AND INDIAN OCEAN

1. "Trans-Atlantic Slave Trade Database", David Eltis, "Coverage of the Slave Trade" (2018); https://www.slavevoyages.org/voyage/about#methodology/coverage-of-the-slave-trade/1/en/ (accessed 4 April 2021); Campbell and Stanziani, eds. 2015.
2. UNESCO, "Records of the Indian Indentured Labourers"; http://www.unesco.org/new/en/communication-and-information/memory-of-the-world/register/full-list-of-registered-heri-

tage/registered-heritage-page-7/records-of-the-indian-inden-tured-labourers/ (accessed 22 Feb. 2021).

3. Prashad 2002; Hardeen 2012.
4. Drewal 1988.
5. Hagenbeck 1911.
6. Ibid., p. 20.
7. Ibid., p. 91.
8. Drewal 1988; Rush 2008.
9. Ashalatha 2016.
10. Pinney 2004; Uberoi 1990.
11. Krishnan 2012.
12. Rush 2008, pp. 155–8.
13. Hofmeyr 2013; Desai and Vahed 2015.
14. Jain and Thomas 2007; Saeed 2018.
15. Nauriya 2012, p. 54.
16. Newell 2011, p. 29.
17. Blyden 1869, pp. 78–9.
18. July 1964, pp. 73–86.
19. Ibid., pp. 78–9.
20. Ibid.
21. Hofmeyr 2013.
22. Nauriya 2012.
23. Desai and Vahed 2015.
24. Zimmerman 2012.
25. Harlan 1966, p. 448.
26. Ibid., p. 449.
27. July 1964, p. 76.
28. Lal and Vahed 2013, p. 2.
29. Wendt 2007, pp. 546–7.
30. Blyden 1869, p. 79.
31. Danielson 2003.
32. Cabrita 2012, p. 439.
33. Ayandele 1971.
34. Danielson 2003.

35. Guha 2018.
36. Curtis IV 2002, pp. 21–43.
37. Marr 2006; Aidi 2005.
38. Singleton 2009.
39. Quoted in ibid., p. 376.
40. Ibid.
41. Asamoah-Gyadu 2011, p. 344; Singleton 2009, p. 10. While Singleton seems to suggest that Agbebi saw Europeans pushing Africans towards Islam and feared the disdain of Europeans towards African Christians, as Quilliam also expressed, African Muslim-Christian animosity was not the same as Christian Islamophobia in the late nineteenth century. African Christians, like Bishop Samuel Ajayi Crowther, admired their Muslim counterparts and sought to expand religious interactions. Shankar 2014.
42. Germain 2007, p. 126.
43. Metcalf 2008; Osondu-Oti 2015; Barnes 2003.
44. Singleton 2009, p. 380.
45. Jonker 2014.
46. Germain 2007, p. 133.
47. Ryad 2015.
48. Ahmad 1961, p. v.
49. Howell 2014, p. 76.
50. Duffield 1971, pp. 77–8.
51. Ibid., p. 77.
52. Ibid.
53. Muhammad Bashir Mahmud Ahmad, Head of the Ahmadiyya Community, to Private Secretary to Viceroy and Gov Gen of India, Delhi through Gov of Punjab , 30 March 1920, Home/Public/267-73, National Archives of India, New Delhi.
54. Ibid.
55. Howell 2014, p. 80.
56. Haddad and Smith 1993, p. 9.
57. Curtis IV 2002.

58. Ahmad 2007, pp. 7–8.
59. Ibid., p. 15.
60. Ramnath 2011, p. 13.
61. Paton 1923, p. 88.
62. Nance 2002.
63. Howell 2014, p. 82.
64. Nance 2002, p. 158.
65. Deslippe 2014, pp. 43–4.
66. Howell 2014, p. 70.
67. Bald 2013, p. 47.
68. Howell 2014, p. 82.
69. Nance 2002, p. 126.
70. Howell 2014, p. 85.
71. Haddad and Smith 1993, p. 63.
72. Hanson 2017, p. 63; Green 2014.
73. Matory 1999, p. 84.
74. Omenka 2004.
75. Ibid.
76. Matory 1999, p. 82.
77. Hanson 2017, pp. 131–8.
78. Adeloye 1974, p. 288.
79. Oduntan 2012, p. 14.
80. Ramos 1941.
81. Micots 2012, p. 26.
82. Notes on Ahmadiyya, 30 Dec. 1929, CO/40256/22 Nigeria, National Archives, Kew.
83. Ibid.
84. Hanson 2017; Reichmuth 1996, pp. 371–2.
85. Loimeier 1997.
86. Letter to Mr Bingham from E. F. Rice, Kano in *The Evangelical Christian and Missionary Witness* (April 1922, News from all Lands, p. 135), 16 Dec. 1921, SIM Archives, Fort Mill, South Carolina, Kano Miscellaneous 1934–45 No. Sr-18/A; Correspondence between Abdul Rahman Nayyar to E. J. Arnett, Aug. to Oct.

1922, Papers of E. J. Arnett, correspondence, etc., MSS. Afr.s.952, 1902–1940, 2/2 (Box 2, folder 2), Rhodes House Library, Oxford University.

87. Isa 2018, pp. 2–3.
88. Ibid.
89. W. R. S. Miller, Report on Kano CMS, June 1929, CMS/ACC237 F5, Papers, etc. of W. R. S. Miller, University of Birmingham Library Special Collections. The Anglican missionary Walter Miller reported on the presence of Ahmadis in Kano far earlier than scholarly accounts date their arrival.
90. Holmes 1926.
91. Ahmad 1961, p. i.
92. "Islamic Culture: Causes of its Rise and Decline", *The Moslem Outlook*, 28 Jan. 1927, p. 1.
93. "The Negro Problem: A Tale of Woe", *The Moslem Outlook*, 19 Feb. 1927, p. 4.
94. Ibid.
95. Ibid.
96. Abdul Fayaz Khan Sahib Ahmady, "Brotherhood of Man", *The Moslem Outlook*, 16 April 1927, p. 1.
97. Thursby 1975; Hardiman 2007. On the efforts of resistance in the Ismaili community, see Virani 2011.
98. Matory 1999, p. 90.
99. Slate 2012b; Iyengar 2018.
100. Martin 1977.
101. Desai and Gill 2018.

2. FEARS OF INDIAN INDEPENDENCE

1. The Problems of Northern Nigeria as the Natives See it, Account of an Interview with Lord Lugard, by Abubakar Imam, 1943, Margery Perham Papers, Rhodes House Library, Oxford.
2. From Abubakar Imam to Lugard, 9 Sept. 1944, Perham Papers, Rhodes House Library, Oxford.

NOTES

3. Marzagora 2020; Green 2015; Green 2013.
4. Devji 2012; Devji 2013.
5. Aiyar 2011; Brennan 2012.
6. Aiyar 2015.
7. Ibid., p. 121.
8. Scott 1978; Kebret 2001, pp. 83–4.
9. Foreign and Polit/N Branch/Abyssinia, 1935, Confidential/ Private offers of financial help from British Indian Subjects to the Emperor of Ethiopia, National Archives of India, New Delhi (hereafter NAI).
10. Markovits 2000; Harre 2017; Kebret 2001.
11. Confidential, Extract from Addis Ababa Report, 1945, External Affairs Branch, NAI.
12. Ibid.
13. Østebø 2013, p. 1037.
14. Purohit 2016.
15. General Staff Branch (Censor Section) Subject: Treatment of Indians in Tanganyika, 3 Nov. 1941, NAI.
16. Devji 2013. On Indian Muslim-Hind tensions in Kenya, see Aiya 2015, pp. 148–52.
17. From Dr Nazir Ahmed, c.o. Nathoo Moolji, Addis Ababa to Khalifatul, 29 Nov. 1944, External Affairs/Middle East/Progs., NAI.
18. Ethiopia – Report of the Indian Goodwill Mission to Ex Affairs, 13 Dec. 1948, NAI.
19. M. Nazir Ahmad to Chief Commissioner of the Northern Territories of Gold Coast, 25 June 1931; Chief Commissioner to Colonial Secretary, 10 Sept. 1934, Public Records and Archives Administration Department, Accra, Ghana (hereafter PRAAD).
20. Malam Usmanu Bala, translated from Hausa, 31 Dec. 1934, PRAAD.
21. Hassan 2015, p. 42.
22. Ahmadiya Movement in Islam, File ID 1/34/271, Arewa House Archives, Kaduna, Nigeria.

23. Ibid.
24. Alhaji Maulvi F. R. H. Hakeem, Head of the Nigeria Branch of the Sadr Anjuman Ahmadiyya, Qadian, to Chief Commissioner and Resident of Zaria, 5 April 1947, File ID 1/34/271, Arewa House Archives, Kaduna, Nigeria.
25. Aiyar 2015, pp. 210–11.
26. Merani and Van der Laan 1979.
27. Markovits 2000, p. 267.
28. Ibid.
29. Indian Ministry of External Affairs, Ex Affairs/XP (P) section 1953/Anti-Indian Propaganda and Counter Propaganda in East Africa, NAI, Correspondence, 30 April 1953, Danger from the East, from a "Kenya Africa" to the Editor, "Comment".
30. Special Report on Ashanti, Information Service of India, p. 3, File no.-37 (35)/55/AfriII3, NAI.
31. Vahed 2015.
32. Sherwood 2019, pp. 101–35.
33. Soske 2017, p. 103.
34. Zulu 1971.
35. Ramamurthi 1994, p. 545.
36. Ibid.; Edward A. Ulzen Memorial Foundation, "January 26, 1948: Chief Nii Kwabena Bonne II Leads Boycott", 26 Jan. 2018; https://www.eaumf.org/ejm-blog/2018/1/26/d3rifcdw-5fm8383gqg35arcftl0bqw (accessed 4 April 2021).
37. Okon 2014.
38. Sherwood 2019, p. 103.
39. Mordi 2019.
40. Roy 2010; Mordi 2019.
41. Bertz 2011.
42. Ibid., p. 75.
43. Indian Government Report, 1953, PRAAD.
44. Dwyer 2006.
45. Saeed 2018.
46. Sinha 2009, p. 291.

47. Sperl and Shackle, eds. 1996, p. 173.
48. Hansen 2005.
49. Indian Institute of Foreign Trade 1983, p. 10.
50. Stolte 2019.
51. Jalal 2007.
52. McCann 2019a, p. 98.
53. Ministry of External Affairs, Africa II, 1953, Africa, Visit of Swami Nisreyasananda of the Ramakrishna mission to Africa, F.AII/53/7242/31, NAI.
54. 8 June 1955 to Kub Chand, Joint Scty ICS, Min of Ex Affairs from Raja J Rameshwar Rao, NAI.
55. Israel 1987, p. 165.
56. Quoted in Vahed 2015, p. 55.
57. Mahesh Jugran Report, Sept. 1955, External Affairs/Special Report on Nigeria 37 (35)/55-AFR II (S) 1955, p. 1, NAI.
58. Ibid., p. 7.
59. Ibid.
60. Ibid., p. 11.
61. "My Hearty Thanks – By Late Maulana Naseem Saifi", *The Truth*, 23 Feb. 2015; https://thetruth.ng/my-hearty-thanks/ (accessed 4 April 2021)
62. Sardar Vallabhai Patel Papers, Copy of a Special Report No. 211 Part III of 1947, 21 Nov. 1947 from the Superintendent of Police, Gurdaspur, NAI.
63. Nadwi 1965, p.72.
64. Ibid.
65. Jugran Report, Sept. 1955, p. 20.
66. Raja Rameshwar Rao, Commissioner of West Africa, to Minister of Foreign Affairs Khub Chand, 13 April 1955, 7; F.18 (6)/55-AFRI, NAI.
67. Jugran, Report, Sept. 1955, p. 9.
68. Ministry of External Affairs, Africa II, 1953, Africa, Visit of Swami Nisreyasananda of the Ramakrishna mission to Africa,

F.AII/53/7242/31 (S), NAI; Rameshwar Rao to Khub Chand, 22 Sept. 1955, NAI.

69. Ministry of External Affairs, Africa II, 1953, Africa, Visit of Swami Nisreyasananda of the Ramakrishna mission to Africa, F.AII/53/7242/31 (S), NAI.
70. Ibid.
71. Wuaku 2013; Atiemo 2017. See also the work in progress of David Amponsah, who is writing a book on Ghanaian-Indian cultural connections.
72. Hackett 1992, p. 221.
73. Shri Apa Pant response, Political report for June 1954, External Affairs/Situation report from Nigeria, F.31-R&I/54 (S), NAI.
74. Shri Apa B. Pant, Africa – notes on certain problems of, 1955, F39-9/55-AFR II (S), NAI.
75. Ministry of External Affairs, Africa II, 1953, Africa, visit of Swami Nisreyasananda of the Ramakrishna mission to Africa, F.AII/53/7242/31 (S), NAI, Serial nos. 53–54 (pp. 49–50).
76. Spooner 2017, p. 224.
77. Pant 1974, pp. 47–59.

3. RACE AS POSTCOLONIAL STRATEGY

1. Vitalis 2013, p. 266.
2. Espiritu 2006.
3. Vitalis 2013, p. 262.
4. Diane and Sankharé 2002.
5. Diagne 2018.
6. Jules-Rosette 2007.
7. Rognoni 2018, pp. 26–7.
8. Diouf and Prais 2013.
9. Senghor 1975.
10. Chatterji 1974, p. 263.
11. Ibid.
12. Spleth 2002.

13. Mohanty 2009, p. 4.
14. Ita 1973.
15. Soyinka 2002, p. 2.
16. Gupta 1978.
17. Ibid., p. 647.
18. Sauldie 1965.
19. Gupta 1970, p. 177.
20. Clarence-Smith 2014, p. 282; Vasudevan 2010.
21. "From Refugees to Tycoons", *Forbes Africa*, 1 March 2012; https://www.forbesafrica.com/focus/2012/03/01/from-refugees-to-tycoons/ (accessed 5 April 2021); Daswani 2021.
22. Gupta 1970.
23. Dubey 2011, p. 191.
24. Kloman 1962.
25. Embassy of India, Dakar, Special Report, Presentation of Credentials in Ouagadougou, Secret, 6 Aug. 1962, by N. V. Rajkumar, National Archives of India (hereafter NAI).
26. External Affairs, XPP, Progs Nos 453 (40)-XPP, 1968, NAI.
27. "Le Sénégal, terre de culture et de dialogue, ne perd pas de vue les enseignements du Mahatma Gandhi à notre époque dominée par les foyers de tension et les luttes fratricides". Articles in Malik's file, External Affairs, XPP, Progs Nos 453 (40)-XPP, 1968, NAI.
28. Harney 2004, p. 13.
29. Dieng 2011, p. 91.
30. Peters 1978.
31. Homburger 1955.
32. Gregersen 1977, pp. 100–1.
33. Thapar 2008, p. 11.
34. Law 2009; Straus 2013; Glassman 2018, p. 199.
35. Senghor 1974a.
36. Rangaswamy 2004.
37. Senghor 1974b.
38. Senghor 1975.

39. UNESCO film, British Pathé; https://www.britishpathe.com/video/VLVA9URNFX4LR5QGNF2Q3PKKX38PM-SENEGAL-MONSIEUR-RENE-MAHEU-DIRECTOR-GENERAL-OF-UNESCO-VISITS-IN (accessed 5 April 2021).
40. Duedahl, ed. 2016.
41. Rangaswamy 2004.
42. Annamalai 2010.
43. Senghor 1974a, p. 2.
44. Manoharan 2020; Ramaswamy 1997.
45. Cummings 1977, p. 38.
46. Ibid.
47. External Affairs 1949 UN-I, Progs Nos 8 (106)-1949, memo, NAI.
48. "Relations Indo-Africaines A Travers Les Ages" (n.d.), p. 35; booklet in Institut Fondamental d'Afrique Noire (IFAN), Cheikh Anta Diop University, Dakar, Senegal.
49. Ssebuwufu 2017, pp. 11–12.
50. Patel 1972, p. 14.
51. Quoted in ibid., p. 14.
52. Mehta 2001, p. 27.
53. Aiyar 2017, p. 62.
54. Nair 2018; Hansen 2012.
55. Mamdani 1993.
56. Reid 2017, p. 236.
57. Gupta 1974.
58. Mouralis 2015, p. 226.
59. Tine 2005.
60. Mouralis 2015, p. 227.
61. Author interview with Dr U. P. Upadhyaya, MGM Regional Resources Centre, Tulu Lexicon Project, Mangaluru, India, 12 Aug. 2015.
62. Upadhyaya and Upadhyaya 1976.
63. Assadi 2016, pp. 145–6.
64. McLaughlin 2008.

65. Upadhyaya interview.
66. Interview with Souleymane Faye, Cheikh Anta Diop University, Head of Serer Division, Centre for Applied Linguistics, Dakar, Senegal, 17 June 2016.
67. B. Kolappan, "Tamil Scholar and Educationist K. P. Aravanan Dead", *The Hindu*, 24 Dec. 2018; https://www.thehindu.com/news/national/tamil-nadu/tamil-scholar-and-educationist-kp-aravanan-dead/article25815220.ece (accessed 5 April 2021).
68. Echeruo 1993.
69. Diagne 2010, p. 248.
70. Ibid., p. 246.
71. Apter 2016.
72. Swan 2018.
73. Souleymane Faye interview.
74. Interview with Mamadou N'Diaye, Cheikh Anta Diop University, Administration, Dakar, Senegal, 18 June 2015.
75. Vander Steene 2008.
76. Souleymane Faye interview.
77. Interview with Indian consular officer, Embassy of India, Dakar, Senegal, 7 Jan. 2016. Due to unrest in Burkina Faso, the staff from India's office there had relocated to Dakar.
78. Ziad Maalouf, "2-Bollywood Teranga: les médias 'indophiles' au Sénégal", *Les voix du monde*, 20 April 2013; http://atelier.rfi.fr/profiles/blogs/bollywood-teranga (accessed 5 April 2021).
79. Slate 2012a; Prashad 2000; Omvedt 2006; Beteille 1990; Omvedt 2012.
80. Anasuya Menon, "Pride and Prejudice", *The Hindu*, 18 Jan. 2020; https://www.thehindu.com/entertainment/art/negritude-a-show-of-african-american-art-explores-the-black-identity/article30592687.ece (accessed 5 April 2021).
81. Winters 2010; Winters 2008; Winters 2006; Hromnik 1991.
82. Ownby 1982.

4. THIRD WORLD SCIENCE

NOTES

1. Osseo-Asare 2019, p. 2; Isaacman and Isaacman 2014; Graboyes 2015.
2. "Brief History of the Edward Bouchet Abdus Salam Institute (EBASI)"; https://ebasi.org/history.html (accessed 5 April 2021).
3. Mtingwa, Mickens, and Valentine 2017; Mickens, ed. 2002.
4. Allotey 2017.
5. Felder 2015, p. 6.
6. Mickens, ed. 2002, chapter 1.
7. Allotey 2017, p. 3.
8. Hanson 2017.
9. Samwini 2006, pp. 70–96.
10. Saifi 1955.
11. Saeed 2007; Devji 2013.
12. Qasmi 2015, p. 94.
13. Ghosh 2014.
14. Dombey 2011, pp. 5–6.
15. Fraser 2008.
16. De Greiff 2006a, p. 230.
17. Ibid.
18. Osseo-Asare 2019, pp. 4–5.
19. Julie Medlock, Accra World Assembly, to Abdus Salam, Imperial College, London, 13 Nov. 1964, ICTP Archives, Trieste, Italy (hereafter ICTP Archives).
20. Ibid.
21. Medlock to Salam, 23 March 1965, ICTP Archives.
22. Sutherland and Meyer 2000.
23. Allman 2008.
24. Ahmed 1987, p. 87.
25. Ahmad 1962, p. 3.
26. Ibid., 27.
27. Ibid., 37.
28. "Nusrat Jehan Project", Ahmadiyya Muslim Community; https://

www.alislam.org/book/brief-history-ahmadiyya-muslim/nusrat-jehan-project/ (accessed 5 April 2021)

29. *Africa Speaks* 1972, p. 18.
30. Ahmad 2006, p. xiv.
31. Ibid.
32. Ibid.
33. Personal communication with Huzaifa Dokaji about Nigeria and George Osei about Ghana, 12 March 2021.
34. Saifi 1957, p. 20.
35. Nadwi 1965, p. 72.
36. Ahmad 2006.
37. Ibid., p. 23.
38. Ibid., p. xiii.
39. Ibid., p. 8.
40. Allotey 2017, p. 3.
41. See, for instance, newsletters of the Ahmadiyya movement auxiliary organisations, like Ahl Nahl in the United States. In 2010, the biography of Syed Sajid Ahmad, manager of engineering services at a university in North Dakota, shows that he was born in Gujarat, Pakistan, and lived in Ghana for several years in the 1970s teaching at Ahmadiyya schools; http://ansarusa.org/publications (accessed 5 April 2021).
42. Balzani 2020, p. 4.
43. Farooq and Ahmad 2017.
44. Tayo 1978, p. 4. Tayo worked in Georgetown, Guyana, where he became embroiled in an ongoing conflict with the local Ahmadi head.
45. Thurston 2014; Kobo 2016.
46. Dombey 2011, p. 7.
47. Hecht 2006, p. 33.
48. De Greiff 2002, p. 39.
49. Ibid., pp. 39–40.
50. Ibid, p. 52.
51. Boaten to Salam, 15 March 1966, ICTP Archives.

52. Akyeampong 1999, p. 31.
53. M. A. Virasoro to Paolo Budini, 30 April 1976, ICTP Archives.
54. Bernard R. Cooper and John Parmentola, "APS Aids Oppressed Physicists", *Physics Today* 31, no. 8 (1978): 9.
55. Ibukun to Abdus Salam, 24 April 1975, ICTP Archives.
56. Pessoa, Freire, and De Greiff 2008.
57. Gidron 2020, chapter 2.
58. De Greiff 2006b, p. 101.
59. Ibid., p. 102.
60. Ibid., p. 109.
61. Imber 1989.
62. Abdus Salam to Olu-Ibukun, 20 June 1975, ICTP Archives.
63. Scientists from Developing Member States in Africa who have participated in the research and training for research activities of the ICTP, as at 1977-4-13, ICTP Archives; Scientific Visitors with Affiliation Nigeria in the Research and Training-for-Research Activities of the ICTP 1970–1978, ICTP Archives.
64. Abdus Salam to Ibukun, 2 Sept. 1975, ICTP Archives.
65. D.1235 Tanzania 1984–6, A.S. to A. Forti of UNESCO's Div of Scientific Res and Higher Ed, 10 July 1984, ICTP Archives.
66. P. E. Mugambi to Budini, 24 May 1977, ICTP Archives.
67. African Mathematical Union; https://www.africamathunion.org/index.php (accessed 5 April 2021).
68. Letter to Abdus Salam from Marembo Karemera from Lumumbashi, Zaire and Mbaro-Saman Lubuma in Algeria Univ of d'Annaba and Kinshasa, 9 April 1990, ICTP Archives.
69. Abdus Salam to Mbaro-Saman Lubuma, 26 June 1991, ICTP Archives.
70. African Physical Society; https://www.africanphysicalsociety.org/about-the-african-physical-society/ (accessed 5 April 2021).
71. F.86 Symposium on Utilization of Indigenous Scientists in National Development, 1–6 June 1986, Nairobi, Drought, Desertification and Food Deficit Study-Project, ICTP Archives.
72. Dalafi and Hassan 1994, p. ix.

73. Abdus Salam, "Islam and Science, Concordance or Conflict?" Invited address delivered at Meeting of "Islam and the West", UNESCO House, Paris, 27 April 1984, 10, ICTP Archives.

74. Pervez Hoodbhoy, "Unfulfilled Expectations – Abdus Salam and Science in Pakistan", ICTP Archives., p. 112.

75. Al Sadiq Al Mahdi to Abdus Salam, 2 June 1981, ICTP Archives.

76. Mtingwa, Mickens, and Valentine 2017.

77. Johnson to Abdus Salam, 14 December 1989, ICTP Archives.

78. Telephone interview with Ronald Mickens, 14 May 2020.

79. Ibid.

80. Gasman and Nguyen 2015, p. 9.

81. Abdus Salam welcome to 2nd Bouchet International Conference: Physics and High Tech for the Development of Africa through the 1990s; ICTP Archives.

82. Johnson to Gallieno Denardo, 6 May 1991, D.669, ICTP Archives.

83. Makhubu 1999, pp. 91–2.

84. Bhabha 2011.

85. Asabere-Ameyaw, Dei, and Raheem, eds. 2012.

86. Thubauville 2013; Thubauville and Amare 2020.

87. Mkandawire, ed. 2005, pp. 1–9.

88. Spight 1974.

89. Ibid., p. 11.

5. HINDUISM'S BLACK ATLANTIC ITINERARY

1. Swami Ghananandji Saraswati, "Africa is Ripe for a Strong Hindu Future", *Hinduism Today*, Aug. 1998, pp. 1–3, 2.

2. See Dennis Laumann's unpublished research on the history of Bhakti Tirtha Swami; also https://btswami.com/ (accessed 7 April 2021).

3. Lavina Melwani, "The Story of *Hinduism Today*", *Hinduism Today*, Feb. 2008; https://www.hinduismtoday.com/modules/wfchannel/index.php?page=0&cid=17 (accessed 7 April 2021).

4. Forsthofel and Humes, eds. 2005.

5. Basu 2020.
6. Atiemo 2017.
7. Veena Sharma, "An African Hindu Swami", Ananda Kutir Ashrama newsletter, Nov. 2011–Feb. 2012, Cape Town, South Africa.
8. Sharma 2015; Sharma 2019, p. 190.
9. Shankar 2021.
10. Shroff 2013.
11. Nadeem F. Paracha, "From Legend to Science: The Crocodiles of Manghopir", *Dawn*, 26 Feb. 2016; https://www.dawn.com/news/1241847 (accessed 7 April 2021).
12. Ahmed 1989.
13. Basu 1993, p. 289.
14. Mallampalli 2004, chapter 5.
15. Ram 1946; Ram 1956.
16. Quoted in Dixie and Eisenstadt 2011, p. 70.
17. Ibid., p. xv.
18. Thurman, Fluker, and Tumber 1998.
19. McLucas and Sharpe 2016, pp. 85–6.
20. Coates 2018, pp. 200–7.
21. Ibid., p. 205.
22. Lucht 2011.
23. Sharma, "An African Hindu Swami".
24. Ibid.
25. Atiemo 2017; Sharma 2019.
26. Aryeh 2020, p. 313.
27. Notice in *The Daily Graphic*, 5 July 1952, p. 4.
28. Lease agreement in Swami Ghanananda's personal papers, Hindu Monastery of Africa, Odorkor, Greater Accra, Ghana.
29. Sharma 2019.
30. Israel 1987, pp. 159–60.
31. Killingray and Plaut 2012, pp. 248, 251; Wuaku 2013, pp. 42–5.
32. Israel 1987, p. 167; Coates (n.d.).
33. Wuaku 2013, p. 406.

34. Amrith 2009, p. 560.
35. Sri Swami Sivananda, "Ayurveda – Theory and Practice", *Health and Long Life* 6, no. 3 (Nov.–Dec. 1956): 33–7, 34.
36. Osseo-Asare 2016.
37. Quoted in ibid., p. 81.
38. "Construction of 'Kutir' at Sivanandanagar", *Health and Long Life* 9, no. 7 (Mar. 1960): 113.
39. Sharma, "An African Hindu Swami".
40. Ibid.
41. Ghanananda 2001, p. 47.
42. Sharma, "An African Hindu Swami".
43. Swami Sivananda, "Japa Yoga" (Uttaranchal: The Divine Life Trust, 2005), p. 35.
44. Twumasi 1979.
45. Shankar 2021.
46. Chang 2016, p. 60.
47. Madhava Smullen, "Temple Profile: Lagos, Nigeria", ISKCON News, 6 Aug. 2011; https://iskconnews.org/temple-profile-lagos-nigeria,2802/ (accessed 7 April 2021).
48. Brahmananda Svami, "How the Hare Krishna Movement Came to Africa", *Back to Godhead* 10, no. 12 (Dec. 1975): 10–15, 15.
49. Bhakti Tirtha Swami biographies; https://shashankrao-84497.medium.com/black-and-hindu-the-story-of-bhakti-tirtha-swami-3fd2b99ac1b2; https://paw.princeton.edu/memorial/john-edward-favors-%E2%80%9972 (both accessed 7 April 2021). See also the research of Dennis Laumann, in progress.
50. Smullen, "Temple Profile: Lagos".
51. Wuaku 2012, p. 342.
52. Ibid. See also Wuaku 2009, pp. 409–10.
53. Atiemo 2017, p. 412.
54. Vande Berg and Kniss 2008, pp. 84–6.
55. Ibid., p. 88.
56. Letter (author's name withheld to preserve anonymity), 11 April

1999, Swami Ghanananda's personal papers, Hindu Monastery of Africa, Odorkor, Greater Accra, Ghana.

57. Svami, "How the Hare Krishna Movement Came to Africa".

58. Vande Berg and Kniss 2008, p. 84.

59. Williams 2015.

60. Ibid., p. 383.

61. Edwards 2008, pp. 127–9.

62. The North Scale Education and Research Institute, Home Study Course brochure, p. 1, personal effects of Swami Ghananananda, 21 Jan. 2019, Hindu Monastery of Africa, Odorkor, Greater Accra, Ghana.

63. Food and Agricultural Organization of the United Nations, "Traditional Crops: Moringa"; http://www.fao.org/traditional-crops/moringa/en/ (accessed 7 April 2021).

64. History of Church World Service; https://cwsglobal.org/about/history/ (accessed 7 April 2021); Edwards 2008, p. 132.

65. Langwick 2018, pp. 155–71.

66. Kali Sichen biography, Mama Moringa; http://www.mamamoringa.com/kali_bio.html (accessed 7 April 2021).

67. Edwards 2008, p. 139.

68. Bennu Farms was formed first, and then Nebedaye Farms as an offshoot; https://www.bennugardens.org/moringa-farm-project (accessed 7 April 2021).

69. Lauren Seibert, "In Senegal, A Tree of Life Nurtures the Poor", *The Culture-ist* (n.d.); https://www.thecultureist.com/2014/09/19/senegal-moringa-tree-food-poor/ (accessed 7 April 2021).

70. Morton 1991.

71. Emeagwali and Dei, eds. 2014, p. x.

72. Roberts 2010.

73. Makhubu 1998, pp. 41–2.

74. Asante and Avornyo 2013.

75. Alter 2015.

76. Kumar 2008, pp. 27–9.

77. Bajpai 1976, p. 442.

78. Ibid.

79. Subramaniam 2019, p. 6.

80. Venkatachalam 2021.

81. Modi and Taylor 2017, p. 11. Emphasis added.

6. *NÉGRITUDE* BEATS BOLLYWOOD

1. David Zizzo, "Gentle Road Warrior Seeks World Peace", 27 Oct. 1991; http://oklahoman.com/article/2373461/gentle-road-warrior-seeks-world-peace (accessed 7 April 2021).

2. Interview with Somnath Mukherjee, Fann, Dakar, West African Research Centre, 11 Jan. 2016.

3. Dakar Biennale 2016, "Somnath Mukherjee"; https://biennaledakar.org/2016/somnath-mukherjee/#! (accessed 7 April 2021).

4. Sayantan Bera, "One Dollar, One Language, One World", *Down To Earth*, 15 Nov. 2013; https://www.downtoearth.org.in/coverage/one-dollar-one-language-one-world-42583 (accessed 7 April 2021).

5. Ibid.

6. Somnath Mukherjee interview.

7. Ghosh 2016.

8. Somnath Mukherjee interview.

9. Abdul Qadir, "Cycling Around the World for 22 Years", *Times of India*, 27 Jan. 2004; https://timesofindia.indiatimes.com/city/patna/Cycling-around-the-world-for-22-years/articleshow/445086.cms (accessed 7 April 2021).

10. Interview with Vidya Diaité, Dakar, 16 June 2015.

11. McLaughlin 1997, p. 577.

12. Mamadou Wathy, "Dans l'antre des Indophile du Sénégal", *Seneplus*, 17 June 2013; https://www.seneplus.com/article/dans-l%E2%80%99antre-des-indophiles-du-s%C3%A9n%C3%A9gal (accessed 7 April 2021).

13. Vernière 1973.
14. Enz and Bryson 2018, pp. 333–5.
15. Wathy, "Dans l'antre des Indophiles du Senegal".
16. Mukherjee 2007.
17. Vander Steene 2008.
18. "Indafrique: le Bollywood, une passion sénégalaise", *Jeune Afrique*, 1 Dec. 2011; https://www.jeuneafrique.com/178304/societe/indafrique-le-bollywood-une-passion-s-n-galaise/ (accessed 7 April 2021).
19. Larkin 1997; 2008.
20. Versluys 2008.
21. Buchanan 2018, p. 166.
22. Gadjigo 2010.
23. Quoted in Burgin 2013.
24. Ibid.
25. Harney 2004, p. 219.
26. Quoted in Burgin 2013.
27. Larkin 2008, p. 183.
28. Desai 2008.
29. *Dakar-Bombay*, uncut film by Mansour Sora Wade.
30. Gilroy 1993, p. xi.
31. Bourdié 2015; Despres 2019.
32. Warren 2006, p. 109.
33. Quoted in Klein 2019, p. 15.
34. Ibid.
35. Sorgel 2020.
36. Barlet 2010, p. 127.
37. Ibid., p. 136.
38. Young 2021.
39. Quoted in Barlet 2010, pp. 138–9.
40. Quoted in ibid., p. 139
41. Quoted in ibid., p. 138.
42. Quoted in ibid., p. 139.
43. Bertz 2019.

44. Hansen 2005.
45. Arjun Chaudhuri, "Hindi TV Queen Touches Nerve with African Women", Reuters, 1 Feb. 2010; https://www.reuters.com/article/idUKLDE6101QI (accessed 7 April 2021).
46. Jedlowski 2018, p. 20 ; Sylvanus and Eze-Emaeyak 2018.
47. "Nollywood meets Bollywood", *Shadow and Act*, 29 Oct. 2012; https://shadowandact.com/nollywood-meets-bollywood-in-first-co-production-between-both-industries-j-u-d-e (accessed 7 April 2021).
48. "Emem Isong's Love is in the Hair in Cinema", *Guardian Saturday Magazine*, 16 Jan. 2016; https://guardian.ng/saturday-magazine/emem-isongs-love-is-in-the-hair-in-cinema/ (accessed 7 April 2021).
49. Jedlowski 2018.
50. Precious 'Mamazeus' Nwogu, "Netflix's New Romance 'Namaste Wahala' is an Abysmal Trial and Error", *Pulse Nigeria*, 15 Feb. 2021; https://www.pulse.ng/entertainment/movies/netflixs-new-romance-namaste-wahala-is-an-abysmal-trial-and-error-pulse-movie-review/0n0cmzv (accessed 7 April 2021).
51. Daswani 2021.
52. Barlet 2010, p. 142.
53. Anum Chandani, Marvi Ahmed, and Hira Hashmi, "'Fair & Lovely,' Skin Whitening and the Pitfalls of Performative Allyship", *Washington Post*, 28 July 2020.
54. Nadeem 2014.
55. Mahita Gajanan, "Unilever Will Drop the Word 'Fair' from its Skin-Lightening Creams", *Time*, 26 June 2020.
56. Barlet 2010, p. 127.
57. "How Indians Learned to Embrace Natural Skin", *Asia Society*, 25 March 2016; https://asiasociety.org/blog/asia/how-indians-learned-embrace-natural-skin (accessed 7 April 2021).
58. Hunter 2011, p. 143.
59. Nadeem 2014, p. 225.
60. Ibid., 146; Thomas 2020.

61. Pierre 2012, chapter 4; Thomas 2020.

62. Ted Stansfield, "Ghana Bans the Sale of Skin Bleaching Products", *Dazed* digital, 3 June 2016; https://www.dazeddigital.com/fashion/article/31377/1/ghana-bans-sale-of-skin-bleaching-products (accessed 7 April 2021).

63. Helene Cooper, "Where Beauty Means Bleached Skin" *New York Times*, 26 Nov. 2016; https://www.nytimes.com/2016/11/26/fashion/skin-bleaching-south-africa-women.html (accessed 7 April 2021).

64. Sally Hayden, "Black Lives Matter Puts Focus on Skin Bleaching in Africa and Asia", *Irish Times*, 23 June 2020; https://www.irishtimes.com/news/world/africa/black-lives-matter-puts-focus-on-skin-bleaching-in-africa-and-asia-1.4286559 (accessed 7 April 2021).

65. Pande 2020.

66. Jacobs 2016.

67. Faria and Jones 2020.

68. Ibid., p. 67.

69. Lasco and Hardon 2020.

70. Kasana 2014.

71. Grabski 2017.

72. Clarke House Initiative, 2016; https://m.facebook.com/clarkhouseinitiative/posts/980747261972785:0 (accessed 7 April 2021).

73. Somnath Mukherjee; https://www.institutfrancais.com/en/work/non-aligned-non-alignes-by-aurelien-froment; https://biennaledakar.org/2016/somnath-mukherjee/ (accessed 7 April 2021); Olga Speakes and Anna Stielau, "The Dakar Biennale, 2014, 20 June 2014"; http://artthrob.co.za/Feature/The_Dakar_Biennale_2014_by_Olga_Speakes__Anna_Stielau_on_20_June.aspx (accessed 7 April 2021).

CONCLUSION

NOTES

1. Hofmeyr 2012; Balachandran 2014.
2. Pavithra Rao and Franck Kuwonu, "India, Africa Rekindle Trade Ties", *Africa Renewal*, Aug.–Nov. 2016; https://www.un.org/africarenewal/magazine/august-2016/india-africa-rekindle-trade-ties (accessed 7 April 2021); Davis 2018.
3. Davis 2018, p. 244.
4. Sylviane Diouf, "Africans in India, Then and Now", New York Public Library, 17 Oct. 2014; https://www.nypl.org/blog/2014/10/17/africans-india-then-and-now (accessed 7 April 2021).
5. "Africans in India", New York Public Library Announcement, 2014.
6. Harshini Vakkalanka, "Africa, India and Royalty", *The Hindu*, 21 Dec. 2015; http://www.thehindu.com/features/metroplus/african-legacy-in-india-begins-even-before-the-mughal-period/article8014097.ece (accessed 7 April 2021).
7. Siddharth Varadarajan, "Upward Mob-ility: As India Prospers, it is Getting More Racist", *Times of India*, 5 Oct. 2014; https://timesofindia.indiatimes.com/home/stoi/all-that-matters/Upward-mob-ility-As-India-prospers-it-is-getting-more-racist/articleshow/44372945.cms (accessed 7 April 2021).
8. "Racism in India: If We Were Racist, Why Would We Live with South Indians, Black People Around Us: BJP's Tarun Vijay", *Scroll-in*, 7 April 2017; https://scroll.in/latest/833983/if-indians-were-racist-why-would-we-live-with-black-people-in-the-south-says-bjps-tarun-vijay (accessed 7 April 2021).
9. "India-Africa Summit … PM Narendra Modi's Speech", *Times of India*, 29 Oct. 2015; https://timesofindia.indiatimes.com/india/India-Africa-summit-Read-full-text-of-PM-Narendra-Modis-speech/articleshow/49577890.cms (accessed 7 April 2021).
10. Subramaniam 2019.
11. TVC News, Trends Episode 134, "#GandhiMustFall"; https://

www.abibitumi.tv/v/1755611322/TRENDS-EPISODE-134----GandhiMustFall (accessed 7 April 2021).

12. Bikash Mohapatra, "'Study in India' and India's African Dilemma", *The Diplomat*, 10 June 2019; https://thediplomat.com/2019/06/study-in-india-and-indias-african-dilemma/ (accessed 7 April 2021).

13. Mampilly 2013, p. 363.

14. Vahed and Desai 2019, p. 273.

15. Subramanian 2019, p. 285.

16. Yengde 2015.

17. Kwame Anthony Appiah, "What We Can Learn from the Rise and Fall of 'Political Blackness'", *New York Times*, 7 Oct. 2020; https://www.nytimes.com/2020/10/07/opinion/political-blackness-race.html (accessed 7 April 2021).

18. Schulze-Engler 2020, p. 126; Rastogi 2005, p. 540.

19. Otten 1992, p. 240.

20. Akwaeke Emezi, "Transition", *The Cut* (n.d.); https://www.the-cut.com/2018/01/writer-and-artist-akwaeke-emezi-gender-transition-and-ogbanje.html (accessed 7 April 2021).

21. Ibid.

22. Schulze-Engler 2020, p. 119.

23. Harris 2019, p. 6.

24. "Why Does Kamala Harris Care More about Human Rights than her Indianness?", *Sabrang*, 14 Aug. 2020; https://sabrangindia.in/tags/vice-president (accessed 7 April 2021).

25. Interview with Indian consular officer, Embassy of India, Dakar, Senegal, 7 Jan. 2016.

BIBLIOGRAPHY

Archives and Libraries

Arewa House Archives, Kaduna, Nigeria.
Burke Library, Union Theological Seminary, Columbia University, New York, USA.
Hindu Monastery of Africa, Odorkor, Greater Accra, Ghana.
Institut Fondamental d'Afrique Noire, Cheikh Anta Diop University, Dakar, Senegal.
International Centre for Theoretical Physics, Marie Curie Library, Trieste, Italy.
MGM Regional Resources Centre, Tulu Lexicon Project, Mangaluru, India.
National Archives, Kew, Richmond, UK.
National Archives of India, Janpath, New Delhi.
Nehru Memorial Museum and Library, New Delhi, India.
Public Records and Archives Administration Department, Accra, Ghana.
Rhodes House Library, Oxford University, UK.
Schomburg Center for Research in Black Culture, New York Public Library, USA.
Senghor Foundation, Dakar, Senegal.

BIBLIOGRAPHY

Archival Sources

SIM Archives, Fort Mill, South Carolina, USA.
University of Birmingham Library Special Collections, Birmingham, UK.

Secondary Sources

Adibe, Jideofor. (2017) "Impact of Xenophobic Attacks against Africans in India on Afro-India Relations." *Journal of African Foreign Affairs* 4, no. 1/2: 85–97

Adeloye, Adelola. (1974) "Some Early Nigerian Doctors and Their Contributions to Modern Medicine in West Africa." *Medical History* 18, no. 3: 275–93.

Africa Speaks. (1972) Rabwah, West Pakistan: Majlis Nusrat Jahan Tahrik-i-Jadid.

Ahmad, Mirza Mubarak. (1961) *Our Foreign Missions.* Qadian: Ahmadiyya Muslim Foreign Missions.

— (1962) *Islam in Africa.* Rabwah: Ahmadiyya Muslim Foreign Missions.

Ahmad, Hadrat Mirza Bashiruddin Mahmood. (2007) *Ahmadiyyat or The True Islam*, trans. Zafrullah Khan. Tilford, Surrey: Islam International Publications Ltd.

Ahmad, Hadrat Mirza Nasir. (2006) *Message of Love and Brotherhood to Africa.* Tilford, Surrey: Islam International Publications Ltd.

Ahmed, Syed Salahuddin. (1987) "Pakistan–Nigeria Relations, A Study in Bilateral Relations." *Pakistan Horizon* 40, no. 2: 84–94.

Ahmed, Feroz. (1989) "Africa on the Coast of Pakistan", *New Directions* 16, no. 4: 22–31.

Aidi, Hisham D. (2005) "Let Us Be Moors: Islam, Race, and 'Connected Histories'." *Souls* 7, no. 1: 36–51.

Aiyar, Sana. (2011) "Empire, Race and the Indians in Colonial Kenya's Contested Public Political Sphere, 1919–1923." *Africa* 81, no. 1: 132–54.

— (2015) *Indians in Kenya.* Cambridge, MA: Harvard University Press.

— (2017) "Out of India: East Africa and its South Asian Diasporas."

In *Routledge Handbook of the Indian Diaspora*, ed. Radha Sarma Hegde and Ajaya Kumar Sahoo. New York: Routledge, pp. 62–73.

Akyeampong, Daniel. (1999) "Abdus Salam and Africa." In *Tribute to Abdus Salam*, ed. A. M. Hamende. Trieste: Abdus Salam International Centre for Theoretical Physics, pp. 29–32.

Ali, Omar. (2016) *Malik Ambar: Power and Slavery Across the Indian Ocean.* New York: Oxford University Press.

Allman, Jean. (2008) "Nuclear Imperialism and the Pan-African Struggle for Peace and Freedom: Ghana, 1959–1962." *Souls* 10, no. 2: 83–102.

Allotey, Francis Kofi A. (2017) "Prof. Abdus Salam, My Teacher and Mentor: The Role of ICTP in Africa." *International Journal of Modern Physics A* 32, no. 8: 231–41.

Alpers, Edward. (2000) "Recollecting Africa: Diasporic Memory in the Indian Ocean World." *African Studies Review* 43, no. 1: 83–99.

— (2017) "Africa and Africans in the Making of Early Modern India." In *The Indian Ocean in the Making of Early Modern in India*, ed. Pius Malekandathil. New York: Routledge, pp. 61–74.

Alpers, Edward, and Chhaya Goswami, eds. (2019) *Transregional Trade and Traders: Situating Gujarat in the Indian Ocean from Early Times to 1900.* New York: Oxford University Press.

Alter, Joseph S. (2015) "Nature Cure and Ayurveda: Nationalism, Viscerality and Bio-ecology in India." *Body & Society* 21, no. 1: 3–28.

Amrith, Sunil. (2009) "Tamil Diasporas across the Bay of Bengal." *American Historical Review* 114, no. 3: 547–72.

Annamalai, E. (2010) "The Political Rise of Tamil in the Dravidian Movement in South India." In *Handbook of Language and Ethnic Identity*, Vol. 2, ed. J. A. Fishman and O. Garcia. New York: Oxford University Press, pp. 230–41.

Appadurai, Arjun. (1990) "Disjuncture and Difference in the Global Cultural Economy." *Theory, Culture & Society* 7, no. 2/3: 295–310.

Apter, Andrew. (2016) "Beyond Négritude: Black Cultural Citizenship and the Arab Question in FESTAC 77." *Journal of African Cultural Studies* 28, no. 3: 313–26.

Aryeh, Daniel Nii Aboagye. (2020) "Religion and Urban Life: Space and

Patronage for Prophetic Ministry in Cities in Ghana." *Alternation* Special Edition 30: 311–34.

Asabere-Ameyaw, Akwasi, George J. Sefa Dei, and Kolawole Raheem, eds. (2012) *Contemporary Issues in African Sciences and Science Education*. Leiden and Rotterdam: Brill/Sense.

Asamoah-Gyadu, J. Kwabena. (2011) "'Get Up ... Take the Child ... and Escape to Egypt': Transforming Christianity into a Non-Western Religion in Africa." *International Review of Mission* 100, no. 2: 337–54.

Asante, Emmanuel, and R. Avornyo. (2013) "Enhancing Healthcare System in Ghana through Integration of Traditional Medicine." *Journal of Sociological Research* 4, no. 2: 256–72.

Ashalatha. (2016) "Raja Ravi Varma and Colonial Eyeing." *Malayala Pachcha* 3, no. 3: 112–30.

Assadi, Muzaffar. (2016) "Regions within Regions and their Movements in Karnataka: Nuances, Claims and Ambiguities." In *Rethinking State Politics in India: Regions within Regions*, ed. Ashutosh Kumar. New Delhi: Routledge, pp. 131–52.

Atiemo, Abamfo Ofori. (2017) "'Returning to our Spiritual Roots': African Hindus in Ghana Negotiating Religious Space and Identity." *Journal of Religion in Africa* 47, no. 3: 405–37.

Ayandele, E. A. (1971) "James Africanus Beale Horton, 1835–1883: Prophet of Modernization in West Africa." *African Historical Studies* 4, no. 3: 691–707.

Aydin, Cemil. (2017) *The Idea of the Muslim World: A Global Intellectual History*. Cambridge, MA: Harvard University Press.

Bajpai, S. D. (1976) "Patterns of Mathematical Thinking are Much the Same as the Fundamental Patterns of Life." *International Journal of Mathematical Educational in Science and Technology* 7, no. 4: 441–5.

Balachandran, Gopalan. (2014) "Atlantic Paradigms and Aberrant Histories." *Atlantic Studies* 11, no. 1: 47–63.

Bald, Vivek. (2013) *Bengali Harlem and the Lost Histories of South Asian America*. Cambridge, MA: Harvard University Press.

Balzani, Marzia. (2020) *Ahmadiyya Islam and the Muslim Diaspora: Living at the End of Days*. London: Routledge.

BIBLIOGRAPHY

Barlet, Olivier. (2010) "Bollywood/Africa: A Divorce?" *Black Camera* 2, no. 1 (n.s.): 126–43.

Barnes, Andrew E. (2003) "Aryanizing Projects, African 'Collaborators,' and Colonial Transcripts." In *Antinomies of Modernity: Essays on Race, Orient, Nation*, ed. Vasant Kaiwar and Sucheta Mazumdar. Durham, NC: Duke University Press, pp. 62–97.

Basu, Anustup. (2020) *Hindutva as Political Monotheism*. Durham, NC: Duke University Press.

Basu, Helene. (1993) "The Siddi and the Cult of Bava Gor in Gujarat." *Journal of the Indian Anthropological Society* 28, no. 3: 289–300.

Bertz, Ned. (2011) "Indian Ocean World Cinema: Viewing the History of Race, Diaspora and Nationalism in Urban Tanzania." *Africa* 81, no. 1: 68–88.

— (2019) "Bollywood in Africa." In *Oxford Research Encyclopedia of Asian History*, ed. David Ludden. New York: Oxford University Press; https://doi.org/10.1093/acrefore/9780190277727.013.333

Beteille, Andre. (1990) "Race, Caste and Gender." *Man* 25, no. 3 (n.s.): 489–504.

Bhabha, Homi K. (2011) *Our Neighbours, Ourselves: Contemporary Reflections on Survival*. New York: Walter de Gruyter.

Bhatt, Purnima Mehta. (2019) *The African Diaspora in India: Assimilation, Change and Cultural Survivals*. New York: Routledge.

Blyden, Edward Wilmot. (1869) *The Negro in Ancient History*, reprinted from the *Methodist Quarterly Review*. New York: G. Lane & P. P. Sanford.

Bora, Papori. (2019) "The Problem Without a Name: Comments on Cultural Difference (Racism) in India." *South Asia: Journal of South Asian Studies* 42, no. 5: 845–60.

Bourdié, Annie. (2015) "'Moderniser' la danse en Afrique. Les enjeux politiques du centre Mudra à Dakar." *Recherches en Danse* 4: 1–18.

Brennan, James. (2012) *Taifa: Making Nation and Race in Urban Tanzania*. Athens: Ohio University Press.

Brennan, Lance. (1998) "Across the *Kala Pani*: An Introduction" *South Asia: Journal of South Asian Studies* 21, no. 1: s1–18.

BIBLIOGRAPHY

Buchanan, Sarah. (2008) "'Amul Yakar, c'est moi': Entretien avec Mansour Sora Wade." *Nouvelles Études Francophones* 33, no. 1: 165–77.

Burgin, Alice. (2013) "The Dialectics of Négritude in Francophone African Film: Mansour Sora Wade's 'Ndeysaan'." In *Contesting Historical Divides in Francophone Africa*, ed. Claire Griffiths. Chester: University of Chester Press, pp. 204–28.

Burton, Antoinette. (2012) *Brown over Black: Race and the Politics of Postcolonial Citation*. Gurgaon: Three Essays Collective.

Cabrita, Joel. (2012) "Patriot and Prophet: John Dube's 1936 Biography of the South African Churchman Isaiah Shembe." *Journal of Southern African Studies* 38, no. 3: 433–50.

Campbell, Gwyn, and Alessandro Stanziani, eds. (2015) *Bonded Labour and Debt in the Indian Ocean World*. New York: Routledge.

Chang, Yongkyu. (2016) "Making of Mami Wata: Diasporic Encounter of African, European and Asian Spirits." *Asian Journal of African Studies* 39: 53–70.

Chatterji, Suniti Kumar. (1974) "Léopold Sedar Senghor: Address of Welcome." *Indian Literature* 17, no. 1/2 (Jan.–June): 257–66.

Chatterji, Indrani, and Richard M. Eaton, eds. (2006) *Slavery and South Asian History*. Bloomington: Indiana University Press.

Clarence-Smith, William G. (2014) "The Textile Industry of Eastern Africa in the *Longue Durée*." In *Africa's Development in Historical Perspective*, ed. Emmanuel Akyeampong et al. New York: Cambridge University Press, pp. 264–94.

Coates, Oliver. (2018) "Between Image and Erasure: Photographs of West African Soldiers in India, 1944–1946." *Radical History Review* 132: 200–7.

— (2019) "World War II and West African Soldiers in Asia, 1943–1947." In *Exploitation and Misrule in Colonial and Postcolonial Africa*, ed. Kenneth Kalu and Toyin Falola. London: Palgrave Macmillan, pp. 191–215.

— (n.d.) "The West African Military Presence in World War Two India: An Historical Geography, 1943–6." Unpublished.

Contursi, Janet A. (1993) "Political Theology: Text and Practice in a Dalit Panther Community." *Journal of Asian Studies* 52, no. 2: 320–39.

BIBLIOGRAPHY

Cummings, Robert. (1977) "The Dakar Symposium: An Analysis." *New Directions* 4, no. 3: 38.

Curtis IV, Edward E. (2002) *Islam in Black America: Identity, Liberation, and Difference in African-American Islamic Thought.* Albany, NY: SUNY Press.

Dalafi, H. R., and M. H. A. Hassan. (1994) *Renaissance of Sciences in Islamic Countries.* London: World Scientific Publishing.

Dalit Camera. (2020) "'Indian Racism Towards Black People is almost Worse than White Peoples' Racism': An Interview with Arundhati Roy." (8 June); https://www.dalitcamera.com/indian-racism-towards-black-people-is-almos t-worse-than-white-peoples-racism/

Danielson, Leilah C. (2003) "'In My Extremity I Turned to Gandhi': American Pacifists, Christianity, and Gandhian Nonviolence, 1915–1941." *Church History* 72, no. 2: 361–88.

Das, Ranajit, and Priyanka Upadhyai. (2017) "Unraveling the Population History of Indian Siddis." *Genome Biology and Evolution* 9, no. 6: 1385–92.

Daswani, Girish. (2021) "This is not Namaste Wahala." *Everyday Orientalism* (blog); https://everydayorientalism.wordpress.com/2021/02/23/this-is-not-namaste-wahala-on-silences-hisstories-and-ghanas-oldest-south-asian-family/

Davis, Alexander. (2018) "Solidarity or Hierarchy? India's Identification with Africa and the Postcolonial Politics of Race." *India Review* 17, no. 5: 242–62.

Davis, Alexander E., and Vineet Thakur. (2016) "Walking the Thin Line: India's Anti-Racist Diplomatic Practice in South Africa, Canada, and Australia, 1946–55." *International History Review* 38, no. 5: 880–99.

De Greiff, Alexis. (2002) "The Tale of Two Peripheries: The Creation of the International Centre for Theoretical Physics in Trieste." *Historical Studies in the Physical and Biological Sciences* 33, no. 1: 33–59.

— (2006a) "Abdus Salam: A Migrant Scientist in Post-Imperial Times." *Economic and Political Weekly* 41, no. 3: 228–34.

— (2006b) "The Politics of Noncooperation: The Boycott of the International Centre for Theoretical Physics." *Osiris* 21, no. 1: 86–109.

BIBLIOGRAPHY

Desai, Ashwin, and Goolam Vahed. (2015) *The South African Gandhi: The Stretcher-Bearer of Empire*. Palo Alto, CA: Stanford University Press.

— (2019) *A History of the Present: A Biography of Indian South Africans, 1990–2019*. New York: Oxford University Press.

Desai, Jigna. (2008) "'Ever Since You've Discovered the Video, I've Had No Peace': Diasporic Spectators Talk Back to Bollywood Masala." In *The Bollywood Reader*, ed. Rajinder Dudrah and Jigna Desai. Maidenhead: McGraw-Hill, pp. 229–42.

Desai, Manan, and Tizarat Gill. (2018) "H. G. Mudgal: Harlem Editor." South Asian American Digital Archive; https://www.saada.org/tides/article/hg-mudgal-harlem-editor

Deslippe, Philip. (2014) "The Hindu in Hoodoo: Fake Yogis, Pseudo-Swamis, and the Manufacture of African American Folk Magic." *Amerasia Journal* 40, no. 1: 34–56.

Despres, Altaïr. (2019) "The Emergence of Contemporary Dance in Africa: A History of *Danse l'Afrique danse!* Biennale." *Journal of African Cultural Studies* 31, no. 3: 334–51.

Devji, Faisal. (2012) *The Impossible Indian: Gandhi and the Temptation of Violence*. Cambridge, MA: Harvard University Press.

— (2013) *Muslim Zion: Pakistan as a Political Idea*. Cambridge, MA: Harvard University Press.

Diagne, Souleymane Bachir. (2010) "In Praise of the Post-Racial: Négritude Beyond Négritude." *Third Text* 24, no. 2: 241–8.

— (2018) "Négritude." *Stanford Encyclopedia of Philosophy*; https://plato.stanford.edu/entries/negritude/

Diane, Alioune, and Oumar Sankharé. (2002) "'Dans la nuit tamoule ...': Le poète, la mort et l'ordre sacral des signes." *Ethiopiques* 69: 174–5.

Dieng, Amady Aly. (2011) *Mémoires d'un étudiant Africain*, Vol. 1. Dakar: CODESRIA.

Diop, Cheikh Anta. (1987) *Precolonial Black Africa*, trans. Harold Salemson. New York: Lawrence Hill Books, 1987.

Diouf, Mamadou, and Jinny Prais. (2013) "'Casting the Badge of Inferiority Beneath Black Peoples' Feet': Archiving and Reading the African Past, Present, and Future in World History." In *Global*

Intellectual History, ed. Samuel Moyn and Andrew Sartori. New York: Columbia University Press, pp. 205–27.

Dixie, Quinton Hosford, and Peter Eisenstadt. (2011) *Visions of a Better World: Howard Thurman's Pilgrimage to India and the Origins of African American Nonviolence*. Boston, MA: Beacon Press.

Dombey, Norman. (2011) "Abdus Salam: A Reappraisal: Part I: How to Win the Nobel Prize." Unpublished MS; https://arxiv.org/pdf/1109.1972.pdf

Drewal, Henry. (1988) "Performing the Other: Mami Wata Worship in Africa." *TDR* 32, no. 2: 160–85.

Dubey, Ajay. (2011) "Looking West 3: Africa." In *Handbook of India's International Relations*, ed. David Scott. London: Routledge, pp. 189–200.

Duedahl, Poul, ed. (2016) *A History of UNESCO: Global Actions and Impacts*. New York: Springer.

Duffield, Ian. (1971) "Duse Mohamed Ali and the Development of Pan-Africanism, 1866–1945." Unpublished doctoral dissertation, University of Edinburgh.

Dwyer, Rachel. (2006) *Filming the Gods: Religion and Indian Cinema*. New York: Routledge.

Echeruo, Michael. (1993) "Négritude and History: Senghor's Arguments with Frobenius." *Research in African Literatures* 24, no. 4: 1–13.

The Economist. (2019) "The New Scramble for Africa: This Time, the Winners Could Be Africans Themselves." (7 March); https://www.economist.com/leaders/2019/03/07/the-new-scramble-for-africa

Edwards, Michelle LeAnne. (2008) "A New Pan-Africanism: Diaspora Transnational Entrepreneurs and Philanthropy Between Ghana and Atlanta, USA." Unpublished doctoral thesis, Gainesville, University of Florida.

el Nabolsy, Zeyad. (2020) "*Lotus* and the Self-Representation of Afro-Asian Writers as the Vanguard of Modernity." *Interventions*: 1–25.

Eltringham, Nigel. (2006) "'Invaders Who have Stolen the Country': The Hamitic Hypothesis, Race and the Rwandan Genocide." *Social Identities* 12, no. 4: 425–46.

BIBLIOGRAPHY

Emeagwali, Gloria, and George J. Sefa Dei, eds. (2014) *African Indigenous Knowledge and the Disciplines*. New York: Springer.

Enz, Molly Krueger, and Devin Bryson. (2018) "Forging a New Path: Plurality, Social Change, and Innovation in Contemporary Senegalese Cinema." *Black Camera* 9, no. 2: 333–5.

Espiritu, Augusto. (2006) "'To Carry Water on Both Shoulders': Carlos P. Romulo, American Empire, and the Meanings of Bandung." *Radical History Review* 2006, no. 95: 173–90.

Faria, Caroline V., and Hilary Jones. (2020) "A Darling® of the Beauty Trade: Race, Care, and the Imperial Debris of Synthetic Hair." *Cultural Geographies* 27, no. 1: 85–99.

Farooq, Samina, and Eatzaz Ahmad. (2017) "Brain Drain from Pakistan: An Empirical Analysis." *Forman Journal of Economic Studies* 13: 55–81.

Felder, Pamela Petrease. (2015) "Edward A. Bouchet: A Model for Understanding African Americans and their Doctoral Experience." *Journal of African American Studies* 19, no. 1: 3–17.

Forsthoefel, Thomas A., and Cynthia Ann Humes, eds. (2005) *Gurus in America*. Binghamton, NY: SUNY Press.

Fraser, Gordon. (2008) *Cosmic Anger: Abdus Salam – The First Muslim Nobel Scientist*. New York: Oxford University Press.

Frenz, Margret. (2014) "Transimperial Connections: East African Goan Perspectives on 'Goa 1961'." *Contemporary South Asia* 22, no. 3: 240–54.

— (2019) "Complicating Decolonisation: Mozambican Indian Experiences in the Twentieth Century." *Journal of Imperial and Commonwealth History* 47, no. 5: 999–1020.

Gadjigo, Samba. (2010) *Ousmane Sembène: The Making of a Militant Artist*. Bloomington: Indiana University Press.

Gandhi, Rajmohan. (2015) "Independence and Social Justice: The Ambedkar-Gandhi Debate." *Economic and Political Weekly* 50, no. 15 (11 April): 35–44.

Gasman, Marybeth, and Thai-Huy Nguyen. (2015) "Myths Dispelled: A Historical Account of Diversity and Inclusion at HBCUs." *New Directions for Higher Education*, no. 170: 5–15.

Germain, Eric. (2007) "Southern Hemisphere Diasporic Communities in the Building of an International Muslim Public Opinion at the Beginning of the Twentieth Century." *Comparative Studies of South Asia, Africa and the Middle East* 27, no. 1: 126–38.

Ghanananda. (2001) *Some Basic Ideas about Hinduism.* Accra: Hindu Monastery of Africa.

Ghosh, Devleena. (2016) "Burma-Bengal Crossings: Intercolonial Connections in Pre-Independence India." *Asian Studies Review* 40, no. 2: 156–72.

Ghosh, Papiya. (2014) *Partition and the South Asian Diaspora: Extending the Subcontinent.* New York: Routledge.

Gidron, Yotam. (2020) *Israel in Africa: Security, Migration, Interstate Politics.* London: Zed Books.

Gilroy, Paul. (1993) *The Black Atlantic: Modernity and Double Consciousness.* Cambridge, MA: Harvard University Press.

Glassman, Jonathan. (2018) "Ethnicity and Race in African Thought." In *A Companion to African History,* ed. William Worger, Charles C. Ambler, and Nwando Achebe. New York: Blackwell, pp. 199–244.

— (2021) "Toward a Comparative History of Racial Thought in Africa: Historicism, Barbarism, Autochthony." *Comparative Studies in Society and History* 63, no. 1: 72–98.

Goyal, Yogita. (2014) "Africa and the Black Atlantic." *Research in African Literatures* 45, no. 3: v–xxv.

Graboyes, Melissa. (2015) *The Experiment Must Continue: Medical Research and Ethics in East Africa, 1940–2014.* Athens: Ohio University Press.

Grabski, Joanna. (2017) *Art World City: The Creative Economy of Artists and Urban Life in Dakar.* Bloomington: Indiana University Press.

Green, Nile. (2013) "Forgotten Futures: Indian Muslims in the Trans-Islamic Turn to Japan." *Journal of Asian Studies* 72, no. 3: 611–31.

— (2014) *Terrains of Exchange: Religious Economies of Global Islam.* London: Hurst.

— (2015) "The *Hajj* as its Own Undoing: Infrastructure and Integration on the Muslim Journey to Mecca." *Past & Present* 226, no. 1: 193–226.

Gregersen, Edgar. (1977) *Language in Africa: An Introductory Survey.* Abingdon: Taylor & Francis.

Guha, Ramachandra. (2018) "Setting the Record Straight on Gandhi and

Race." *The Wire*, 23 Dec. https://thewire.in/history/setting-the-record-straight-on-gandhi-and-race

Gupta, Anirudha. (1970) "A Note on Indian Attitudes to Africa." *African Affairs* 68, no. 275: 170–8.

— (1974) "Uganda Asians, Britain, India, and the Commonwealth." *African Affairs* 73, no. 29: 312–34.

— (1978) "India and Africa South of the Sahara." *International Studies* 17, no. 3/4: 639–55.

Hackett, Rosalind I. J. (1992) "New Age Trends in Nigeria: Ancestral and/ or Alien Religion?" In *Perspectives on the New Age*, ed. James Lewis and J. Gordon Melton. Albany, NY: SUNY Press, pp. 215–31.

Haddad, Yvonne Yazbeck, and Jane Idleman Smith. (1993) *Mission to America: Five Islamic Sectarian Communities in North America.* Gainesville: University of Florida Press.

Hagenbeck, Carl. (1911) *Beasts and Men: Being Carl Hagenbeck's Experiences for Half Century Among Wild Animals* (abridged), trans. Hugh S. R. Elliot and A. G. Thacker. London: Longmans.

Hall, Bruce S. (2011) *A History of Race in Muslim West Africa, 1600–1960.* New York: Cambridge University Press.

— (2020) "Reading Race in Africa and the Middle East." *Anthropologia* 7, no. 1 (n.s): 33–44.

Hansen, Thomas Blom. (2005) "In Search of the Diasporic Self: Bollywood in South Africa." In *Bollyworld: Popular Indian Cinema through a Transnational Lens*, ed. Raminder Kaur and Ajay Sinha. New Delhi: Sage, India, pp. 239–60.

— (2012) *Melancholia of Freedom: Social Life in an Indian Township in South Africa.* Princeton University Press.

Hanson, John. (2017) *The Ahmadiyya in the Gold Coast: Muslim Cosmopolitans in the British Empire.* Bloomington: Indiana University Press.

Hardeen, Devi. (2012) "The Brown Atlantic: Re-thinking Post-Slavery." Black Atlantic Resource Debate, University of Liverpool; https://www.liverpool.ac.uk/media/livacuk/csis/blackatlantic/BARD-Essay-1-1.pdf

Hardiman, David. (2007) "Purifying the Nation: The Arya Samaj in

Gujarat, 1895–1930." *Indian Economic and Social History Review* 44, no. 1: 41–65.

Harlan, Louis. (1966) "Booker T. Washington and the White Man's Burden." *American Historical Review* 71, no. 2: 441–67.

Harney, Elizabeth. (2004) *In Senghor's Shadow: Art, Politics, and the Avant-Garde in Senegal, 1960–1995.* Durham, NC: Duke University Press.

Harre, Dominique. (2017) "Exchanges and Mobility in the Western Indian Ocean: Indians between Yemen and Ethiopia, 19th–20th Centuries." *Chroniques du Manuscrit au Yémen* 1: 42–69.

Harris, Kamala. (2019) *The Truths We Hold: An American Journey.* New York: Penguin.

Hassan, Ibrahim Haruna. (2015) "An Introduction to Islamic Movements and Modes of Thought in Nigeria." PAS/ISITA Working Paper no. 1. Evanston, IL: Northwestern University.

Hecht, Gabrielle. (2006) "Negotiating Global Nuclearities: Apartheid, Decolonization, and the Cold War in the Making of the IAEA." *Osiris* 21, no. 1: 25–48.

Hodgson, Dorothy, and Judith Byfield, eds. (2017) *Global Africa: Into the Twentieth-First Century.* Berkeley: University of California Press.

Hofmeyr, Isabel. (2007) "The Black Atlantic Meets the Indian Ocean: Forging New Paradigms of Transnationalism for the Global South – Literary and Cultural Perspectives." *Social Dynamics* 33, no. 2 (2007): 3–32.

— (2012) "The Complicating Sea: the Indian Ocean as Method." *Comparative Studies of South Asia, Africa and the Middle East* 32, no. 3: 584–90.

— (2013) *Gandhi's Printing Press: Experiments in Slow Reading.* Cambridge, MA: Harvard University Press.

— (2015) "Styling Multilateralism: Indian Ocean Cultural Futures." *Journal of the Indian Ocean Region* 11, no. 1: 98–109.

Holmes, Mary Caroline. (1926) "Islam in America." *Muslim World* 16, no. 3: 262–6.

Homburger, Lilias. (1955) "L'Inde et l'Afrique." *Journal des Africanistes* 25, no. 1: 13–18.

BIBLIOGRAPHY

Horne, Gerald. (2009) *The End of Empires: African Americans and India.* Philadelphia, PA: Temple University Press.

Howe, Stephen. (1998) *Afrocentrism: Mythical Pasts and Imagined Homes.* London: Verso.

Howell, Sally. (2014) *Old Islam in Detroit: Rediscovering the Muslim American Past.* New York: Oxford University Press.

Hromnik, Cyril. (1991) "Dravidian Gold Mining and Trade in Ancient Komatiland." *Journal of Asian and African Studies* 26, no. 3/4: 283–90.

Hunter, Margaret L. (2011) "Buying Racial Capital: Skin-Bleaching and Cosmetic Surgery in a Globalized World." *Journal of Pan African Studies* 4, no. 4: 142–64.

Imber, Mark F. (1989) *The USA, ILO, UNESCO and IAEA: Politicization and Withdrawal in the Specialized Agencies.* New York: Springer.

Indian Institute of Foreign Trade. (1983) *Market Survey of Books and Publications in Kenya, Nigeria and Tanzania.* New Delhi: IIFT.

Irvine, Judith T. (2017) "Language and Social Hierarchy in West Africa." In *Oxford Research Encyclopedia of Linguistics*; https://doi.org/10.1093/acrefore/9780199384655.013.239

Isa, Kabiru Haruna. (2018) "A Religious Minority in Search for Space and Identity: A History of Ahmadiyya Community in Kano, Nigeria." Unpublished paper in author's possession.

Isaacman, Allen F., and Barbara S. Isaacman. (2014) *Dams, Displacement, and the Delusion of Development: Cahora Bassa and its Legacies in Mozambique, 1965–2007.* Athens: Ohio University Press.

Israel, Adrienne. (1987) "Measuring the War Experience: Ghanaian Soldiers in World War II." *Journal of Modern African Studies* 25, no. 1: 159–68.

Ita, J. M. (1973) "Frobenius, Senghor and the Image of Africa." In *Modes of Thought: Essays on Thinking in Western and Non-Western Societies*, ed. Robin Horton and Ruth Finnegan. London: Faber & Faber, pp. 306–36.

Iyengar, Malathi. (2018) "Afro-Asian-Caribbean Connections in Transnational Circulation: The Harlem Ashram as Chronotope." In *Afro-Asian Connections in Latin America and the Caribbean*, ed. Luisa

Marcela Ossa and Debbie Lee-DiStefano. New York: Rowman and Littlefield, pp. 61–88.

Jacobs, Evan. (2016) "Keratin Kapital: Black Hair and the Economy of Otherness: Understanding the State of Black Hair in South Africa through the Import of Indian Hair." MA thesis, Anthropology, University of the Witwatersrand.

Jain, Kajri, and Nicholas Thomas. (2007) *Gods in the Bazaar: The Economies of Indian Calendar Art*. Durham, NC: Duke University Press.

Jalal, Ayesha. (2007) "Striking a Just Balance: Maulana Azad as a Theorist of Trans-National *Jihad*." *Modern Intellectual History* 4, no. 1: 95–107.

Jayasuriya, Shihan da Silva, and Richard Pankhurst, eds. (2003) *The African Diaspora in the Indian Ocean*. Trenton, NJ: Africa World Press.

Jayawardene, Sureshi. (2013) "Pushing the Paradigm: Locating Scholarship on the Siddis and Kaffirs." *Journal of Black Studies* 44, no. 7: 687–705.

Jedlowski, Alessandro. (2018) "Post-Imperial Affinities and Neoliberal Convergences: Discourses and Practices of Collaboration between the Nigerian and the Indian Film Industries." *Media, Culture & Society* 40, no. 1: 23–40.

Jonker, Gerdien. (2014) "A Laboratory of Modernity – the Ahmadiyya Mission in Inter-War Europe." *Journal of Muslims in Europe* 3, no. 1: 1–25.

Jules-Rosette, Benetta. (2007) "Jean-Paul Sartre and the Philosophy of Négritude: Race, Self and Society." *Theory and Society* 36, no. 3: 265–85.

July, Robert. (1964) "Nineteenth-Century Negritude: Edward W. Blyden." *Journal of African History* 5, no. 1: 73–86.

Kasana, Mehreen. (2014) "Feminisms and the Social Media Sphere." *Women's Studies Quarterly* 42, no. 3/4: 236–49.

Kebret, Negash. (2001) "Ethiopia-India Relations: A Historical Perspective." *Africa Quarterly* 41, no. 3: 76–89.

Killingray, David, and Martin Plaut. (2012) *Fighting for Britain: African Soldiers in the Second World War*. Woodbridge, Suffolk: Boydell and Brewer.

Klein, Gabriele. (2019) "Artistic Work as a Practice of Translation on the

BIBLIOGRAPHY

Global Art Market: The Example of 'African' Dancer and Choreographer Germaine Acogny." *Dance Research Journal* 51, no. 1: 8–19.

Kloman, Erasmus H. (1962) "African Unification Movements." *International Organization* 16, no. 2: 387–404.

Kobo, Ousman Murzik. (2016) "Islamic Institutions of Higher Learning in Ghana: The Case of the Islamic University College." In *Muslim Institutions of Higher Education in Postcolonial Africa*, ed. Mbaye Lo and Muhammed Haron. New York: Palgrave Macmillan, pp. 179–91.

Kooria, Mahmood. (2020) "Introduction: Narrating Africa in South Asia." *South Asian History and Culture* Special Issue 11, no. 4: 351–62.

Krishnan, Madhu. (2012) "Mami Wata and the Occluded Feminine in Anglophone Nigerian-Igbo Literature." *Research in African Literatures* 43, no. 1: 1–18.

Kumar, Ravindra (2008) *How to be One with God: An Autobiography of a Scientist Yogi*. New York: Sterling Publishers.

Kwoba, Brian, Roseanne Chantiluke, and Athinangamso Nkopo, eds. (2018) *Rhodes Must Fall: The Struggle to Decolonise the Racist Heart of Empire*. London: Zed Books.

Lal, Vinay, and Goolam Vahed. (2013) "Hinduism in South Africa: Caste, Ethnicity, and Invented Traditions, 1860–Present." *Journal of Sociology and Social Anthropology* 4, no. 1/2: 1–15.

Langwick, Stacey. (2018) "Healing in the Anthropocene." In *The World Multiple: The Quotidian Politics of Knowing and Generating Entangled Worlds*, ed. Keiichi Omura, Grant Jun Otsuki, Shiho Satsuka, and Atsuro Morita. Abingdon: Taylor & Francis, pp. 155–71.

Larkin, Brian. (1997) "Indian Films and Nigerian Lovers: Media and the Creation of Parallel Modernities." *Africa* 67, no. 3: 406–40.

— (2008) "Itineraries of Indian Cinema: African Videos, Bollywood, and Global Media." In *The Bollywood Reader*, ed. Rajinder Dudrah and Jigna Desai. Maidenhead: McGraw-Hill, pp. 216–28.

Lasco, Gideon, and Anita P. Hardon. (2020) "Keeping Up with the Times: Skin-Lightening Practices Among Young Men in the Philippines." *Culture, Health & Sexuality* 22, no. 7: 838–53.

Law, Robin. (2009) "The 'Hamitic Hypothesis' in Indigenous West African Historical Thought." *History in Africa* 36, no. 1: 293–314.

BIBLIOGRAPHY

Lee, Christopher J. (2021) "Decolonizing 'China-Africa Relations': Towards a New Ethos of Afro-Asianism." *Journal of African Cultural Studies* 33, no. 2: 230–7.

Lee, Christopher J., ed. (2010) *Making a World after Empire: The Bandung Moment and its Political Afterlives.* Athens: Ohio University Press.

Loimeier, Roman. (1997) *Islamic Reform and Political Change in Northern Nigerian.* Chicago, IL: Northwestern University Press.

Lucht, Hansa. (2011) *Darkness before Daybreak: African Migrants Living on the Margins in Southern Italy Today.* Berkeley: University of California Press.

Mahajan, Karan. (2019) "'State Capture': How the Gupta Brothers Hijacked South Africa Using Bribes instead of Bullets." *Vanity Fair* (3 March).

Makhubu, Lydia. (1998) "Bioprospecting in an African Context." *Science* 282, no. 5386: 41–2.

— (1999) "Third World Women Scientists." In *Tribute to Abdus Salam,* ed. A. M. Hamende. Trieste: Abdus Salam International Centre for Theoretical Physics, pp. 91–5.

Mallampalli, Chandra. (2004) *Christians and Public Life in Colonial South India, 1863–1937.* New York: Routledge.

Mamdani, Mahmood. (1993) "The Ugandan Asian Expulsion: Twenty Years After." *Journal of Refugee Studies* 6, no. 3: 265–73.

— (2009) *Saviors and Survivors: Darfur, Politics and the War on Terror.* New York: Crown Books.

Mampilly, Zachariah. (2013) "India's Sojourn to Africa." In *Handbook of Africa's International Relations,* ed. Tim Murithi. Abingdon: Routledge, pp. 356–66.

Manoharan, Karthik Ram. (2020) "In the Path of Ambedkar: Periyar and the Dalit Question." *South Asian History and Culture* 11, no. 2: 136–49.

Markovits, Claude. (2000) *The Global World of Indian Merchants, 1750–1947: Traders of Sind from Bukhara to Panama.* New York: Cambridge University Press.

Marr, Timothy. (2006) *The Cultural Roots of American Islamicism.* New York: Cambridge University Press.

BIBLIOGRAPHY

Martin, Tony. (1977) "Carter G. Woodson and Marcus Garvey." *Negro History Bulletin* 40, no. 6: 774–7.

Marzagora, Sara. (2020) "Refashioning the Ethiopian Monarchy in the Twentieth Century: An Intellectual History." *Global Intellectual History* 5, no. 1: 1–25.

Matory, J. Lorand. (1999) "The English Professors of Brazil: On the Diasporic Roots of the Yorubá Nation." *Comparative Studies in Society and History* 41, no. 1: 72–103.

Mawdsley, Emma, and Gerard McCann, eds. (2011) *India in Africa: Changing Geographies of Power*. Cape Town: Pambazuka Press.

McCann, Gerard. (2013) "From Diaspora to Third Worldism and the United Nations: India and the Politics of Decolonizing Africa." *Past & Present* 218, no. 8: 258–80.

— (2019a) "Where was the Afro in Afro-Asian Solidarity? Africa's 'Bandung Moment' in 1950s Asia." *Journal of World History* 30, no. 1/2: 89–123.

— (2019b) "Possibility and Peril: Trade Unionism, African Cold War, and the Global Strands of Kenyan Decolonization." *Journal of Social History* 53, no. 2: 348–77.

McLaughlin, Fiona. (1997) "Islam and Popular Music in Senegal: The Emergence of a 'New Tradition'." *Africa* 67, no. 4: 560–81.

— (2008) "The Ascent of Wolof as an Urban Vernacular and National Lingua Franca in Senegal." In *Globalization and Language Vitality: Perspectives from Africa*, ed. Cécile Vigoroux and Salikoko S. Mufwene. London: Continuum, pp. 142–70.

McLucas, Karla, and Rhonda Vonshay Sharpe. (2016) "African Americans, Dalits and Tribals: A Comparative Analysis of Subaltern Communities in India and the USA." *Review of Black Political Economy* 43, no. 2: 85–6.

Mehta, Jagat S. (2001) "Negotiating Compensation for Indians with Idi Amin's Government." *India International Centre Quarterly* 28, no. 3: 25–46.

Menon, Dilip. (2017) "Was Mohandas Gandhi a Racist?" *Africa is a Country* (10 March); https://africasacountry.com/2017/03/was-mohandas-gandhi-a-racist

Merani, H. V., and H. L. Van der Laan. (1979) "The Indian Traders in Sierra Leone." *African Affairs* 78, no. 311: 240–50.

Metcalf, Thomas R. (2008) *Imperial Connections: India in the Indian Ocean Arena, 1860–1920*. Berkeley: University of California Press.

Mickens, Ronald E., ed. (2002) *Edward Bouchet: The First African-American Doctorate*. Singapore: World Scientific Publishing Company.

Micots, Courtnay. (2012) "Performing Ferocity: Fancy Dress, Asafo, and Red Indians in Ghana." *African Arts* 45, no. 2: 24–35.

Mills, Greg, Olusegun Obasanjo, Hailemariam Desalegn, and Emily van der Merwe. (2020) *The Asian Aspiration: Why and How Africa Should Emulate Asia – and What it Should Avoid*. New York: Oxford University Press.

Mkandawire, Thandika, ed. (2005) *African Intellectuals: Rethinking Politics, Language, Gender and Development*. London: CODESRIA/Zed Books.

Modi, Renu, and Ian Taylor. (2017) "The Indian Diaspora in Africa: The Commodification of Hindu Rashtra." *Globalizations* 14, no. 6: 911–29.

Mohanty, Seema. (2009) *The Book of Kali*. New York: Penguin.

Mordi, E. N. (2019) "Nigerian Forces Comforts Fund, 1940–1947: 'The Responsibility of the Nigerian Government to Provide Funds for the Welfare of Its Soldiers'." *Itinerario* 43, no. 3: 516–42.

Morton, Julia. (1991) "The Horseradish Tree, *Moringa pterygosperma* (*Moringaceae*) – A Boon to Arid Lands?" *Economic Botany* 45, no. 3: 318–33.

Mouralis, Bernard. (2015) "L'usage de l'Antiquité chez Cheikh Anta Diop et l'ombre menaçante de Senghor." *International Journal of Francophone Studies* 18, no. 2/3: 215–34.

Moyn, Samuel, and Andrew Sartori, eds. (2013) *Global Intellectual History*. New York: Columbia University Press.

Mtingwa, Sekazi, Ronald Mickens, and Jami Valentine. (2017) "Obituary of Joseph Andrew Johnson III." *Physics Today* (28 July).

Mukherjee, Madhuja. (2007) "Early Indian Talkies: Voice, Performance and Aura." *Journal of the Moving Image* 6: 39–61.

Mullen, Bill, and Cathryn Watson, eds. (2005) *W. E. B. Du Bois on Asia: Crossing the World*. Jackson: University Press of Mississippi.

Mungai, Christine. (2015) "15 Facts about the Indian Diaspora." *Agenda*,

BIBLIOGRAPHY

World Economic Forum/*Mail & Guardian Africa* (25 June); https://www.weforum.org/agenda/2015/06 /15-facts-about-the-indian-diaspora -in-africa/

Myburgh, Pieter-Louis. (2017) *The Republic of Gupta: A Story of State Capture.* New York: Penguin.

Nadeem, Shehzad. (2014) "Fair and Anxious: On Mimicry and Skin-Lightening in India." *Social Identities* 20, no. 2/3: 224–38.

Nadwi, S. Abul Hasan. (1965) *Qadianism: A Critical Study: The Pseudo-Religious Movement of Mirza Ghulam Ahmad (Qadian) The Claimant to the Prophethood.* Lahore: Sh. Muhammad Ashraf.

Nair, Savita. (2018) "Despite Dislocations: Uganda's Indians Remaking Home." *Africa* 88, no. 3: 492–517.

Nance, Susan. (2002) "Mystery of the Moorish Science Temple: Southern Blacks and American Alternative Spirituality in 1920s Chicago." *Religion and American Culture: A Journal of Interpretation* 12, no. 2: 123–66.

Nauriya, Anil. (2012) "Gandhi and Some Contemporary African Leaders from KwaZulu-Natal." *Natalia* 42: 45–64.

Ndlovu-Gatsheni, Sabelo J. (2015) "Decoloniality as the Future of Africa." *History Compass* 13, no. 10: 485–96.

Newell, Stephanie. (2011) "Articulating Empire: Newspaper Readerships in Colonial West Africa." *New Formations* 73: 26–42.

Ngugi wa Thiong'o. (2012) "Asia in My Life." *Journal of Contemporary Thought* Forum: "From Indian Literature to World Literature" (Aug.): 35–9.

Obeng, Pashington. (2003) "Religion and Empire: Belief and Identity Among African Indians of Karnataka, South India." *Journal of the American Academy of Religion* 71, no. 1: 99–120.

— (2007) *Shaping Membership, Defining Nation: The Cultural Politics of African Indians in South Asia.* Lanham, MD: Lexington Books.

Oduntan, Babatunde Oluwatoyin. (2012) "Beyond 'The Way of God': Missionaries, Colonialism and Smallpox in Abeokuta." *Lagos Historical Review* 12: 1–22.

Okon, Etim E. (2014) "Kwame Nkrumah: The Fallen and Forgotten Hero of African Nationalism." *European Scientific Journal* 10, no. 17: 50–77.

Omenka, Nicholas. (2004) "The Afro-Brazilian Repatriates and the

Religious and Cultural Transformation of Colonial Lagos." *Abia Journal of the Humanities and the Social Sciences* 1, no. 1: 27–45.

Omvedt, Gail. (2006) *Dalit Visions: The Anti-Caste Movement and the Construction of an Indian Identity.* New Delhi: Orient BlackSwan.

— (2012) "Andre Beteille's Dream World: Caste Today." (20 March); Countercurrents.org; https://www.countercurrents.org/omvedt200312.htm

Osondu-Oti, Adaora. (2015) "An Appraisal of India-Nigeria Historical and Contemporary Relations." *Alternation* Special Edition 15: 102–26.

Osseo-Asare, Abena Dove. (2016) "Writing Medical Authority: The Rise of Literate Healers in Ghana, 1930–70." *Journal of African History* 57, no. 1: 69–91.

— (2019) *Atomic Junction: Nuclear Power in Africa after Independence.* New York: Cambridge University Press.

Østebø, Terje. (2013) "Islam and State Relations in Ethiopia: From Containment to the Production of a 'Governmental Islam'." *Journal of the American Academy of Religion* 81, no. 4: 1029–60.

Otten, Thomas J. (1992). "Pauline Hopkins and the Hidden Self of Race." *ELH* 59, no. 1: 227–56.

Ownby, Carolan Postma. (1982) Review: "The Indian Rope Trick: *Indo-Africa. Towards a New Understanding of the History of Sub-Saharan Africa* by Cyril A. Hromnik." *Journal of African History* 23, no. 3: 415–16.

Pande, S. (2020). "Impact of Bleaching Syndrome: The Inexorable Predicament of Dark-Skinned Indian Women." In *The Routledge Handbook of Exclusion, Inequality and Stigma in India*, ed. N. M. P. Verma and Alpana Srivastava. New York: Taylor & Francis, pp. 284–97.

Pant, Shri Apa B. (1974) *A Moment in Time.* Bombay: Orient Longman.

Patel, Hasu H. (1972) "General Amin and the Indian Exodus from Uganda." *Issue: A Journal of Opinion* 2, no. 4: 12–22.

Paton, William. (1923) "Indian Moslems and the Khalifate." *International Review of Mission* 12, no. 1: 82–97.

Pessoa, Osvaldo, Olival Freire Jr., and Alexis De Greiff. (2008) "The Tausk Controversy on the Foundations of Quantum Mechanics: Physics, Philosophy, and Politics." *Physics in Perspective* 10, no. 2: 138–62.

Peters, Jonathan. (1978) *A Dance of Masks: Senghor, Achebe, Soyinka.* Washington, DC: Three Continents Press.

Peterson, Derek R. (2017) "Nonconformity in Africa's Cultural History." *Journal of African History* 58, no. 1: 35–50.

Pierre, Jemima. (2012) *The Predicament of Blackness: Postcolonial Ghana and the Politics of Race.* University of Chicago Press.

Pinney, Christopher. (2004) *"Photos of the Gods": The Printed Image and Political Struggle in India.* London: Reaktion Books.

Prashad, Vijay. (2000) "Afro-Dalits of the Earth Unite!" *African Studies Review* 43, no. 1: 189–201.

— (2002) *Everybody was Kung Fu Fighting: Afro-Asian Connections and the Myth of Cultural Purity.* Boston, MA: Beacon Press.

Prestholdt, Jeremy. (2020) "The Ends of the Indian Ocean: Notes on Boundaries and Affinities across Time." In *Reimagining Indian Ocean Worlds*, ed. Smriti Srinivas, Bettina Ng'weno, and Neelima Jeychandran. Abingdon: Routledge, chapter 1.

Purohit, Teena. (2016) "Muhammad Iqbal, Mirza Ghulam Ahmad, and the Accusation of Heresy." *Comparative Studies of South Asia, Africa and the Middle East* 36, no. 2: 246–55.

Qasmi, Ali Usman. (2015) *The Ahmadis and the Politics of Religious Exclusion in Pakistan.* London: Anthem Press.

Quirin, James. (1998) "Caste and Class in Historical North-West Ethiopia: The Beta Israel (Falasha) and Kemant, 1300–1900." *Journal of African History* 39, no. 2: 195–220.

Ram, Augustine Ralla. (1946) "The Christian Church in the India of Today and Tomorrow." *Theology Today* 2, no. 4: 472–87.

— (1956) "Organic Church Unity: A Comment from India." *Ecumenical Review* 8, no. 3: 243–8.

Ramamurthi, T. G. (1994) "Lessons of Durban Riots." *Economic and Political Weekly* 29, no. 10 (5 Mar.): 543–6.

Ramaswamy, Sumathi. (1997) *Passions of the Tongue: Language Devotion in Tamil India, 1891–1970.* Berkeley: University of California Press.

— (2004) *The Lost Land of Lemuria: Fabulous Geographies, Catastrophic Histories.* Berkeley: University of California Press.

Ramnath, Maia. (2011). *Haj to Utopia: How the Ghadar Movement Charted*

BIBLIOGRAPHY

Global Radicalism and Attempted to Overthrow the British Empire. Berkeley: University of California Press.

Ramos, Arthur. (1941) "Acculturation among the Brazilian Negroes." *Journal of Negro History* 26, no. 2: 244–50.

Rangaswamy, Nimmi. (2004). "Making a Dravidian Hero: The Body and Identity Politics in the Dravidian Movement." In *Confronting the Body: The Politics of Physicality in Colonial and Post-Colonial India*, ed. James Mills and Satadru Sen. London: Anthem Press, pp. 135–45.

Rastogi, Pallavi. (2005) "From South Asia to South Africa: Locating Other Post-Colonial Diasporas." *MFS Modern Fiction Studies* 51, no. 3: 536–60.

Rawat, Vidya Bhushan. (2020). "Ambedkar is More Relevant to Africa than Gandhi says Dr Obadele Kambon." (11 Sept.), Countercurrents.org; https://countercurrents.org/2020/09/ambedkar-is-more-relevant-to -africa-than-gandhi-says-dr-obadele-kambon/

Reichmuth, Stefan. (1996) "Education and the Growth of Religious Associations Among Yoruba Muslims – the Ansar-Ud-Deen Society of Nigeria." *Journal of Religion in Africa* 26, no. 4: 365–405.

Reid, Richard. (2017) *A History of Modern Uganda*. New York: Cambridge University Press.

Robb, Peter, ed. (1995) *The Concept of Race in South Asia*. New York: Oxford University Press.

Roberts, Dorothy. (2010) "Race and the New Biocitizen." In *What's the Use of Race? Modern Governance and the Biology of Difference*, ed. Ian Whitmarsh and David S. Jones. Cambridge, MA: MIT Press, 259–76.

Rognoni, Maria Stella. (2018) "The Conundrum of Entanglement: India's Participation in UN Peacekeeping Missions in the Congo." *Afriche e Orienti* 20, no. 1/2: 24–40.

Roy, Kaushik. (2010) "Discipline and Morale of the African, British and Indian Army Units in Burma and India during World War II: July 1943 to August 1945." *Modern Asian Studies* 44, no. 6: 1255–82.

Rush, Dana. (2008) "The Idea of 'India' in West African Vodun Art and Thought". In *India in Africa, Africa in India: Indian Ocean Cosmopolitanisms*, ed. John Hawley. Bloomington: Indiana University Press, pp. 149–80.

BIBLIOGRAPHY

Ryad, Umar. (2015) "Salifiyya, Ahmadiyya and European Converts to Islam in the Interwar Period." In *Muslims in Interwar Europe: A Transcultural Historical Perspective*, ed. Bekim Agai, Umar Ryad, and Mehdi Sajid. Leiden: Brill, pp. 47–87.

Saeed, Sadia. (2007) "Pakistani Nationalism and the State Marginalisation of the Ahmadiyya Community." *Studies in Ethnicity and Nationalism* 7, no. 3: 132–52.

Saeed, Yousuf. (2018) *Muslim Devotional Art in India*. Abingdon: Taylor & Francis.

Saifi, Naseem. (1955) *An Outline of Islam*. Lagos: Islamic Literature.

— (1957) *Our Movement*. Lagos: Islamic Literature.

Samwini, Nathan. (2006) *The Muslim Resurgence in Ghana since 1950: Its Effects upon Muslims and Muslim-Christian Relations*. Munster: LIT Verlag.

Sanders, Edith. (1969) "The Hamitic Hypothesis: Its Origin and Functions in Time Perspective." *Journal of African History* 10, no. 4: 521–32.

Sauldie, Madan M. (1965) "India and Africa: An Indian's Assessment." *Africa Report* 10, no. 1: 15–17.

Schulze-Engler, Frank. (2020) "Entangled Solidarities: African-Asian Writers' Organisations, Anti-Colonial Rhetorics and Afrasian Imaginaries in East African Literature." In *Reconfiguring Transregionalisation in the Global South: African-Asian Encounters*, ed. Ross Anthony and Uta Ruppert. Basingstoke: Palgrave Macmillan, pp. 117–39.

Scott, William. (1978) "Black Nationalism and the Italo-Ethiopian Conflict, 1934–1936." *Journal of Negro History* 63, no. 2: 118–34.

Senghor, Léopold Sédar. (1974a) "Négritude and Dravidian Culture." *Journal of Tamil Studies* 1: 1–12.

— (1974b) "Négritude." *Indian Literature* 17, no. 1/2: 269–73.

— (1975) "Why Create a Department of Indo-African Studies at Dakar University?" *International Journal of Dravidian Linguistics* 4, no. 1: 1–13.

Shankar, Shobana. (2014) *Who Shall Enter Paradise? Christian Origins in Muslim Northern Nigeria, c.1890–1975*. Athens: Ohio University Press.

— (2020) "A Tale of Two Gandhis in Ghana." In *Black Ambassadors of Politics, Religion, and Jazz in India: Afro-South Asia in the Global African*

Diaspora, Vol. 3, ed. Omar H. Ali, Kenneth X. Robbins, Beheroze Schroff, and Jazmin Graves. Greensboro, NC and Ahmedabad: University of North Carolina and Ahmedabad Sidi Heritage and Education Center, pp. 49–55.

— (2021) "Hindu Devotional Music in Ghana: Singing and Sensing the Unknown." *Yale Journal of Music & Religion* Vol. 6, no. 2, Special Issue, ed. Margarethe Adams and August Sheehy.

Sharma, Veena. (2015) *Advaita Vedanta and Akan: Inquiry into an Indian and African Ethos*. Shimla: Indian Institute of Advanced Study.

— (2019) "Building a More Sensitive World Through Religious Tourism." In *Peace Journeys: A New Direction in Religious Tourism and Pilgrimage Research*, ed. Ian S. McIntosh, Nour Fara Haddad, and Dane Munro. Cambridge: Cambridge Scholars Press, pp. 176–91.

Shepherd, Verene. (1988) "Indians and Blacks in Jamaica in the Nineteenth and Early Twentieth Centuries: A Micro-Study of the Foundation of Race Antagonisms." *Immigrants & Minorities* 7, no. 1: 95–112.

Sherwood, Marika. (2019) *Kwame Nkrumah and the Dawn of the Cold War: The West African National Secretariat, 1945–48*. London: Pluto Press.

Shroff, Beheroze. (2013) "'Goma is Going On': Sidis of Gujarat." *African Arts* 46, no. 1: 18–25.

Singleton, Brent D. (2009) "'That Ye May Know Each Other': Late Victorian Interactions between British and West African Muslims." *Journal of Muslim Minority Affairs* 29, no. 3: 369–85.

Sinha, Babli. (2009) "'Lowering Our Prestige': American Cinema, Mass Consumerism, and Racial Anxiety in Colonial India." *Comparative Studies of South Asia, Africa and the Middle East* 29, no. 2: 291–304.

Slate, Nico. (2012a) "The Dalit Panthers: Race, Caste, and Black Power in India." In *Black Power Beyond Borders: The Global Dimensions of the Black Power Movement*, ed. Nico Slate. New York: Palgrave Macmillan, pp. 127–43.

— (2012b) *Colored Cosmopolitanism: The Shared Struggle for Freedom in the United States and India*. Cambridge, MA: Harvard University Press.

Sorgel, Sabine. (2020) *Contemporary African Dance Theatre: Phenomenology, Whiteness, and the Gaze*. New York: Springer.

BIBLIOGRAPHY

Soske, Jon. (2017) *Internal Frontiers: African Nationalism and the Indian Diaspora in Twentieth-Century South Africa.* Athens: Ohio University Press.

Soyinka, Wole. (2002) "Senghor: Lessons in Power." *Research in African Literatures* 33, no. 4: 1–2.

Sperl, Stefan, and Christopher Shackle, eds. (1996) *Qasida Poetry in Islamic Africa and Asia*, Vol. 1: *Classical Traditions and Modern Meanings.* Leiden: Brill.

Spight, Carl. (1974) "Towards Black Science and Technology." *Black Books Bulletin* 5, no. 3: 6–11.

Spleth, Janice. (2002) "The Arabic Constituents of 'Africanité': Senghor and the Queen of Sheba." *Research in African Literatures* 33, no. 4: 60–75.

Spooner, Kevin. (2017) "'Awakening Africa': Race and Canadian Views of Decolonizing Africa." In *Dominion of Race: Rethinking Canada's International History*, ed. Laura Madokoro, Francine McKenzie, and David Meren. Vancouver: University of British Columbia Press, pp. 206–27.

Ssebuwufu, John Pancras Mukasa. (2017) *Managing and Transforming an African University: Personal Experience at Makerere University, 1973–2004.* Dakar: CODESRIA.

Stolte, Carolien. (2019) "Introduction: Trade Union Networks and the Politics of Expertise in an Age of Afro-Asian Solidarity." *Journal of Social History* 53, no. 2: 331–47.

Straus, Scott. (2013) *The Order of Genocide: Race, Power, and War in Rwanda.* Ithaca, NY: Cornell University Press.

Subramaniam, Banu. (2019) *Holy Science: The Biopolitics of Hindu Nationalism.* Seattle: University of Washington Press.

Subramanian, Ajantha. (2019) "Meritocracy and Democracy: Indian Reservations and the Politics of Caste." *Public Culture* 31, no. 2: 275–88.

Sutherland, Bill, and Matt Meyer. (2000). *Guns and Gandhi in Africa: Pan-African Insights on Nonviolence, Armed Struggle and Liberation.* Trenton, NJ: Africa World Press.

Swan, Quito. (2018) "Blinded by Bandung? Illumining West Papua,

Senegal, and the Black Pacific." *Radical History Review* 2018, no. 131: 58–81.

Sylvanus, Emaeyak Peter, and Obiocha Purity Eze-Emaeyak. (2018) "The Business of Film Music in Mainstream Nollywood: Competing without Advantage." *Journal of Cultural Economy* 11, no. 2: 141–53.

Tamari, Tal. (1991) "The Development of Caste Systems in West Africa." *Journal of African History* 32, no. 2: 221–50.

Tayo, Haji Salahuddin. (1978) "Facts about the Ahmadiyya Movement." Riyadh: Al-Nasser Press.

Thakur, Vineet. (2014) "The Colonial Origins of Indian Foreign Policymaking." *Economic & Political Weekly* 49, no. 32: 58–64.

— (2018) *Postscripts on Independence: Foreign Policy Ideas, Identity, and Institutions in India and South Africa.* New York: Oxford University Press.

Thapar, Romila. (1996) "The Theory of Aryan Race and India: History and Politics." *Social Scientist* 24, no. 1/3: 3–29.

— (2008) *The Aryan: Recasting Constructs.* Gurgaon: Three Essays Collective.

Thomas, Lynn. (2020). *Beneath the Surface: A Transnational History of Skin Lighteners.* Durham, NC: Duke University Press.

Thubauville, Sophia. (2013) "Indian Academics in Ethiopia: South-South Migration of Highly Skilled Indians." *Diaspora Studies* 6, no. 2: 123–33.

Thubauville, Sophia, and Hanna Getachew Amare. (2020) "Migration of Indian Educators to Ethiopia: Between Solidarity and Global Capitalism." In *Afrasian Transformations: Transregional Perspectives on Development Cooperation, Social Mobility and Cultural Change,* ed. Ruth Achenbach, Jan Beek, John Njenga Karugia, Rirhandu Mageza-Bethel, and Frank Schulze-Engler. Leiden: Brill, pp. 218–32.

Thurman, Howard, ed. Walter E. Fluker, and Catherine Tumber. (1998) *A Strange Freedom: The Best of Howard Thurman on Religious Experience and Public Life.* Boston, MA: Beacon Press.

Thursby, G. R. (1975) *Hindu-Muslim Relations in British India: A Study of Controversy, Conflict and Communal Movements in Northern India, 1923–1928.* Leiden: Brill.

BIBLIOGRAPHY

Thurston, Alexander. (2014) "The Era of Overseas Scholarships: Islam, Modernization, and Decolonization in Northern Nigeria, c.1954–1966." *Journal of Religion in Africa* 44, no. 1: 62–91.

Tine, Antoine. (2005) "Léopold Senghor et Cheikh Anta Diop face au panafricanisme: deux intellectuels, même combat mais même conflit des idéologies?" In *Intellectuels, nationalisme et idéal panafricain: perspective historique*, ed. Thierno Bah. Dakar: CODESRIA, pp. 129–57.

Twumasi, Patrick A. (1979) "A Social History of the Ghanaian Pluralistic Medical System." *Social Science & Medicine. Part B: Medical Anthropology* 13, no. 4: 349–56.

Uberoi, Patricia. (1990) "Feminine Identity and National Ethos in Indian Calendar Art." (28 April) *Economic & Political Weekly* 25, no. 17: WS41–WS48.

Uche, Chibuike U. (2012) "British Government, British Businesses, and the Indigenization Exercise in Post-Independence Nigeria." *Business History Review* 86, no. 4: 745–71.

Upadhyaya, U. P., and S. P. Upadhyaya. (1976) "Affinités ethno-linguistiques entre Dravidiens et les Nègro-Africain." *Bulletin de l'IFAN* 38, no. 1: 127–57.

Vahed, Goolam. (2015) "'Nehru is Just Another Coolie': India and South Africa at the United Nations, 1946–1955." *Alternation* Special Edition 15: 54–84.

Vande Berg, Travis, and Fred Kniss. (2008) "ISKCON and Immigrants: The Rise, Decline, and Rise Again of a New Religious Movement." *Sociological Quarterly* 49, no. 1: 79–104.

Vander Steene, Gwenda. (2008) "'Hindu' Dance Groups and Indophilie in Senegal: The Imagination of the Exotic Other." In *India in Africa, Africa in India: Indian Ocean Cosmopolitanisms*, ed. John C. Hawley. Bloomington: Indiana University Press, pp. 117–48.

Van Stipriaan, Alex. (2003) "Watramama/Mami Wata: Three Centuries of Creolization of a Water Spirit in West Africa, Suriname and Europe." *Matatu* 27, no. 1: 321–37.

Vasudevan, Parvathi. (2010) "The Changing Nature of Nigeria–India Relations." Chatham House Programme Paper AFP 2010/02.

Venkatachalam, Meera. (2021) "The Indian Political Right, Soft Power, and the Reimagining of Africa." In *India's Development Diplomacy and Soft Power in Africa*, ed. Kenneth King and Meera Venkatachalam. Oxford: James Currey, chapter 3.

Vernière, Marc. (1973) "Pikine, 'ville nouvelle' de Dakar, un cas de pseudo-urbanisation." *L'Espace Géographique* 2, no. 2: 107–26.

Versluys, Eline. (2008) "Multilingualism and the City: The Construction of Urban Identities in Dakar (Senegal)." *City & Society* 20, no. 2: 282–300.

Virani, Shafique. (2011) "*Taqiyya* and Identity in a South Asian Community." *Journal of Asian Studies* 70, no. 1: 99–139.

Vitalis, Robert. (2013) "The Midnight Ride of Kwame Nkrumah and other Fables of Bandung (Ban-doong)." *Humanity: An International Journal of Human Rights, Humanitarianism, and Development* 4, no. 2: 261–88.

Vittorini, Simona, and David Harris. (2011) "New Topographies of Power? Africa Negotiating an Emerging Multipolar World." In *African Engagements*, ed. Ton Dietz, Kjell Havnevik, Mayke Kaag, and Terje Oestigaard. Leiden: Brill, pp. 280–99.

Ware, Rudolph. (2014) *The Walking Qur'an: Islamic Education, Embodied Knowledge, and History in West Africa*. Chapel Hill: University of North Carolina Press.

Warren, Vincent. (2006) "Yearning for the Spiritual Ideal: The Influence of India on Western Dance, 1626–2003." *Dance Research Journal* 38, no. 1/2: 97–114.

Wendt, Simon. (2007) "'They Finally Found Out that We Really Are Men': Violence, Non-Violence and Black Manhood in the Civil Rights Era." *Gender & History* 19, no. 3: 543–64.

Wilkerson, Isabel. (2020) *Caste: The Origins of Our Discontents*. New York: Random House.

Williams, Justin. (2015) "The 'Rawlings Revolution' and Rediscovery of the African Diaspora in Ghana (1983–2015)." *African Studies* 74, no. 3: 366–87.

Winters, Clyde. (2006) Correspondence: "Did the Dravidian Speakers Originate in Africa?" *BioEssays* 29, no. 5: 497–8.

— (2008) "Origin and Spread of Dravidian Speakers." *International Journal of Human Genetics* 8, no. 4: 325–9.

BIBLIOGRAPHY

— (2010) "9 bp and the Relationship Between African and Dravidian Speakers." *Current Research Journal of Biological Sciences* 2, no. 4: 229–31.

Wuaku, Albert. (2009) "Hinduizing from the Top, Indigenizing from Below: Localizing Krishna Rituals in Southern Ghana." *Journal of Religion in Africa* 39, no. 4: 403–28.

— (2012) "Selling Krishna in Ghana's Religious Market: Proselytising Strategies of the Sri Radha Govinda Temple Community of Ghana." *Journal of Contemporary African Studies* 30, no. 2: 335–57.

— (2013) *Hindu Gods in West Africa: Ghanaian Devotees of Shiva and Krishna.* Leiden: Brill.

Yengde, Suraj Milind. (2015) "Caste Among the Indian diaspora in Africa." (12 Sept.) *Economic & Political Weekly* 50, no. 37: 65–8.

— (2019) *Caste Matters.* New Delhi: India Viking.

Young, Katie. (2021) "Hindi Films, Bollywood, and Indian Television Serials: A History of Connection, Disconnection, and Reconnection in Tamale, Northern Ghana." *Journal of African Cultural Studies*, DOI: 10.1080/13696815.2020.1868291.

Zia-Ebrahimi, Reza. (2011) "Self-Orientalization and Dislocation: The Uses and Abuses of the 'Aryan' Discourse in Iran." *Iranian Studies* 44, no. 4: 445–72.

Zimmerman, Andrew. (2012) *Alabama in Africa: Booker T. Washington, the German Empire, and the Globalization of the New South.* Princeton University Press.

Zulu, Zakhele. (1971) "Why I Joined the Communist Party – 1: Impact of the Durban Riots." *African Communist* 46, no. 3: 50–3.

INDEX

INDEX

Ahmad, Hazrat Hafiz Mirza Nasir, 123–5

Ahmad, Bashiruddin Mahmud, 37, 39, 40, 75, 125, 126–7

Ahmad, Mirza Ghulam, 36–7, 60

Ahmad, Mirza Mubarak, 122

Ahmadiyya headquarters, 74–5

Ahmadiyya Indian Muslim movement (1889), 18, 36–44, 46, 47, 48–9, 50, 59–60, 69, 74, 118, 122–8, 138, 142

Ahmadiyya Nusrat Jehan, 124

Ahmady, Abdul Fayaz Khan Sahib, 49–50

Ahmed, Nazir, 57–8, 59

Ahrar Party, 119

Ahuja, Hamisha Daryani, 198

Aiyar, Sana, 103

Akanni, Niji, 197

Akyeampong, Daniel, 129–30

Al Hilal, 68

Al-Asuli, Bokhara, 137

Ali Nadwi, Sheikh Sayyid Abul Hassan, 126

Ali, Duse Muhammad, 37–8, 39, 42, 43

Ali, Muhammad, 74

Ali, Noble Drew, 42

Al-Jazeera, 207

All African Healing Arts Society, 169

Allotey, Francis K. A., 116, 122, 137

al-Mahdi, Sadiq, 137–8

Amal, 119

"American impositions", 15

American National Science Foundation, 138

American Physical Society, 131

Amin, Idi, 18, 20, 102–3, 104, 110, 209–10

"Amis des Inde" club, 180–1

Amistad slave ship revolt, 116

Ampofo, Oku, 171

An Outline of Islam, 118

Anarkali, 68

Andoh, Anthony Kweku, 167–9, 171

Andoh, Joseph Emmanuel, 167

Andrews, C. F., 157

Annadurai, C. N., 100

Annamalai University (Chidambaram), 86, 106, 180

anti-Ahmadi riots, 119

anti-apartheid movement, 13, 69, 85, 138, 157

anti-China sentiment, 91

anti-Indian feelings, 101

anti-Indian propaganda, 64

anti-Indian riots (Durban, 1949), 11

Anti-Inflation Campaign Committee, 64

anti-racism, 13

anti-racist politics, 11

anti-white feeling, 58

apartheid, 2, 11, 63, 91, 94, 202, 209

Appah, Adoagyir Mahdi, 44

Appiah, Kwame Anthony, 210

INDEX

INDEX

INDEX

INDEX

European imperialism, 34, 54
European race-making, 14
European racial ideologies, 5–6, 7

Fair & Lovely (skin-lightening cream product), 199–200, 201
Fancy Dress masquerade-parade, 46
Fanon, Frantz, 120
Farishta Ya Qatil (film), 184
Faye, Souleymane, 106, 110–11
film piracy, 195
films, 65–9, 112, 180, 181–9, 193–6
Floyd, George, 201
Fluker, Walter, 152–3
Forest Academy, 157
Freshwater (Emezi), 210, 211
Friday *khutbah* (prayer), 126
Friends of India, 181, 182
"Friends of Krishna", 164–5
Frobenius, Leo, 88–9, 109
Froment, Aurélien, 204
Front National Sénégalais, 105

Gadjigo, Samba, 187
Gallardo, J. C., 131
Gandhi, Indira, 91, 176
Gandhi, Mohandas K., 2–3, 9, 22, 24, 25–32, 51, 54–5, 61, 94–5, 156, 212
Gandhi, Rajmohan, 15
Gandhian movement, 54
Gandhian politics, 17
#GandhiMustFall, 2, 14–15, 208

Garvey, Marcus, 22, 38, 43, 49
Gaskiya Ta Fi Kwabo (newspaper), 53
Gatheru, R. Mugo, 70
General Conference of UNESCO (1974), 132
Ghadar movement, 22, 41
Ghana, 11, 64, 68, 80, 120–1, 127, 132, 149, 158, 163, 166, 168, 171, 200, 212
Ghanaian Hinduism, 19, 167, 172
Ghanananda Saraswati, Swami (Kwesi Essel), 145–8, 153, 154–7, 158–63, 165, 166, 171, 174, 179
ghazal (poem), 68
Gheirawani, Mohammad, 34–5
Ghosh, Amitav, 210
Gilroy, Paul, 22, 189
Godrej, 201
Gokhale, Krishna, 27
Gold Coast, 23, 44, 45, 48, 62–3, 65, 66, 71, 79, 156, 159
Graham, Billy, 123
Green, Nile, 44
Greiff, Alexis De, 120
Guha, Ramachandra, 3
Gujarat, 5, 6, 149, 151
Gupta brothers, 2
Gupta, Anirudha, 90, 104

Habshis, 6, 9, 149–50
Hackett, Rosalind, 79
Hagenbeck, Carl, 22, 23

INDEX

INDEX

Indian films, 65–9, 112, 180, 181–9, 193–6

Indian High Commission's office, 64

Indian iconography, 24–5

Indian indentured labourers, 21

Indian Institute of Technology, 209

Indian materialism, 8–9

Indian Muslims, 34, 36, 44, 50, 51, 50–1, 57, 58

Indian National Academy of Letters, 86

Indian Ocean, 3, 5, 7, 16, 18, 20, 21, 112, 205

Indian Opinion, 24, 27–8

Indian racial origin, 9–10

Indian railway workers, 55

Indira Gandhi National Centre, 206

Indo-Aryan languages, 96

Indo-Aryan myth, 7

Indo-European language family, 96

Indo-Pakistan conflict (1965), 89

Indouphilie, 112, 178, 179, 180–5, 194–5

Indus Valley, 95, 97

Inkanyiso Yase Natal (journal), 27

Institut Fondamental d'Afrique Noire (IFAN), 86, 105, 178

International Atomic Energy Agency (IAEA), 119, 128, 129, 144

International Centre for

Theoretical Physics (ICTP), 17, 115, 117, 121, 128, 129, 131, 132, 133, 135, 138, 142, 143, 174

Iqbal, Muhammad, 57

Irele, Abiola, 188

ISKCON (International Society for Krishna Consciousness), 146, 163, 164–7

"Islam in Africa", 122

Islam, 6, 33, 44, 45, 54

Islamic aid, 125–6

Islamic World (newspaper), 35

Israel, 88, 132–3

Italian invasion of Ethiopia (1935), 56

J.U.D.E. (film), 197

Jackson, Jesse, 153

jamaat, 151

Jamaica, 10

Jews, 62

"jinn films", 183

Jinnah, Muhammad Ali, 118, 119

Johnson, Anthony, 138

Johnson, Joseph Andrew, III, 116, 138

Johnson, Lynette E., 138

Johnston, Harry, 97

journalism, 69

Jugran, Mahesh, 72–4, 75, 76

Justice Party, 100

Kali (goddess), 85, 87, 88

INDEX

INDEX

INDEX

négritude, 52, 84, 85–7, 113–14,
    185–9, 191, 192–3, 202
Negro in Ancient History, The
    (Blyden), 26–7
Negro World (Du Bois), 51
Nehru administration, 81, 93
Nehru, Jawaharlal, 5, 12, 13, 63,
    64, 69–70, 76, 81, 83, 85, 91
neocolonialism, 142
Netflix, 199
New Asian-African Strategic
    Partnership (2005), 11
New Delhi, 90, 198, 206
New Haven, 116
New York Public Library, 206
Ngugi wa Thiong'o, 1–2, 4, 8,
    15–16, 210
Nigeria, 46–8, 53–4, 72–4, 76, 79,
    126, 127, 130, 133–4, 196–7
Nigerian Ahmadis, 59, 126
Nigerian Broadcasting
    Corporation, 74
Nigerian forces, 66
Nigerian National Research
    Council, 133
Nigerian Youth Association, 47
Nisreyasananda, Swami, 71, 77
Nkrumah, Kwame, 5, 13, 63, 65,
    84–5, 120, 122, 124, 130
Nollywood, 180, 195, 196–9
Nollywood-Bollywood nexus,
    196–9
Non-Aligned Movement confer-
    ence I (Belgrade, 1961), 5, 83
Non-Aligned Movement, 198

non-violence, 29, 31
North Scale Education and
    Research Institute (NSERI),
    167–9
Northcott, Cecil, 123
Nyasaland, 57

Obote, Milton, 102
Odhiambo, T. R., 136, 137
*Of One Blood: Or, The Hidden
    Self* (Hopkins), 210
Office de Radio et Télévision du
    Mali (ORTM), 194
ogbanje (Emezi), 210–11
Oklahoman, The, 175
Olcott, Henry Steel, 97
Olu-Ibukun, 131, 132, 133, 134,
    135
Onwurah, Rita, 197–8
Organization of African Unity
    (OAU), 18, 85, 103, 121, 131
Orient Review (journal), 38
Orthodox Christian monarchy, 6
Osakwe, Chukwuma, 197

Pakistan, 11, 85, 118–21, 123,
    128, 142
Pam, Mamadou, 184, 185, 196
Pan-Africanism, 4–5, 12, 26, 27,
    30, 41, 50, 51, 88, 142, 144,
    192, 204, 209
Pan-Africanist antiracism, 13, 17
Pan-Islamism, 32–44, 50, 138
Pant, Apa, 79–80, 81
Patani, A. A., 133

INDEX

INDEX

INDEX

INDEX